Jolette

a memoir

*Call Girl, Soldier,
Drug Smuggler, Survivor*

By J. Mitchell

Jolette, A Memoir

Text Copyright 2023 by J. Mitchell

ISBN: 978-0-9899194-3-2

All rights reserved.

Book Design: Manuela Gomez Rhine

To Naomi Pearl

Twice the miracle in my life.

Once when you were born.

Then when we met so many years later

and you let me into your life.

With love always.

Jolette

1

Seattle, 1980

Helen was answering phones, "Elite Massage." She had a sexy voice, was personable over the phone with clients and maternal and protective with the girls. She called me baby and honey in such a nice way it made my heart soft. I loved Helen. She was trying to teach me how to enjoy oral sex.

"I hate it," I told her. "Gross."

"Listen baby, I know, honey. But you have to detach the man from the penis. Just take the man out of the picture. Just love the penis and take care of it."

Sometimes Helen was way beyond me. Penises were ugly and unappealing. There was no way I wanted to suck on that thing. It wasn't going to help to mentally detach it from the man. But giving head was also part of the job. "And I don't get it. How are you supposed to put a rubber on with your mouth?" I asked Vicky, the gorgeous Asian girl who got a ton of requests but a ton of rejections too. Some guys loved Asian women and others wouldn't see them. There was barely any middle ground. Vicky leaned forward. We were sitting on a couch in the office. "You keep it in the back of your mouth, put your mouth down on his cock and you use your tongue and put the rubber on the head and then push it down with your lips. They won't even know they're wearing it."

"Oh gimme a break. Are you kidding? That sounds hard."

Helen and Vicky both looked at me. "You'll get it, honey," Helen said.

"Helen?" I asked tentatively switching the subject.

"What baby?"

"It's a crescent moon tonight."

"Oh shit, Jolette. Do not tell me you're not working because it's a crescent moon."

"I can't help it. Crescent moons are bad for me. I always have bad nights with crescent moons."

"Oh my god, Jolette."

"I know. It's weird. I already know that, but I can't help it," I whined.

"Honey, you're going to miss so much business. It's always busy on Fridays."

"I know. But I just can't."

My name is Jolette though I used the names Michelle, Danielle, and Camille for work. Funny how quickly one can adapt to a new name. You wouldn't really guess it. We get so attached to our name and never really think about it, but it can switch easily enough. When I changed my name to Michelle it took a few days but then I was Michelle. After a handful of years as Michelle, I changed to Danielle and pretty quickly I was Danielle. Jolette took a backseat and on the rare occasion when someone called me by my real name it felt like Jolette was someone who lived far away.

It was 1980 and I'd just moved to the soggy city of Seattle, the flourishing hub which had its beginnings some 14,000 years ago after a gigantic glacier withdrew its icy clasp, carving the terrain left behind into mountains, hills, bluffs, and ridges. I knew this from reading tourist pamphlets. Named after Chief Seattle, head of the Suquamish and Duwamish tribes, the burgeoning city grew up on many of those hills, giving strong calf muscles to those who would choose to ascend its streets by foot. I found a one-room studio apartment on one of the steep hills and set out to find a phone booth. I needed to make money and I knew how. Pushing open a filthy phone booth door, I flipped open an enormous, unwieldy telephone book that hung from a wire noose, its body heavy, thick with thin pages permeated with ink — the phone numbers of every single person and business in Seattle. I had to ignore my first instinct not to touch this anvil, this breeding ground of bacteria, evidence of spills and grime smeared randomly throughout the monolithic volume, and submitted my fingers into its midst finding their way to the yellow pages. There were only two ads for outcall massage. I chose Elite Massage and dialed the number. A friendly girl invited me to the office when I asked about a job.

Working as a call girl fit me like a glove. I'd just moved to Seattle from Hawaii where I'd worked outcall in Waikiki for close to a year. I was glad I'd stumbled into the work, one day while desperate for a job, walking down Kalakaua Avenue. There was an edge, which I liked, and an escape from the claustrophobia of conformity, which I really liked. I had more free time. I had more money, and it wasn't hard to have sex with strangers. I could do it easily, at least in the beginning. And I didn't mind that sex for hire was illegal. I liked being an outlaw.

The Boren Street Apartment building sat in a rundown neighborhood, a poor cousin to the adjacent more affluent downtown, resembling a prison more closely than a docile dwelling with its uniformed rows of squinty windows and vomit yellow exterior. The interior hallway floors were decorated with items of indistinguishable origin. A strong ammonia smell guaranteed nearby urine. I watched my footing, negotiating down the hallway to apartment 47, and knocked on the door. It opened to a woman of mid-sized girth, her blonde hair stiff with hairspray, her blue eyes looking out from under a heavy lid of blue eyeshadow and thick false lashes, immediately assessing me.

"Hi, I'm Jolette," I said, it sounded like a question.

"I'm Marilyn. Come in." The woman stood aside to reveal a sparse room with a shabby couch and a desk with a clunky black phone manned by a young woman. "This is Carol." Carol looked up and threw me a friendly smile. She had thick dark hair that fell to her shoulders, freckles running across her nose, and was sort of chubby. I liked her right away.

"Hi," I smiled back.

"So you've worked outcall before?" Marilyn asked, a glob of glue staring at me from one of her false eyelashes. I had to resist the urge to point it out, nodding, "Yes."

"Okay. My fee is fifty dollars. Whatever else is between you and the client. Anything extra is extra. Don't agree to anything verbally. Talk to the other girls. We'll book you with Douglas. He always sees our new girls first. Carol, call Douglas and see if he wants to see Jolette. Or do you want to use a different name? You probably should."

"Um, yes, Michelle."

"Okay. See if Douglas wants to see Michelle tonight. Douglas calls once a week at least, sometimes twice."

"He'll love you," Carol smiled. "He likes thin brunettes."

"He likes anybody," Marilyn said.

"Well, yes, true. But especially brunettes." Carol smiled again.

"Okay, thank you. Do I need to know how to massage?" I couldn't keep my eyes off Marilyn's eyelids.

"No, not for Douglas, but I want you to know the basics. Come in tomorrow at noon and I'll teach you."

That night I steered through the incessant wet, a steady drizzle pattering against my windshield, aimed towards Douglas. The rain had slowed, was only slightly spitting as I pulled up in front of a modest home just south of Seattle. I knocked on the door that opened to a very tall, thin man who was hunched over, his head hanging as though a burden his shoulders refused. He lifted his head to register me, his eyes two holes of sadness, and attempted a weak smile but could barely lift his lips — a modern day Boo Radley.

"Hi Douglas, I'm Michelle." I offered my hand and with the speed of a tortoise he reached forward to take it. I held his clammy hand gently. "Thank you for inviting me over. How are you this evening?"

"Oh, I'm good. I don't know. Come on in." He shuffled aside and I saw an immaculate and sterile living room, obligatory sofa, chair, and table.

Jolette

"I love your place," I said, stepping inside. "It's so comfortable."

"Oh yes, it's okay," he said.

"Do you live here alone?"

"Well, yes, now I do. My girlfriend left me a year ago." He lifted his head to look at me.

"Oh no. I'm so sorry. Are you doing okay?"

"Well, yes. No. I'm really not okay. I miss her. Those were her canisters." He pointed to a line of canisters on the kitchen counter.

"Oh!" I exclaimed.

"She had those canisters for sugar, and flour, and you know, some candies and coffee."

"They're really pretty. Did she decorate your home?"

"Yes. Look. She put these pictures up." He pointed to the wall.

"Oh, those are beautiful," I said. "This is really nice. Would you mind if I used your phone to check in with the agency?"

He turned and led the way to the telephone and I called Carol.

"Elite Massage," Carol's voice apple pie friendly.

"Hi, it's Michelle. I'm checking in with Douglas."

"Alright. Call me in an hour."

"Would you like something to drink?" he asked.

"Sure. I don't drink alcohol, but anything else is good."

"Would you like orange juice?"

"Yes, thank you." I sat on the couch. "So you work at Boeing?"

"Yes, yes I do."

"Do you like working there?"

"Yes. I don't know. I guess I like it." He brought me the orange juice and sat down beside me, well-practiced in a malfunctioning way.

I turned to face him. "How long have you been there?"

"Ahh…sixteen years."

"What is it you do exactly?" I smiled.

"I design various components of the jet engine."

"Oh really?" A display of enthusiasm. "That would be interesting. Pretty important work, I would think."

"Yes, it is in fact. But, well, my girlfriend…uh my ex-girlfriend…she didn't think it was too interesting," he said.

"Oh, jeez. I'm sorry about her."

"Yea. She's been gone a year now."

"Oh gosh. You've had a hard time?"

"Yes."

"I'm so sorry. You'll get through it though. You'll be okay."

"I don't know."

"I know it's tough." I leaned towards him and kissed his cheek. "I'm so sorry."

"Yes, I'm sorry too." His eyes filled and before he could flood, I placed a gentle hand on his arm to keep him present. "Could I use your bathroom please?"

"Sure, let me take you."

I followed him down a hallway. "Oh, there's your bedroom?"

"Yes," he nodded.

I lightly pulled his arm and drew him towards me, kissed the fragile man softly on his mouth. "Do you wanna just meet me there in a minute?"

"Yes."

"Okay. Good."

I walked into the bathroom, looked into the mirror, stretched, yawned, and slipped out of my dress before returning to Douglas where he obediently assented to my tender lead.

2

Seattle, 1981

Why is it immoral to be paid for an act that is perfectly legal if done for free.
Gloria Allred, b. 1941, American Women's Rights Attorney.

Marilyn seemed way too old to be working outcall. At least that's what we all thought. She was forty-something – two unfathomable decades older than the rest of us girls – and was sort of attractive in a heavier, less fresh, lots of blue eye shadow kind of way.

The girls and I would shake our young heads. "Marilyn is too old to be working."

But she ran the business and if she wanted to work, I guess that was her prerogative. Sometimes if a guy called and complained about a girl he'd just seen Marilyn would get all in a tizzy and end up offering a free visit and whatever else to mollify the customer. The guy would naturally agree to be solaced by a freebie and then she would go to whatever hotel or motel room he was in and deliver. She'd be briefly mad at whatever girl had upset the precious client but all was soon forgotten as the girl resumed going on calls and making money. Marilyn could do what she wanted. I mean, she could sort of do what she wanted. Selling sex was illegal so you didn't want to get arrested. You had to be careful. You couldn't agree to anything verbally — that was grounds for arrest, a misdemeanor charge called Offer and Agree, more commonly known as O & A – and was the first step undercover police would attempt to secure a bust.

Semantics was key. We were all careful with what we said and stuck with, "Anything extra is extra." "How much extra?" the client would ask.

"One hundred dollars," we would say.

Which it was in those days. I was very polite upon meeting the new client and benevolent if complied with.

"May I see your driver's license and plane ticket please?"

Most guys already knew the routine and didn't ask anything directly but of course there would be those who would have to say, "What do I get for a hundred dollars?"

"You get my time and attention."

"Yea, but what's included?"

"Don't worry, I think you'll be happy."

If he was so dense or uncooperative that he couldn't or wouldn't read between the lines, well, that was just annoying, and if he pursued that avenue further I couldn't stop the irritation that flooded through me, prompting, "You know, I don't think this is working out. You should probably see someone else."

Some fast back peddling and a welcome display of docility ensued. "No, no. It's okay. Here's my ID. Is there anything else? My plane ticket? Could I get you a drink?"

Then I'd roost at the little round table, a hotel room staple, and make conversation. My comfort level determined the length of superficial conversation, ranging from five to twelve minutes, longer if I was still unsure of the client or if I was being punitive for the earlier undesirable behavior or if the conversation was actually interesting.

Police and weirdos were the two main reasons identity had to be established. Checking ID was a must.

"I just need to know you are who you say you are," I would smile to still any indignant feathers. "It's just routine."

"I understand. You have to be careful," was the normal response.

While not a guarantor of safety, at least the correct ID offered a modicum of security but of course it was no insurance against undesirable encounters with weirdos or police and later in my career I would fall prey several times to traps set by the Seattle Police Department.

Besides learning to tap dance around the legal system, there was also the weirdo category to contend with, the spectrum ranging from irritating to terrifying.

Irritating and annoying behaviors could be overlooked if I was feeling tolerant but were nails on a chalkboard other times. For instance, when a client gurgled, "Why do you need to see my ID? Do I get to see your ID too? That only seems fair." Most times I managed to respond with a smile and gently laugh, "Yes, well, it doesn't work that way." But sometimes I allowed the words," Is this going to be a problem?" to shoot through my lovely lipsticked mouth, eyebrow raised. Then, a sweet smile, the words, "I hope not," leaving the client confused but more compliant.

Being called "honey" by clients who tossed the word at me dismissively, as if I were an inflatable doll with convenient holes, was also annoying. It meant I had to say, "I don't like being called honey," before I scratched their eyes out. But those were mere irritants born of ill-bred clients, my impatience, and society's skewed judgment, which viewed clients as normal, call-girls less than.

Unfortunately, mainstream society subscribed to this skewed viewpoint and unwittingly so did many working girls, myself included, although my personal spin was to consider myself unconventional and a notch superior to humdrum normal. Still, society's taint permeated, derogatory labels abounded, and at the very least, subjected a substantial number of sex workers to a camouflaged existence, avoiding judgment.

At the spectrum's far other end, lurked a far more deadly threat, one that transformed all else into a holiday, for, in the 1980s of Seattle, prostitutes were the target of a serial killer. Most victims were young women between fourteen and twenty-five, working the streets, their strangled bodies recovered near the Green River, some twenty miles south of Seattle, giving the elusive killer his newspaper headline title — the Green River killer.

The Green River killer was notorious, frustrating authorities and working girls alike, with his ability to evade capture for several decades. As the number of vanished street girls increased, authorities found it odd that the presumed alert street girls were so susceptible. The killer was someone who didn't raise their normally sharpened antennas, leading some to speculate the killer may have been a police officer. Back in the 80s he roamed free, targeting the working girls who strolled the strip near Sea-Tac Airport where the bright lights of the Red Lion, the Marriott Hotel, the Doubletree, and other major hotels — hotels I frequented — illuminated only the hotel skirt, leaving the rest of the strip engulfed in darkness, an oasis for snatching girls unseen. My nightly ventures brought me far too close to these killing grounds.

Police were predictably motivated to amp their arrest quota, make the department look good, at election times, but the weirdos were less calculable. You just never knew when they might hit, although it's possible that the gravitational pull of the full moon compelled a flourish of unstable behavior. The human body, after all, is sixty percent water, which would be subject to tidal activity. That was the reason I was anxious with full and crescent moons, irritating Carol or Helen or Barb, the girls who answered the phones and set up the appointments, when I would shun work depending on the moon phase. "Carol, the moon is full tonight." "Oh god, please do not tell me you're not going to work." "I can't help it. It scares me." They would sigh, mildly exasperated but never pushy, and I would frequently stay tucked into the safety of my apartment while the moon indulged its extremes.

Ultimately, the majority of clients were non threatening and amiable, some more interesting than others. After my initial ten to twelve minute conversation with a client, I would politely ask to use the restroom. "Could you put the fee on the table please?" I would say as I high-heeled to the bathroom, shut the door and looked in the mirror where I would then give myself a thirty-second break from the call girl routine, stretching, assessing my young face. It was an aesthetic face, light brown eyes above high cheekbones. A wave of auburn hair fell to my shoulders. It was naturally curly, normally unruly but subdued with gel and a hair blower and I was happy that I'd lost a ten pound chunk and now flaunted a slender frame. I would pull off my dress, adjust the underlying lingerie, leaving heels and nylons attached, then make my grand reentry.

The next steps were routine. Over to the guy, murmur something inane like hi, a kiss on the cheek then to the mouth, no tongue, that was a rule, press against him, push him onto the bed, undress him and myself, push him onto his back, kiss his nipples, kiss down his stomach unless the stomach was an undesirable spot for my lips and then I would just trail a finger down his stomach, put condom on — hopefully I'd gotten non-lubricated because the lubrication was god-awful to taste — quickly count to thirty as I gave head, the time I allotted, then lay on top of the guy for a second, pull him over on top of me, make appropriate noises, have him enter me, give five minutes of thrusting and then work to the climax. Eight to ten minutes for sex, then a sigh and relaxation.

"That was nice," I would say as if delightfully surprised and give a thirty-second cuddle. Detach and regretfully say, "You have to get up early tomorrow." Then smile and add — cue for laugh — "And I don't."

Guy would agreeably laugh. "Yes, I do have to get up early." I would dress and give him a kiss on the cheek. Guy would be relaxed and grateful. "Thank you, Michelle (or Danielle or whatever name I was using) for a nice evening." I would smile, "You're welcome. It was nice meeting you." Then out the door in under an hour unless there were any initial hitches, or I stayed longer because the guy was caressing my back which I could never resist.

Word choice was an important element when working as a call girl. Like it is in any aspect of life. As a call girl the importance was attached to what words could not be said but the main point here is the power of words. Every word you chose indicates perspective and a choice of interpretation. What words you chose to speak and think with will change perspective, will alter life. Amazing. It's so simple. Relatively simple. I frequently remind myself of that. It's all your choice. In this case, as I write this, it's my choice.

3

Seattle, 1981

Grown men should not be having sex with prostitutes unless they are married to them.
Jerry Falwell, 1933-2007, televangelist, conservative activist.

It was Friday, money drop day at the office.

"You know what I hate?" I said to Liz, Nadine, and Trudy, who were sitting on the couch. I dropped my envelope with money for Marilyn on the desk and turned to face the girls. "I hate it when they lay there and bob their cock. It's so disgusting."

"Ew, I hate it too," Trudy said.

"I wanna say, 'Oh, is something wrong? Here, let me just cut this thing off.'" I mimic a cutting motion and the girls burst into laughter.

"Penises are ugly," I said. "No wonder no one's wife wants to suck them."

"That's where all the business comes from," Trudy said, her voice loud and shrill. She always said whatever she wanted. That's why I liked her. "The business comes from the wives that won't suck cock," Trudy continued. She sat forward on the couch and emptied her purse on the table to clean it out.

"I don't think penises are ugly. They're kinda cute," Liz said.

I groaned. "Oh god, Liz."

"They are and I like sex." Liz had the most baby face of all the girls. Her lashes were dark and sweeping, her cheeks full and rosy, with dark hair and delicate tendrils framing her features.

"You like it with clients?" I asked and plopped down on the only chair in the room.

"Sometimes," Liz said. "You do too." She looked at me.

"I like David. He's the only one," I said. David was a young musician with Rod Stewart hair and big green eyes.

"He's a cutie," Liz said.

"He sure is," Nadine said. "But damn, he's always getting me on the floor and it kills my back."

"I know! I barely get inside and we're already down on the carpet. I get rug burn every time," I said.

"Where does he get his money? He must call three times a week," Trudy said. "Helen, how many times a week does David call?"

"Girls, that boy calls almost every day." Helen looked up from the desk. "Not always to make an appointment, but he likes to know who's working."

"That's creepy," Nadine said, and got up to use the smallest bathroom ever seen on the North American continent. She turned on the light, looked into the mirror.

"You're still gorgeous," I called to her.

"Yes, I am," Nadine smiled, and pulled out her makeup.

"And so humble," I said.

"Hey Michelle, do you take your school books to appointments?" Nadine grinned. "Trudy said you do."

"No, I don't."

"Yes, you do," Trudy said. "Remember when we went to see Clifford? You brought in all your school books." She laughed. "He thought we were doing a study session."

Jolette

"Oh, that's right, I did. I couldn't get the car window up and didn't want the books to get wet."

"When are you graduating anyway?" Liz asked.

"Two years."

"That's a long time," Nadine said. She was outlining her lips. "What are you going to do after you graduate?" she asked, admiring herself in the mirror.

"Be a foreign correspondent."

"A what?" Nadine turned.

"Michelle is going to be a reporter. She's going to all the places where there's wars and shit and she's going to be a reporter and write stories. Right?" Trudy looked at me. I was closer to Trudy than the rest of the girls.

"Yea, that's right," I said.

"Damn girl. You crazy to want to do that," Nadine said.

"I think it's neat," Liz said.

The phone rang. "Elite Massage," Helen's voice sweet as syrup. "Well, hello Ted. Yes we do. What hotel are you in this evening?"

"I'm not going out. I'm done for the day," Trudy said. Helen frowned at her. She was always too loud.

"Sure, Ted. We have one blonde girl working this evening. Her name is Christine. She is a lovely girl. Where did you fly in from Ted? Oh I see," Helen laughed. "And what is your last name? Oh, is that Norwegian?" Helen was born personable. "Well, Christine will need to see your driver's license and your plane ticket when she gets there, Ted. Um hum. That's right. Yes, she should be there within the hour. You have a nice evening too, Ted." Helen hung up the phone.

"Christine doesn't like nights," Liz said. "She's a daytime girl. Does she get the most requests?"

"No, she doesn't. Does she?" I asked. "June gets the most requests, doesn't she?"

Jolette

"June definitely gets the most requests," Helen said. "Everyone loves June."

"Did you know June speaks five different languages including Russian?" I said.

"It's because her father was a diplomat and she traveled a lot," Helen said. "I have to check this guy out. He's from Boise. What is the area code for Boise? Let's see." She checked the phone book. "Okay, here it is."

"Christine is going to be pissed. She doesn't like working past ten," Trudy said.

"What are we doing for Christmas you guys?" Nadine asked.

"Yes, could I get the number for Ted Lindbloom?" Helen's voice in the background.

"Should we draw names for secret Santa?" I asked.

"Yea," Trudy said. "We can get together at my apartment. I'm getting a tree tomorrow. We can decorate it."

"Can I bring a friend?" Nadine asked.

"No, let's have it just be us girls and then we can go out after," Liz said.

"Yea, that sounds good," I agreed. "You know what I hate about going out? I hate it if I go home with a guy and have sex. I always feel like he should be paying me. I feel like I'm working for free."

"You know what I hate?" Nadine said. "I hate when they want to take me to dinner for free. Like that guy Mitchell. He won't leave it alone. He's always wanting to take me to dinner. I do not want to sit and talk and have dinner with Mitchell. And most definitely not for free," Nadine said.

"That's the problem with regulars," I said. "They always want too much. The more time you spend with them the more they want your time for free. I don't like regulars."

"They're safer," Trudy pointed out.

"Yea, they're way safer," Liz agreed.

"They're too much work," I said.

16

"Are you guys leaving yet?" Nadine asked.

"Yea, I'm going," Trudy said and I nodded, "Yea."

"Did you smell that piss in the hallway?" Liz asked.

"Yes! "I said. "Can't Marilyn afford a better place than this?"

"Marilyn is cheap," Trudy said.

"She sure is," I agreed. "See you later Helen. I'm on call. Beep me if you need me."

4

Seattle, 1982

It's speculated that the Green River killer murdered seventy or eighty women between 1982 and 1998. Forty-nine bodies were recovered. Some were found placed next to each other. Some far apart. Most of the women were between the ages of fourteen and twenty-five and were street prostitutes or runaways. Most were picked up along a dispirited strip of the Seattle Pacific Highway where small motels burrowed in between the larger Marriott and Red Lion Hotel. The girls were strangled, the body dumped, and the killer would return for post-mortem sex. While the Green River killer was busy murdering girls who worked that strip, I was frequently visiting the larger more expensive hotels and though I was not a street girl, I did not escape him. Because the Green River killer made me nervous always.

Jolette

My car crept down a long narrow road, through a thick forest of trees, headlights nervously searching the road ahead, the bordering Evergreens tall and statue still, silent witnesses to any transgressions that occurred in the deep belly of the woods. I was afraid of the dark. I didn't like the way it snuck up from behind and whispered on my neck. A shadow of huddled buildings was suddenly illuminated by my glancing headlights. It was enough for me to catch the words on a dismal sign – Green River Motel. With an inward grimace I swung into the parking lot.

"Oh god," I had moaned to Carol. "Really? The Green River Motel on the Green River? It's gonna be a funky-assed place in the middle of nowhere right next to the Green River."

"Oh come on. It doesn't mean anything," Carol had said. "But if you don't want to go, maybe June will go instead."

"Oh crap. No, I'll go." I had to get my money.

There were certain guidelines I followed. Number One: It was always my money already. I was just going to go get it. The man had the money. I would go to the man to get my money.

Number Two: I didn't wear necklaces, ever. I didn't want to be strangled by a necklace. It would probably break anyway, but still you never knew, so I never wore a necklace.

Number Three: Keep my eyes on the client's hands. Know where the client's hands are at all times. Self-explanatory.

Number Four: No other person allowed in the room. Never two men.

Number Five: Be ready to push my fingers into client's eyes during sex if there was any inkling of foul play. Stay alert, fingers on stand-by, ready for action. This would be an extreme measure and I had weighed in on my actual ability to push my fingers into someone's eyeballs. It would depend on the incentive I figured. Should a knife suddenly appear I might be able to at least shoving my fingertips into their eyes. Done with impact it could be effective. It would be one of those things you couldn't think about too long. You just had to do it. Period.

The Green River killer is not going to check into the Green River motel right in front of the Green River, I thought as I switched off the ignition, the darkness immediately swallowing me. I was just being paranoid, but how would I know what anyone was going to do, especially someone who enjoyed killing prostitutes? Serial killers usually followed an MO, but what if something changed? What if?

Stop it, I told myself. This is going to be fine. Just go get your money. My shoulders tightened as I forced myself through the dark parking lot to one of the small motel cottages. My gears shifted into automatic as I knocked on the motel door that opened to a slim man, slightly shorter than me.

"Stanley?" I smiled, "I'm Michelle. How are you this evening?"

Stanley was the color of caramel, his hair dark and slicked back, with brown eyes that darted up at me, then skirted off.

"Fine," he said. He opened the door. I took a careful step in.

"Great. What brings you here to the middle of the woods?" I asked.

"Just traveling through for work," he said, looking away.

It wasn't a nervous glance away. I would have liked it better if it were. I preferred slightly nervous clients. But his glance was not that kind of nervous. He didn't meet my eyes for some other reason. Not exactly nervousness.

I surveyed the motel room. There were two rooms, one to the right holding a bed and suitcase, nothing glaringly out of place, and the other room to the left offered a couch, chair, and a few tables. Modest.

"Oh. This is a comfortable place. I like it. How long are you staying here?" I took another step in.

"Til tomorrow."

"Oh. Okay. And then you're off to work?"

He nodded.

"What kind of work do you do?" I smiled, perched on the edge of the couch.

"Deliver goods to hardware stores." He sat in the chair.

"Oh! What kind of goods?"

"Just stuff." He wasn't connecting. I weighed the prospect that he was just uneasy and nervous but wasn't convinced.

"Okay, Stanley, do you mind if I take a look at your ID? Carol probably told you to have it ready?"

"Uh huh, sure." Stanley stood up. His limbs were stiff. His body tense. He walked into the other room. I heard him open his suitcase. I didn't like it. *You're paranoid because it's the Green River motel*, I said to myself.

No, I argued with myself. *I don't like it because I don't like it. He's not connecting. He's deliberately distancing for some reason.*

Then I heard something. I heard what sounded like voices. Was that two voices? In the other room? Or was he talking to himself, or what? Sometimes you have to decide fast. You can't wait to figure out if you're right or wrong.

I was up. My heels rapidly clicked against the floor all the way to the door. I kept my focus on the door. When you have to do something fast and you must succeed, your focus has to be strong and certain and you must move in a direct line. So must your brain.

To the door. It is locked.

Unlock it. Turn the knob and out the door, pull the door closed as I step back into the night. Into the dark. The dark, now a friend who muffles my outline, wraps me into its cloak as I race. Race without running. It's really important not to actually run, that compounds the fear, but race to my car without running.

Open the car door, get in, turn the key in the ignition, lock the doors, headlights push back the dark. My car and I escape.

5

Seattle, 1982

It was supposed to be a stepping stone. It was supposed to get me through college. It wasn't supposed to be twenty-five years.

Jolette

The Westin Hotel on Fifth Avenue had a small dining area near the lobby. It was always quiet and was the perfect spot to drag my books and order a baked potato to study and wait for a call, my beeper set to vibrate snuggled into my purse, which was draped on the chair.

I'd been at the University of Washington for two years, with Elite a little longer. I opened my political science book and began to read, "What does 'following precedent' mean?"

A waitress brought me a steaming potato and I smashed a bunch of butter on it. No sour cream. Too fattening.

Following precedent means the lower courts are bound to follow the caseload of higher courts.

What exactly does "bound" mean?

Restricted by law.

What is the job of the judge versus jury?

Jolette

Judge decides the law. Jury decides the facts.

I scribbled in my notebook and then tested myself on the identities of those in national political office. As a news reporter I would always have to be aware of current affairs and the players.

Who was secretary of state?

George Shultz.

Vice president under Reagan was George Bush.

Who was the secretary of defense?

I couldn't remember the secretary of defense.

The waitress came over. "Is everything okay?"

I nodded. "Yes, hey, do you know who the secretary of defense is?"

She shrugged. "No idea."

A barely discernible whirring sound caught my attention. My beeper vibrating. I grabbed my purse and headed to the lobby phone booth.

"Elite Massage." Carol's voice cozy as flannel pajamas. "It's Michelle, hi."

"Hello there. I have someone new at the Red Lion. Tom Skeward from San Francisco. Room 427. He'll have a plane ticket and papers from work. He's a consultant. He checks out."

"Wow. There are so many consultants I can't believe it."

"I know. Thousands."

"Okay, I'll be there in an hour."

"Alright I'll let him know."

The drive to the Red Lion would take forty minutes. I checked my purse. I had condoms. Trojan, lambskin, non-lubricated. Good. It wasn't raining but it was already getting cold and I didn't linger, clutching my books, heels clacking down the sidewalk to my new red Honda Prelude, shiny and smart, evidence of a comfortable chunk of change. I kept my money in shoeboxes piled on the top shelf in my closet. It had a tendency to pile up if I didn't spend it fast enough. I was on-call five nights a week from 7 p.m. to 1 or 2 a.m. Made one to three hundred a night. Sometimes four or five. Not bad.

I slipped my right heel off and put on my tennis shoe. I'd already ruined way too many high heels pressing on that gas pedal every night — the heel skinned sliding against the rough car floor — turned the ignition and flipped on the radio. *Physical* by Olivia Newton-John. No. Turned the station. *Ain't Nobody*. Chaka Khan. Much better. Slid the car onto the Five South and headed to Sea-Tac, the Red Lion. My car had been on that route so many times it could have driven itself. Traffic was nil and I yawned, stifled the idea of skipping the appointment and going back home to crawl into bed with a book. Go get your money, I commanded myself. My mind wandered. I wondered how Lenny was doing.

Lenny and I grew up in Anoka, a cookie-cutter suburb just north of Minneapolis. I met her in ninth grade where I was drawn to her tough girl stance — she could cut with a simple look and flash of her eyes, shark flat and deadly. Should someone make the mistake of looking her way a moment too long, she'd deliver a hard hitting, "WHAT?"

"Oh sorry," the offending person might say and Lenny would glance them up and down.

"If I looked like you I'd be sorry too."

Mean. Other times her shark eyes would shift to golden brown and she'd bend over backwards to offer help. One night she picked me up in her blue Chevy, her back seat filled with canned food.

"What's all this?" I asked.

"That's for Darleen and her kids. I just emptied my mom's cupboards."

"Your mom is going to shit."

Darleen was a waitress at a hole-in-the-wall restaurant down by the Greyhound bus station, an unsavory block inhabited by those with threadbare pockets and nowhere to go. Lenny had befriended her one night, one of many people in need whom Lenny seemed to attract.

"My mom has plenty of food and Darlene and her kids are hungry," Lenny said and pushed in the car's cigarette lighter with her fat finger —

she hated her fat fingers — her nail gleaming with red polish. She smashed the cigarette lighter against the end of her Kool and we drove towards Darlene's meager one-room apartment.

Lenny and I were suspended from junior high school a couple of times together. It never took much. Not wearing a bra. Smoking in the bathroom. An insolent retort to a teacher. Mr. Reins, the vice principal — short, round, with a large nose and shiny head topped with a few overworked strands – was suspend happy. He and I worked in tandem. We made a good team too. I wanted adventure, didn't mind trouble. He detected those traits and supported them, his response reliable. Like clockwork. Soon I held the record. Twelve times suspended before finally expelled. It was all quite simplistic, beginning on the day I raised my hand in Miss Madison's class. "Can I go to the bathroom?"

"No, you may not." A millisecond of uncertainty was flattened by a puff of courage and I heard myself say, "You want me to pee on the floor?"

And that was it. To the principal's office where Mr. Reins was happy to crow, "Suspended for three days," and I was launched into a series of suspensions elicited by minor infractions. "You were late to class," he'd admonish. "I can guarantee I wasn't missing anything." Suspended again.

One undertaking that brought no repercussions whatsoever was the most audacious, and I can't resist telling. Giving instructions to a willing student - "Take some paper, put it in the sink and light it, leave, and I'll walk in" - this plan fell perfectly into place. I laid in wait near the bathroom, saw the accomplice walk out, and I walked in, took a quick look at the small piece of paper burning in the sink and ran out.

Our science teacher, Mrs. Dalton, happened to be walking down the hall as I ran from the bathroom yelling "Fire, there's a fire!"

Normally unflappable, she charged into the bathroom faster than I'd ever seen her move and though I was on a mission it briefly registered, this incongruous sight, this small woman with the clipped short hair who wrapped herself into a blouse, skirt, nylons, and low-heeled shoes each day as fitting as a tutu on a baseball player, gender identity not to be questioned in those days, who emitted teaching sounds and was otherwise quiet as a mouse, charging into the bathroom stilted yet agile. I noted this even while racing to the red fire alarm and reaching for the prize – the forbidden handle. I grasped the handle and pulled. The alarm burst free, whirling through the halls, signaling the school to evacuate. Which everyone did. I felt giddy with success while wandering through the clump of students gathered outside the building, everyone excitedly chattering. I had to dampen my glee when yanked into the office after the school returned to status quo.

"Next time report the fire to the office first," Reins said. "How about next time I just let the school burn down? You should be thanking me," I said. "Go back to class," Reins only said, without suspending me for a change. He made up for it shortly thereafter.

I was late to class, smelling like cigarettes, sent to the office immediately. Ho hum. Reins was poised to declare yet another suspension, when I, who had grown weary of these lackluster interactions, offered two new words to our conversation. "Fuck you." His eyes widened. "Did you hear that?" he spun his pudgy body around to call out to the secretary. "Did you hear that?" "Fuck you," I repeated in case she hadn't heard. His face reddened. He looked like he was going to pop. "Fuck you," I explored further by yelling. The result was exponential. "Call the police!" he cried. "Call the police! She's hysterical!"

Our last exchange on that rare sunny Minnesota day at Anoka Junior High was a bit anticlimactic. The police arrived, a burst of blue through the school's front doors, two big uniformed men with belts bearing black batons, shiny silver handcuffs and impressive upholstered guns slung around their thickened waists. I stood, subdued and obedient, doing my best to undermine Mr. Reins one final time as he excitedly conveyed to the officers that I was uncontrollably hysterical. He culminated with a furious, "You're expelled," spewed my direction in front of the officers who exchanged glances.

Jolette

"Okay," I said quietly. My quiet demeanor may not have fooled them. I saw them stare down at my bell-bottom jeans where the words Question Authority was splashed in yellow paint across the widest part of the bell and then gaze up to, "A family that smokes together stays together," printed near a bright green marijuana leaf splayed over my thigh.

"Did you call her parents?" the chubbier officer asked Reins.

"Rebecca, quick, call her parents," Reins called to his slack-jawed secretary.

"My dad's working and my mom doesn't have a car," I calmly offered. In fact, I felt extraordinarily calm. A feeling of tranquility had come over me, like a comfortable blanket, like a child who had just witnessed a night of fireworks, then got sleepy.

"We'll take her home and speak with her mother," said the less fat officer. "Come on, let's go."

We all walked out the front door and I acquiesced without any farewell glance although I could feel the heat of Rein's ire following me. "You're the worst student in this school. Even worse than all the boys," he yelled, making me smile as I left the school's confines.

Billie Jean was playing on the radio and I'd heard it so many times I only listened a second before switching the station. *Every Breath You Take*. I sighed and left it. The same songs were played a thousand times a day. The freeway was dark with scarcely any other cars for company. I reached for my pack of gum, popped a stick in my mouth and drifted.

"Do you have enough ciggie butts?" Lenny asked, glancing my way with her super big brown eyes. They were her best feature.

"No, I'm out."

Lenny smoked Kool menthols. I smoked Marlboros. "Okay, well, first thing we have to get you some ciggies."

I loved Lenny's style. She would make it her mission to find someone to buy me a pack of Marlboros at Moby Dick's, a pool hustlers haven on Seventh and Hennepin, our regular hangout even though we were only sixteen. Floyd, the bouncer who carried a big old belly above his belt, had one glass eye and semi-sat on a slim stool guarding the back door, giving dap to all the regulars. He was soft on Lenny and she had a genuine fondness for him too.

"How you doin, Floydie?" she would say, sassy and bright, displaying a huge smile. She had a pretty smile.

"How you doin, Miss Lenny?" he'd respond.

"Better now that I see you," she'd say and Floyd would melt a little and Lenny would shoot the shit with him for a few minutes before we made our entrance.

If any of the bartenders wanted to see our ID, we'd say, "Talk to Floyd," and Floyd would just say, "They alright."

Most of the pool hustlers had names like Slick or Slim or Red or Willy. They lined the walls, fixated on the players who were bent over cue sticks laser-focused on angles and pockets. Lenny had a thing for black men. She never liked the white boys. I was the one who liked the long-haired white boys but they never moved her. We found an open booth, settled in, and swiveled to watch the hustlers. Lenny was eyeballing the crowd, deciding who she would pick to lose her virginity with. She'd decided earlier that day. "I wanna lose my virginity tonight. It has to be someone I don't know or care about at all and that I'll never see again." She nibbled on the end of her straw, then slurped up her coke. "He'll do." Lenny nodded towards a man sporting a green hat, leaning up against the wall behind one of the pool tables. She didn't drink alcohol. I didn't drink much either. Just a shot of Southern Comfort here and there and that was only because I heard that Janis Joplin drank it.

"You sure?" I asked.

"Yeah," she nodded. "He's not a regular."

"Okay. You want me to get him?"

Jolette

"Yeah."

"I'll lead, okay?"

"Yeah. I'll say how cold it is outside if I change my mind," she said.

"Okay."

I turned slightly in the booth and glanced over at the guy with the green hat. He was paying close attention to the pool game but after I'd glanced his way two or three times, he noticed and was on the trail. His eyes stayed on me and I glanced his way, briefly met his stare, glanced away and then back again. Lenny was much better at all of the games we played. She was by far the better hustler, but this, of course, didn't take an expert. He was already on his way over.

"Say there, Miss Lady. How you doin tonight?" He'd reached our table. I looked at Lenny. She was playing meek while I led.

"We're okay," I said. Lenny batted her eyes a little, took a sip of her coke.

"Well, you two ladies shore lookin' fine. Can I sit with yous for a minute?"

"Yea, okay," I said. "That okay with you Len?"

Lenny nodded. I scooted over a bit and he pulled up his long brown coat as he sat down. I saw that his nails shone with clear polish and I could smell some kind of cologne, Brut maybe.

"We picked you out," I said. Lenny shot me a look. I moved too fast.

"Oh, you did now, did you?" green hat said.

"Yea. See, we want your help with something."

"Yea? Whats that?"

"Well, my friend here, she's still a virgin and she wants to lose her virginity tonight. So we picked you."

He paused then laughed. "You twos crazy, you know that. Yous crazy."

"We're serious," I said. "We picked you, but we need a place. You have a place? Cuz if you don't we'll get somebody else."

"Naw, I gotta place," green hat said quickly. "But lemme get this straight. This for real?" He looked at Lenny.

"Yea, it's for real," Lenny said with some snark. She couldn't help herself. Being snarky came easy to her. "And there's not much to say. I don't want to be a virgin anymore and that's it."

He licked his lips and shifted around like he was suddenly a little nervous.

"It's for real. She just wants to lose her virginity and she doesn't want it to be with anyone she knows or cares about. That's all," I said very nicely. "She thought you were perfect." I smiled. I looked at Lenny and she granted him a smile.

Green hat looked at her. "Sounds alright to me." We followed green hat out the front door of Moby's, the cold striking our faces with freezing daggers.

"How far is your room?" I called to him, ducking my head trying to dodge the cold's fury.

"Round the corner."

We followed him until he stopped in front of a dingy-looking doorway with lettering above the door that looked like it'd been written with magic marker – Continental Hotel.

I turned to Lenny. "Is it too cold out here or anything?"

"No, it's okay."

"Alright then." We followed green hat through the lobby down a smelly, skinny hallway to door number seven.

He swung the door open to a small box of a room, fit with a single bed, sheets, and thin disheveled blanket, a sad little dresser off in the corner. Green hat removed his coat and moved towards Lenny. She put her hands up to ward him off. "Hold on. I don't want any kissing or anything."

"Damn woman. You cold," he said.

"She's just nervous, that's all," I said. "Don't be mean, Lenny."

"I'm not kissing," she muttered.

"Where you gonna go?" Green hat looked at me.

"I'm staying here," I said, looking around for a chair but there was none.

"You stayin' here? With us?" he asked.

"Yea. That's the deal. I stay here. Is that a problem?"

"No," he said. "Not a problem at all." He sat down on his messy bed and pulled off his boots.

Lenny shrugged off her coat, removed her boots, then looked at me. I read her mind. "Just get under the blankets and take your clothes off," I said. I knew she hated being naked in front of anybody. She looked at the bed and I also knew she didn't want to get into his unmade dirty bed. "It's okay. Just do it."

She got under the messy sheets, stripped off her shirt, bra, slacks, and underwear, handing them to me. I placed them on the dresser top, turned to see that green hat had removed his hat and stood completely nude, his Afro smashed down where the hat had nested. I couldn't look at Lenny for fear we'd bust out laughing. Stripped of his hustler trappings, his cool demeanor had taken one look and run. Now he was just a skinny, gawky boy with funny hair. I could barely manage the words, "You sure you're not too cold or anything?" Lenny mumbled no and green hat slipped his naked bones under the blankets, climbing on top of her. Lenny was always so composed and tough that it was strange seeing her eyes suddenly look a little unsure. I took her hand and held it. "It's okay. Just try to relax." I sat on the edge of the bed, making them both move over a bit. Green hat glanced at me with a vague look of disbelief before he refocused on Lenny.

There was movement under the sheets and green hat buried his head in her neck, bucked himself up, and pushed Lenny's legs apart. He must have tried to get her ready with his fingers because I saw her face change drastically. She grimaced, "Ow." Then he put both hands up by her head and pushed his torso into her. She opened her mouth and let out a small scream. "Shit that hurts!"

"It'll be okay now," I promised, still managing to hold her hand. But it wasn't okay. She grimaced and he moved up and down on top of her, bouncing the bed, making me readjust. "Try to relax. It's better if you relax," I encouraged. His black arms on either side of her head made her face look even whiter. I caught a rare scared expression in her eyes.

"Hey, hey, stop, that's enough. Stop!" I pushed green hat's shoulder and he stopped. His forehead was sweaty. He let out a frustrated sigh as he rolled off her. "You want me to show you how to do it?" I asked Lenny. She nodded. She got out of bed without caring who saw her bare body. I stripped, climbed in. "Okay," I said to green hat. He slid on top of me. I allowed my body to relax and meld into his. He pushed his erection against me. My body responded. I was able to accommodate him without paying too much attention. I looked at Lenny as I let my body move with his rhythm. "See, you just let your body move with his. You wanna try it again?"

"No!" she was vehement, and I went back to finishing the sex. He came. I jumped up and got my clothes on. "Bye," we tossed over our shoulder as we left green hat sitting on his messy bed muttering what sounded like, "You twos crazy."

"Congratulations, you lost your virginity," I said outside as the cold blasted us, searing any uncovered skin, trying to find entrance into our heavy coats.

"Yea finally," she said. "I'm starving. Are you hungry?"
"Yes! Di'Napolis. Wanna?"

"Yea. Let's split a spaghetti." We tucked our faces into our scarves, the winter posture of every Minnesotan, and slugged through the frozen tundra with visions of warm bread and butter and a plate of steaming spaghetti prompting haste.

I pulled off the freeway and noted the absence of activity. It was getting cold and it was a Tuesday night. A few deserted markets and some lonely motels weakly stood their ground, and I was happy to drive past them towards the brighter lights of my destination.

6

Seattle, 1980

Marriage is for women the commonest mode of livelihood, and the total amount of undesired sex endured by women is probably greater in marriage than in prostitution.
    Bertrand Russell, British philosopher, logician, essayist, political activist, Nobel Laurette, 1872 – 1970.

The Red Lion Hotel lounged comfortably along the Pacific Coast Highway, a hop, skip from Sea-Tac Airport. It's parking lot, the size of a football field, curled snugly around the hotel's perimeter, the hotel elongated enough so that I was able to easily slip in one of the side entrances unseen, avoiding the well-lit lobby. I spit my gum to the ground before making my entrance, cherished the inelegance of that moment, spit it hard, then set off down the plush carpeted halls. Given the frequency of my visits, the Red Lion felt familiar and was a friendly host, graciously greeting me by having the elevator door open and waiting, which I obliged, pushing number four.

 I was already tired and wondered how I was going to get through the hour. I didn't feel like going. The work was boring, plus I always had to push hands off my nipples with some kind of excuse. The clients always wanted to pinch, tweak, pull on nipples and breasts. I was well-practiced in defensive moves. My arm shot up to ward off pinching fingers.

"Oh, jeez, I'm so sensitive I can't handle being touched right now. I'm getting my period."

"You're always getting your period," my regulars would say, and I would respond, "I know! It's awful!" The girls would laugh. Trudy would say, "I don't know how you have so many regulars. They can't touch you anywhere." No fingers allowed in body cavities either. Fingers were too dirty.

I had to give myself an assignment to get through the hour. Learn one new thing. That always made time go faster. It was a good way to deal with depression too, if you had it in you to really find something new to learn. The key was, it had to be completely new, something so new it grabbed all your attention, especially the part of the brain that likes to mope around. Like learning that there was such a thing as quantum physics where certain particles go faster than the speed of light and nothing behaves according to existing rules. I liked that kind of thing. But it could be anything. A new musical instrument you've never heard of, or whatever. I would learn one new thing. Learn two new things? No, stick with one for tonight. Learn one new thing I didn't know anything about.

Room 427 was near the end of the hallway. There were a few trays on the floor, I glanced at the cups, plates, silverware. They always looked so pretty and I considered taking something but nothing was actually irresistible enough to make the effort. Sometimes, when I was tired of being a call girl, a feeling which had recently grown — every job gets tiresome - I would think about the life attached to that tray and wish I could walk through that hotel door into another life.

I lightly tapped on 427. It opened to a face easy on the eyes, a sprinkle of silver running through thick dark hair, blue eyes warm, smile at the ready, no nerves. Definitely not a first timer.

"Hello Tom? I'm Michelle. How are you this evening?" I extended my hand. He congenially responded with a perfect grasp. Warm, dry, firm. I had a thing about hands. Liked masculine hands, no long nails, no manicures, nothing overly attended to. I briefly looked down. Liked his hands a lot. Masculine. Strong.

"Hello Michelle. Please come in." I stepped into room 427, which was a little like stepping into my own living room, I spent so much time in these rooms. The problem with familiarity is that you get a little too comfortable. You couldn't get comfortable when working outcall. You had to stay present, alert.

"Thank you. You're from San Francisco?" Bright smile.

"Yes, Marin County." His tone so easy I could have taken a nap in it.

"Well, welcome to Seattle. You're just in time for some rain as usual," I smiled, waited for him to laugh, which he did.

"Oh yes, I know. It's awfully rainy up here."

"How long are you in our fair city?" I asked.

"Until Thursday."

"And you just got in today?"

"Yes, this afternoon."

"All business or do you get to relax a little?"

"All work, I'm afraid. But I already know Seattle pretty well. I get up here every couple of months or so."

"Yes, it's a nice place." I didn't like it but most people did. "Do you mind if I take a look at your ID and plane ticket? Helen probably already told you to have it ready?" I smiled.

"Oh, of course. Here you are." He picked up his plane ticket from the desk, handed it to me. "Thank you," I murmured, reading the ticket. Name, dates fit. "Great. Perfect. Do you mind if I take a quick look at your driver's license please?"

A couple of business suits hung in the closet space. His suitcase was open on the second bed. A pile of papers lay on the table. I glanced down at the papers as he picked through his wallet. Bain Consulting, San Francisco.

"Here you go." He handed his driver's license to me. I checked the name, address, photo, birthdate, expiration. Born in 1940. He was in his early forties.

"Thanks so much. Are these your work papers?" I gave him back his driver's license and focused on the table. "Do you mind if I take a peek?"

"You are pretty thorough," he said amiably.

I smiled into his face. "Yes, I am."

"I guess you see all kinds," he said.

"Most people are pretty nice." Didn't like that last comment, tacky. I allowed a seepage of disapproval. "May I use your phone to check in with the agency please?"

"Oh, of course. And, um, I'm sorry if I offended you."

"You did," I said in the nicest tone. "That was a little indelicate, don't you think?"

"Yes, it was. I apologize."

I looked at his face. A bit of non-composure.

"It's okay. I'm sensitive sometimes." I walked to the phone. Helen's voice smooth as a silk braid. "Elite Massage."

"Hi, it's Michelle. I'm checking in with Tom at the Red Lion."

"Hi baby. Everything okay?"

"Yes, peachy."

"Call me in an hour, honey."

"Okay."

"How do you like your consulting work?" I smiled. Sat at the little round table.

"Oh, I like it a lot. Can I get you a drink or anything?"

"No, I'm good, thank you. What kind of consulting do you actually do?"

"Well," he sat in the chair opposite me. "Tomorrow I'll go visit a company and address work efficiency."

"Oh, hmm. What does that actually mean?"

Jolette

"Really? Are you interested in this?"

"Yea, I'm curious. Are you what's considered a strategy or a business consultant?"

"Oh," eyebrows raised slightly. "Well, some might consider what I do to be under business consulting, but what I really do is operations."

"And that involves cutting costs?"

"Yes, mainly cutting costs, optimizing profit."

"Oh, I see." I still needed to learn something. "Say, who's the Secretary of Defense?"

"Secretary of Defense? Caspar Weinberger. You like politics?"

"Yes, it's interesting. Shoot, I never remember Caspar Weinberger. It's sort of an odd first name."

"Yes, you don't hear that name often in the states. His mother named him after a good friend of hers. His father nicknamed him Cap."

"Oh really!" Bingo. "How do you know that?"

"Oh, I'm sure I read it somewhere. You know, Caspar originally comes from Gasper, which was an ancient name. It meant treasurer and came from the Persian Gulf. Caspar was also the name of one of the three wise men who traveled to see the baby in the manager, aka Jesus."

"Ha, aka Jesus. Are you religious?"

"Definitely not."

I laughed. "Well, that's interesting. How do you know all of that?"

"I read a lot, especially history."

"Okay, so Caspar comes from Gasper from ancient times, somewhere around the Persian Gulf, wherever that is. Somewhere over there. Okay, good. I will definitely remember his name now." I glanced at his hands. I sure liked those hands. He laughed too.

"Do you want to know where the Persian Gulf is?"

"Yea, where is it?"

Jolette

"It's in Western Asia along the Mediterranean Sea and is bordered by Iran, Kuwait, Qatar, and Saudi Arabia. Are you familiar with those countries?"

"Yes, I am." I sure was. We got a lot of clients from Qatar, Kuwait, and Saudi Arabia, all of them students. I had a regular from Qatar, the smallest Arab nation but maybe the richest thanks to the earth's regional gift of oil. Arabs were not my favorite. Too arrogant, too opinionated, worse than New Yorkers. June said they never showered. She said they just used cologne instead. She would know. She spent a lot of time in their company. She was everyone's favorite, especially Middle Easterners. June had a pretty face. It was soft, just like her voice, and she was unendingly patient and sweet with long dark hair, a fuller figure. She was also intelligent, liked to laugh, and listened well with compassion. She was perfect. Everyone loved her. I did too. Unfortunately, or maybe fortunately, I had much less patience, was edgy with authority. Eventually I just refused to see them. No Arabs and no coke freaks, never ever. Coke freaks were a pain. They would never come, throwing off my choreographed routine, focusing way too much on the penis. It was never an easy one hour appointment. Sometimes they'd book entire nights and never come. I hated it. You could not pay me enough. Older, mild-mannered men ensconced in the white-collar world, most of them consultants, were by far my preference.

"Can I tell you why I like politics?" I was still a little animated what with the Caspar revelation.

"Sure."

"Because it's a magnified version of human behavior. It's human behavior but becomes macroscopic. It turns into the behavior of countries. You know what I mean?"

"Yes, right. That's an interesting perspective."

"And the consequences are extreme. So, it's human behavior magnified, which makes it even more sad and entertaining and lethal. You know."

"Could I ask you a question, Michelle?"

"Oh no, what?"

"Why do you say oh no?"

"What are you going to ask me? Why am I in this business?"

"Well, yes. You could do anything. Why this?"

Even seemingly intelligent men assumed that if a woman had a working brain to any degree, she would not be engaged in prostitution. It seemed ironic to me that selling sex was not deemed appropriate in this sex-saturated, lust-driven, penis-dominated world, due to a bullshit interpretation of morals cast from a patriarchal, overbearing religious cult, Christianity. I'm not talking coerced sexual services or pedophilia or anything damaging like that. I'm just talking two adults, an agreed upon business deal. I sighed. People had so many misconceptions about the sex industry.

"Oh god. It's not that big of a deal really and it just works for me right now. The hours are flexible, pay is good." It was true. I was grateful I'd found work where I could make decent money with easy hours.

"But you could do a lot of other jobs that are less dangerous."

"I don't wanna do a lot of other jobs. I'm not going to do just anything for work. I'm not going to waitress. I already did that a ton. Or be a secretary, ugh. I'm not going to do anything a million hours a day unless I love it."

"So you love this?"

"Ha. Not exactly. But it's not a million hours a day. It's minimum time, maximum pay, kind of what you probably counsel your clients to do." I grinned. "Anyway, it's temporary. It's okay for now."

"But it's not good for you." His blue eyes were kind, still I was mildly irritated. Straight people never understood. Selling sex was always such a big deal. Probably that had something to do with the woman being in control and making a lot of money.

"I'm fine. It's not that bad. Why isn't it good for me? Anyway, I'm going to graduate from UW and then get into journalism." I stood up. "I'm going to use your restroom now. I'll be right back. Don't go anywhere." I smiled, bent slightly to introduce my lips to his. His penis brain immediate-

Jolette

ly took over, the surge of his heat palpable. So much for all the concern about my welfare.

"Sure, go ahead," he murmured.

"Thank you. Could you put the fee on the table please?" I murmured back with my customary exit line as I withdrew to the bathroom. My request for the fee was always made at that precise moment for two reasons. First, someone told me not to touch the money until you were certain the guy wasn't a cop. The minute you touched the money you were agreeing to solicitation, could be arrested on the spot, so I never initially placed a finger on the bills, only requested the fee after all ID had been checked, then money was left on the table until the grand finale concluded. Of course, if you were dealing with police, you'd be busted the minute any sexual act occurred but not touching the money bought you a little time to decide if the guy was safe or not. I made mistakes twice, was arrested in Seattle in 1984 and 1986.

The second reason I always asked for the fee to be put on the table while I was in the bathroom was so I could just scoop it quickly from the table later, not having to watch them fumble with wallets. No punctuation on the moment.

Inside the bathroom I glanced at his toiletries, normal stuff, slipped off my dress, looked into the mirror, yawned at myself, stretched, out the bathroom door and, lights dimmed, the performance began. The ballet de sex, choreographed, harmonious, the beginning, middle, final conclusion, no encore. All in eight to twelve minutes. Perhaps it was true that I felt slight pleasure due to this particular client's pleasing aesthetics combined with compatible congeniality. Plus his attractive hands. Perhaps it was also true that the most pleasing event of the night was the discovery of Caspar Weinberger's name. If I remember correctly, both were true.

7

Anatomy

Too many people think sex is related to love. It rarely is. Mostly it's anatomy. Designed, with bells and whistles, to promote procreation.
                                            Author Unknown

With every client there was a golden moment of opportunity to mitigate my workload profoundly; penetration, that threshold broached, which launched the body into pleasurable orbit, provided a split second which, if utilized with believable sound effects – a gasp, an "oh god" or better yet, a small yelp – could thrust the penis brain into the stratosphere, effectively cutting my efforts to incite explosion by fifty percent. But it had to be believable. Anything less only caused distraction and if one was tired from a busy night, could only muster a heavily whispered, "Oh!" placed into the client's ear, well, that could work, but it had to have at least a salt grain of credibility.

Penetration's sidekick was lubrication. They needed each other like a pen needs paper. What turns on the slippery mucus faucet for women are two pea-sized glands, invisible to the eye, tucked under the skin on either side of the vagina, called Bartholin's glands named after guess who, Mr. Bartholin, a Danish anatomist in the seventeenth century. Somehow – pause here to reflect — he discovered that when the body became aroused, extra quantities of blood were delivered to the genitalia, which encouraged Bartholin's glands to squirt lube as if greasing wheels and, as in Goldilocks and the Three Bears, it couldn't be too much and it couldn't be too little. It had to be just right.

As a young woman, my ability to generate the slick slime was geyser comparable. No K-Y Jelly needed. Seemingly arousal occurred automatically, my body having its own ideas with no regard to my state of mind. As witnessed when I was raped in my teenage years, my body ignored my brain and, to my shock, began to move in response to my attacker's forced penetration. I firmly shut it down but remained stunned by that bodily betrayal. In later years, somewhere around thirty-five and much to my dismay, my vagina went through its own climate change, from lush moist jungle to southwest desert, arid with prickly cacti abrading any penis that might stray into its midst. This was painful to everyone and no amount of K-Y seemed enough to wet the far reaches of my parched vaginal dust bowl. It could have been that my Bartholin's glands had become obstructed but no medical authority ever ventured that explanation. Instead I gooped my vaginal cavity with a variety of synthetic lubricants that proved to be as effective as a single sprinkler in the Mojave Desert.

When, years later, subject to a sudden dry vagina, penetration became painful, work became tougher and sex-for-pleasure almost impossible. I didn't know why there seemed to be a sudden shift in my vaginal environment and gynecologists had no explanation either. I endured by gritting my teeth. Sex was necessary for my work and as part of any intimate relationship. A long-lasting, intimate relationship considered the gold cup, proving you were worthy.

8

The Rapes, 1970, 1972

I could tell you having a penis shoved inside of me without my permission harmed me. I could tell you I cried. That would be well understood. But I didn't cry, and though it was only my second sexual experience, I didn't feel damaged except for my poor face which had been pulverized. I didn't feel that my entity, my prized self, was attached to my sex. I was angry, yes. Furious that I'd been beaten into submission, yes. But it was not a shattering of me. No.

Jolette

There were two rapes, one at fourteen, the second at sixteen.
    Age: Fourteen. Rape location: Donnybrook International Speedway, Brainerd, Minnesota.

Donnybrook was built in 1968 by a Northwest Airlines pilot, George Montgomery, who wanted someplace to break out his 427 Cobra, whatever that was. So he acquired eight-hundred acres, cut a coarse three-mile track featuring a one-mile straight followed by two sharp curves making it the longest straightaway with fastest turns on a racecourse in the United States. That was enough to garner attention from motorsports racing nuts, its notoriety spread like an oil slick. Its party reputation attached like a groupie. I was fourteen when it beckoned.

Jolette

"There's a big party at Donnybrook," I said to my new friend Maude whose blonde hair tumbled mid-back. Her spirit open, humor wry, she was a willing and able hitchhiking partner.

"Let's go, okay?" Maude, a good-natured thumbs-up, met me halfway between her house and mine on Rice Creek Terrace in Anoka, an undulating, winding street where large homes could look out their back windows at the corresponding creek, normally a compatible companion but with a wicked streak for it took the life of a small child one year while a classmate was babysitting him. She was in sixth grade. He was her two-year-old nephew. She went to the bathroom while he played in the backyard. When she came out he was gone, had fallen into the creek. They found his body swept up against the embankment some feet further down. Last I heard she'd pulled out most of her hair and was transferred to a different school.

Maude waved in the distance. We stopped to do our ceremonial greeting, hands circled up, palms met above head, circled down, heads bowed, then wild clapping.

"University or Central?" Maude asked when we met. She smeared chapstick over her mouth. Winter punished everybody's lips. We'd already dispensed the mandatory lie to our parents — we were with a friend and her parents for the weekend, camping up north.

"Central" I responded, and Maude pulled her cap down over her pink-tipped ears, her blonde hair a cascade of movement over her shoulders, shining as if just polished, the only brightness in the day's dismal cast. We walked to Central Avenue where I took first position, out in front, an exhilarated toss of my arm, thumb out, ready for anything. Maude took second, hiding from the disagreeable elements behind me, tucked into her peacoat, head nuzzled into a winter scarf, hands shoved deep into pockets, her nose already red from winter's rough coddling. Donnybrook was 140 miles north, ETA probably three hours.

Nothing was outstanding about the first car that stopped, a four-door Buick, two smiling, friendly guys, hair too short for my taste. Their heads swiveled to greet us as we climbed in the back. They were going all the way to Donnybrook they said. They'd heard about the same party. They broke out some weed. Maude inhaled a few tokes. I shook my head. I didn't like pot. It made me too paranoid. I lit a cigarette instead. We talked a little. Driver guy turned up the radio, *Purple Haze*. I'd already looked at Maude, touched my nose, not interested in these guys. She'd double tapped hers, definitely not interested. It was dark by the time we hit Donnybrook. We found a campfire flanked by a small huddle of people. Nothing much was going on. We were cold. Disappointed. The guy who'd done all the driving approached me.

"We're going to go to a shed to sleep. It should be better here tomorrow. Do you two wanna come with?"

Okay, I shrugged but Maude was resistant. She didn't like the guys, and said no. They talked to her awhile. She relented, and we headed back to the car. The driver sent me a big grin. "How'd ya like to drive?"

"Sure," I said, and got behind the wheel. He instructed my driving. I laughed and drove us far out of town, then off the main highway down a dirt road through a big field with nothing else around. Then kerplunk, the car just stopped.

"Shit," the driver guy said.

"Out of gas, man," said the other.

We can walk the rest of the way, they agreed. By this time the guy who'd let me drive didn't have a big smile anymore. He was getting moody and roughly flung his arm around my shoulders while we stumbled through the dark until reaching a small shed. I ignored the arm around my shoulder but now that we were inside the shed, driver guy started slobbering on me with a wet mouth. I pulled away and he slapped my face with stunning force. I reeled from the sting and surprise but didn't fall.

"Lay down," he growled.

"No," I said, and he backhanded my face, slapped and repeated. My tongue stirred as fluid poured into my mouth. Blood. My rage was hot. It lifted its head, "No!" I screamed. The back of his hand blasted my head again. My head spun. I wobbled. My eyes were open but my head had dropped. All I could see were his legs in jeans and boots. Whomp whomp, backhanded, slapped again. My head and mind became numb. As if I had no feeling at all anymore.

"Leave her alone!" Maude burst from the floor where she sat with the other guy who was muttering something like, Wow man, I've never seen him like this before.

The rapist turned to Maude and whaled a huge slap across her face. She burst into tears. He slapped me again and this time I fell to the floor where he was on me in an instant. My pants were pulled off, not an easy feat, can't pull pants over boots easily, so he pulled off one of my boots, yanked one pant leg off, and jerked his pants down, not taking off his boots. Just slammed his skinny very white butt between my legs. Somehow he managed to shove his smallish parcel into my hard-to-find opening under a tangle of young pubic hair, grunting and pushing. He suddenly yelled, then all motion stopped. He flopped over, a pile of wetness left in my crotch. I lay dead still for two minutes, then pulled my jeans up over the mess, looked at Maude, who was wide-eyed, watching me. We heard snoring, both guys were asleep. We quietly got up and left.

This was my second sexual experience.

The sun was just lifting over the earth's rim, gentle rays beginning to warm the frozen field. Our footsteps crunched with each step. We didn't murmur a word until far out of audio range. "That fucker," I said. "Yea," agreed Maude. "That fucking asshole." She looked at me. "Oh god, your face." I brought a tentative hand to my cheek. My fingers touched puffiness, the pressure of my fingertip was enough to produce pain. It hurt especially around my left eye, which barely opened. "Shit," I said.

"It's really swollen," Maude said, her eyes concerned, her face a shade whiter than usual. She looked shook up.

"How about my lip? Is it cut bad?"

"Yes."

My mouth felt stiff, hard to move, I could taste blood. I looked down the dirt road. "There's the car," I pointed. We wordlessly headed to the car, opened the door. On the floor of the backseat were a few tools, a hammer. I reached for the hammer and looked at Maude. "I'm gonna break the windshield."

"Yes, do it."

Windshields don't break easily. Introduced to the automobile in 1904, they were first made of simple plate glass, a feature which hailed the term "glass necklace" for those whose unfortunate heads went through the windshield. By 1966 the glass had become laminated – a layer of plastic between two sheets of glass – providing better protection to those who were accident prone, trauma caused a yielding, bending of the windshield as opposed to sending shards of glass flying.

Naturally I didn't know that, but was a little unsure while wielding the hammer, staring at the windshield in a moment of contemplation. I was afraid. What if the two guys heard me smashing the glass. Would they come running? I tapped the windshield with the hammer's head, then raised my arm and brought the hammer down harder. It almost bounced off. That fucker, I thought of the driver and raised my arm again, this time delivering a blow with all my might. It jarred my swollen head but I repeated the action a multitude of times, surprised the glass wasn't breaking. Instead it only caved slightly. I continued striking and finally, it yielded to force. Much like I had only an hour earlier. A large portion of the windshield bowed, sending spider-webbed cracks across its horizon, one deft blow caused a hole to appear. I threw the hammer to the ground.

"Let's get out of here," I said to Maude, and with the taste of blood still in my mouth, I left feeling I'd delivered at least a bit of justice.

We hung out for another day at Donnybrook, attached ourselves to a group of people who gasped at the sight of my face, vowing adamantly to protect us should the rapist and his friend return. Maude found ice for my traumatized head and some of the swelling went down.

When I got home, I hid my face. It wasn't hard to do. It wasn't like my family ever really looked at each other anyway. It was more like we avoided each other. That seemed more comfortable.

Jolette

The bruising faded. The semblance of normality resumed.

Age: Sixteen. Rape location: San Jose, California.

The counterculture allure of Berkeley in the early 1970s shone like a beacon promising excitement and adventure. I had quite an interest in those categories and felt no compunction about hitchhiking from Minneapolis to Berkeley one stultifying Minnesota summer. My parents had thrown up their arms, surrendering any protest — having already been through a half dozen runaway ordeals — and gave permission for me to hitchhike to Berkeley. It was futile to impose sanctions. They felt incapacitated with me, their eldest child, and were inept in the face of such constant disobedience. "Fine, go then," they said. I needed no extra assurance, was out the door in a flash with a backpack and my new dog, Kapola, a small shepherd mix puppy from a box of puppies a student was giving away.

Throwing my thumb to the road, I abandoned the unpleasant household — an unfriendly place of cold looks and sharp tongues — that I'd been born into, and took a deep inhale, feeling intoxicated while gazing down a highway, no end in sight, all prospects open, the world brightened with freedom. I would make Colorado, nine hundred miles from Minneapolis, in two days, find a youth hostel to stay in for a few days, then set off again. Kapola and I had a deal. One day we'd eat people food, the next day we'd get him dog food and I'd eat the milk biscuits. He walked beside me down the road with no coaxing, no leash. We shared everything.

We hit Berkeley ten days after leaving Minneapolis. First stop was Telegraph Avenue, a smorgasbord of colorful visuals, the sidewalks packed with a whirlwind of street vendors, crafts set up on tapestries covering the ground, musicians with guitars, drums, harmonicas, flutes, the music vibrating airwaves for blocks, headbands tied over waves of hair, fringe coats, tunics, flowing dresses, peace symbols on ripped jeans and jackets, bare feet the most common footwear, the scent of pot and patchouli permeating the air, psychedelic colors leaving no empty space on the sides of buildings. Kapola and I walked down Telegraph absorbing it all, our senses on overdrive. I knew we had to make money. We were hungry and chose a corner. Kapola sat by my side while I panhandled. "Spare change? Spare change? Spare change so I can feed me and my dog?" We made enough to eat, enough to crash at a nearby youth hostel, a communal room with bunk beds filling up at night with longhaired travelers, the air permeated with patchouli oil. I fell asleep content that I'd entered a new dimension.

On our second day, we met a man playing a flute in People's Park. His hair was dark, curly, and fell over his shoulders. He wore a red headband across his forehead. His jeans hung from his slight frame. I watched as he lifted his flute to his lips and I began to dance. Kapola ran in circles as I lifted my arms and twirled my long thrift store dress worn over shredded jeans, belted with scarves. We struck up a friendship, hung out for the next few days, walking the streets, stealing food from the grocery store, panhandling, spending nights at the youth hostel, sharing a bed, though no sex, not even an inkling that direction, until one day he disappeared into the shadows to stick a needle in his vein.

"You wanna come with?" he asked me. "You wanna try a little heroin?"

"Okay," I agreed, but fell behind while talking with two guys in the Army, dressed in fatigues, hair shorn. When they heard I was going to try heroin, one said to me, "Naw, you don't wanna try that. It's not a good idea."

Something about the sound of his voice, his tone, his words ,struck me as perfectly agreeable. "Okay, I won't," I responded. Heroin flutist disappeared. Kapola and I tucked into the youth hostel for the night. I could hear someone playing the guitar in the street while falling asleep.

By the next day the heroin flutist had not returned to the hostel. Kapola and I sat on a curb, my boots kicking through the dust. I didn't know what to do next. I'd been on Telegraph Avenue for a week. I was tired. Maybe I'd head to LA I felt unsure, and was a bit mopey. I missed heroin flutist, missed having a companion, but he might never return. I threw a thumb out.

The car that stopped had a smashed-in passenger door. It wouldn't open, so I got in the backseat with Kapola. The man, dark-skinned with a big smile, was very friendly. He chattered away, said he was going as far as San Jose, fifty miles south of Berkeley. By the time we got to San Jose I'd moved into the front seat because he was so nice. Stevie Wonder came on the radio. The man smiled, and sang, looking at me. *You are the sunshine of my life, that's why I'll always be around, you are the apple of my eye...* forever linking that song to that day.

The singer said he was going back up to Berkeley after making a few stops in San Jose. I decided I didn't want to go to Los Angeles after all. I wanted to return to Berkeley, to see my heroin flutist friend again. I waited in the car while the singer rapist made his stops.

He'd been gone about an hour, when he returned, he didn't look at me. His mood had completely changed. He seemed flattened. He said he needed gas for his car and knew where to siphon it. He drove us to an industrial area, pulled up to a truck, got a tube from the trunk of the car, stuck it into the truck's gas tank, put his mouth on the end of it, sucked the gas up, got the flow going, inserted the tube's opposite end into his car's gas tank. I'd never seen anything like it; him sucking up gas was as guttural as his voice was starting to sound. I got a lot quieter and was sorry I was in the front seat where I was trapped. I thought about getting in the back seat again. I thought about getting out and running and began to sidle over to the driver's door, Kapola in my arms, when the driver's door opened.

"Move over," he snapped, not nice at all. "Get back over there."

I moved over, looked out the window into the darkness. Where was I? In the middle of San Jose somewhere, in an industrial area. He drove for a bit, then suddenly pulled the car to the side of the road, looked at me, tried to kiss me.

"No," I protested.

His face tightened. "Get in the backseat and take your pants off," he grunted, "or I'll kill your dog." He was unrecognizable from the smiling man who had first offered me a ride. He circled his hands around Kapola's small neck. "Climb over the seat," he said. I obeyed. He let Kapola go, climbed over the seat and climbed on top of me, huffing and puffing like an out of shape marathoner, roughly pulled at my jeans. They came off. I felt pressure on my abdomen as he pushed my legs apart, fumbling around, trying to jam his penis inside of me. My body automatically began to respond. I shut it down. Crazy body. I stiffened my legs. This made him angry. "Relax," he said. I turned my head to the side as far as I could, kept my legs locked. He jerked up and down on me, making frustrated sounds then, exasperated, got off. "You need to relax," he said, mad. I pulled my jeans on as fast as I could. Kapola was in the front seat, quiet, just sitting. "Let's try again," he said. "No!" I screamed. He was angry, yelled, "You bitch," pushed open the back door, and threw my backpack in the street. I stretched into the front seat, grabbed Kapola just as his slimy fingers attached to my back and I was launched out the door, falling into the street, Kapola in my arms. The man, a blur, as he jumped back into the car and it sped off.

The silence was startling, the only sound was the banging of my heart. Must have been around midnight. I stood up, looked around, modest homes under night's blanket were slumbering, except for one house where a front porch light shone and a lamp in the window lent a soft glow. I hesitated briefly and knocked. A surprised woman opened the door a crack.

"I'm sorry to bother you but I've just been raped and thrown out of a car." I was polite and very calm. So calm. As if trauma had a tranquilizing effect.

She stared at me a moment, then invited me in, and called the police. Entrance into her home was like slipping into another universe, her humble square living room was homey with a comfy couch, chairs, and walls proudly bearing pictures of smiling faces. It spoke of family, love, and safety. I wanted to look at all the photos. "You have such a nice home," I said, strolling through her living room with Kapola in my arms, as if in an art gallery. "I really like all of your pictures. I really like your house."

"Thank you," she said, a quiet woman, she said no more.

Jolette

The police arrived. No one believed that I'd been raped. I was too composed, not hysterical at all. I was taken to a juvenile detention center, given a bed and one of the police officers, a female with a nice smile, said she'd take Kapola for the night since he wasn't allowed in juvy.

We were flown back to Minneapolis the next day, suddenly transported back to the land I forever wanted to leave. On the day of my return, my parents pulled me aside. I felt instantly queasy, their discomfort contagious as an illness, crippling my insides, making me hate them for some reason. My father cleared his throat, my mother in attendance, the atmosphere best described as icky.

"I'm only going to ask you this once, then we'll never talk about it again. Were you really raped?"

"Yes," I said indignant, scornfully wrinkling my nose at the question, an intense embarrassment seeped through my body. I covered it with irritation. "God, I can't believe you asked me that."

"Don't use that word, girl," my mother angered at my blasphemy.

"Oh god," I stormed from the room. They were useless as a source of comfort. As anything really. Life was better when I was as far away from them as possible.

Kapola was taken to the vet by my father a week later. He was diagnosed with distemper. The vet said he would die, so my father handed him over to be euthanized. Nobody told me until he was already dead. I was too stunned to cry, too stunned to be angry. He had been my good friend. I had let him play with another dog. That dog had been sick. I shouldn't have let him play with that other dog. I stumbled, my heart hurt. The death of my Kapola far more devastating than, for example, the intrusion of a raging penis into only my flesh.

9

Seattle, 1980

Here's what I tell myself in those moments of uncertainty, of feeling inferior or wrong or so alone. I tell myself it's my world too. Mine for the experience. Mine for the choices. Mine to do what I want to do in this earthly realm of unknown destinations. It's my world too.

Jolette

"I hate it when they want a massage before sex," I complained to Trudy. We were at a club. A little early, the crowd sparse, we kept a casual eye on the door monitoring newcomers. I sipped a heated Grand Marnier brandy from a snifter, which was hard to drink from, my nose bumping into the opposite side of the glass when I lifted it to my lips. "I hate these glasses! How am I supposed to drink from this?" I complained as Trudy slurped a vodka diet seven. She was always trying to lose weight. I told her to quit inhaling entire pizzas at one sitting, but she loved her immediate gratification. "I hate doing massage before sex. It should either be one or the other, but not both," I continued.

"Why? What's the big deal? Just rub their backs," Trudy said, her eyes scouting the darkened room, disco music a mild background throb, not yet full blast.

"Because it's like massage is different from sex. Sex is more basic, like peeing. Massage is, I don't know, just different, so to mix the two is hard."

"You're messing with yourself. Don't get so analytical about the whole thing. Just rub their backs for two minutes," Trudy said. Her teeth were slightly bucked, her chin thrust forward when she spoke. "I give massages all the time," she continued, shrilly confident as was her style. "It's not a big deal. You're overthinking it."

"It's not my thinking that's getting in the way." I glanced at the door. Several men were entering, one stood out, tall with an ebony patina, a face of handsome proportion. A gorgeous smile. Trudy followed my glance. "Um, nice," she said, her eyes filling with purpose.

"It's not my thinking that's the problem," I continued, our eyes pinned on the handsome ebony man. "It's my feelings. It's like, I massage and it's just different energy and I sort of open up and then I'm supposed to just snap right back into penis land, where all the man can think about is coming. It pisses me off."

"You're way overthinking it," Trudy said. We were quiet for a minute, watching the handsome man walk across the floor with his friends. His eyes swept the room, caught us staring at him. I turned my head, but Trudy kept with a bold stare and I saw her engage and smile. "That is one beautiful man. I want him." Trudy said, then abruptly turned to me. "Michelle."

I narrowed my eyes, "What?"

"Come on. Please."

I groaned, "I don't wanna do a freebie. It's my night off and besides I have a problem I didn't get to finish talking about." Of course I knew what she wanted. Because Trudy had slightly bucked teeth and a bit of heft to her hips it was more difficult for her to snatch up the men she desired. Unlike me, she had a robust appetite for sex on her night off. She wanted to use me as bait. If she could mention a threesome to ebony man, she would probably get her wish. It wouldn't be the first time.

Trudy turned to me, gave me her full attention now that she wanted something. "You are just way overthinking the whole thing."

"I told you it's not my thinking that's the problem. It's my feelings. I can't stand it."

"Convince yourself it's not a real massage or something. I don't know. Don't get so emotional about it."

"But I'll know I'm just trying to fool myself. I'm having a hard time with it," I insisted, whining just a little. "I really am, Trud. I don't know how to handle it."

"Then don't do a massage at all. Tell them you don't do massage."

"That won't work either. You're not helping at all."

We both glanced over to handsome ebony man at the same time. He was sitting at a table across the room with a group of guys. He glanced back, smiled.

"Michelle, oh pleeeease."

"Oh, alright."

Trudy tucked her chin down, widened her eyes, her nose pointed straight at ebony like a bloodhound poised for the hunt. Once the line was cast, he was easily reeled to the table where Trudy snared him like the masterful sportswoman she was, her hand constantly touching his arm, smiling up into his face, quips right and left designed to charm, me smiling at her side, adding adorning commentary until Trudy bat her eyes and the words, "Why don't we all go to your place," slid from her red lipsticked mouth. From the disco to his bedroom took under an hour.

His skin, black velvet to the touch, covered a magnificent torso and a gorgeous set of broad shoulders with beautiful biceps, a lovely duo. Ebony leaned in towards me first, his hands everywhere. I responded easily but I didn't have the passion Trudy effused. Her fervor was contagious. She inserted herself and commanded the scene like a zealous director. Soon he and she were coupled in their own hot, sweaty ecosystem. I provided sound effects and small gestures. The moment rose to a swell and achieved climax.

Jolette

"I feel like I just had a big, yummy dessert," Trudy said as we exited ebony's luxury apartment building, balancing like ballet dancers in our very high heels as we maneuvered down the building's front stairs

"You owe me big time," I said.

"You loved it."

"Loved is not the right word."

"Well, you at least liked it. How could you not?"

"I only did it for you. I told you, I don't like doing freebies."

"Thank you. I did love it," Trudy giggled like a third grader.

"Anything to make you happy. I guess." I rolled my eyes.

She circled her arm around mine, her head came close. "He was scrumptious. Did you see how he got going with me? Boom boom boom boom boom."

"Yes, I saw his boom boom boom. Couldn't miss it. The whole bed was shaking."

Compartmentalization. The eukaryotic cell, a cell containing a nucleus, is an organism where the fundamental molecules of life reside. Think mitochondria, ribosomes, golgi apparatus. These fundamental molecules, referred to as organelles, function in separate compartments within the cell, separated by membrane. This compartmentalization allows each organelle to function more efficiently. There is similarity to the functioning of a human in its entity. Compartmentalization. A handy tool utilized for functioning ability, maintaining order and calm to balance overactive emotions. Sex for pleasure, sex for money, sex to help a friend. Each one for me was accorded a distinct room of its own.

Sex for money was the easiest. I understood it perfectly, could perform seamlessly. Sprinkled with a bit of affection and presto, I made in one hour what might otherwise take a few days, could make in one night what might otherwise take a week or longer. Done without compromising my standards, my standards consisted predominantly of not yielding to authority and not working a shit job for minimum pay.

The more difficult compartment, sex for pleasure, blurred into the arena of feelings that delivered a disproportionate level of chaos, thanks to internal uncertainties and confused messaging. But was hard to resist due to nature's instinctual rulings.

Naturally, the compartments were separated with strict boundaries. A client would never become anything more than a client. No exceptions although I spent more time with my regulars than with friends and we knew each other very well. It was the extreme opposite in the sex for pleasure category. Where, just after hello, I was naming our children.

The truth was, being with a man never felt comfortable or natural for me. Yet I subscribed to "happily-ever-after," just like millions of people. The fairy tale would prove elusive and catastrophic for me.

10

Seattle, 1981

> *Prostitutes hire out one tiny portion of their body. Employees sell countless huge portions of their lives.*
>   Mokokoma Mokhonoana, South African author, social critic, philosopher.

Liz and I had an appointment with Clarence, a regular with third-degree burn scars running like tire tracks over his chest and down his abdomen to his scorched pubic. His hands were webbed up pretty good, almost one hundred percent scarred, the tightened skin restricting movement. He was ten years older than me, his eyes intelligent, his mouth quick. "A house fire," Clarence told me when I'd already seen him a few times and lightly traced his scars with my fingertips.

"Does it hurt?" I asked.

"No, not really. Only sometimes in my hands."

I assumed his scarred body was the reason he used outcall, but I was wrong. Outcall was just easy, he explained. But maybe he was also exacting revenge on his girlfriend who was, oddly but true, a call girl at the other massage outcall in town. "Does it bother you that your girlfriend is working outcall?" I asked him on one of my weekly visits.

"No, darlin'. Not at all. She does her thing. I do mine," he said. I didn't believe him.

Liz had the longest eyelashes, like I've already said, and baby soft skin. Clarence, meeting Liz for the first time, was only too happy to put his dark limbs next to hers and entwine. I put my hands on his body in appropriate places while they got to know each other better, and wondered where Clarence got all his money. He called the agency at least a couple of times a week. His apartment was modest but clean, his attire the same. He told me he sold vacuum cleaners. I doubted it. It would be some time later that I learned he was supplying the crack houses in the seamier neighborhoods of Seattle. He told me he didn't use cocaine. Never liked the stuff. It was just business for him, he could make a lot of money. That, I did believe. I'd never seen him high, knew he didn't drink. He liked to remain in control of his faculties. I told him to be careful. "Always," he said. And that, I didn't believe. Sooner or later, shit always happens, especially in the drug world. Everyone knew that.

He was arrested a few years later. Sentenced to fifteen years for possession and dealing cocaine. We stayed in touch for a short time, writing letters. His writing deteriorated. He sounded broken. I felt bad for him. He hadn't seen it coming. Even though he should have.

Clarence was only one of my many regulars. The majority of my clients, company men who were in Seattle for job-related meetings, were pleasure seeking, wanting momentary escape via ejaculation and didn't mind fucking around on their wives. There were thousands of them. I mean truly, there is probably only about two percent of men who haven't paid for sex at some point in their life. That's my opinion. My educated opinion.

One of my favorite clients – I had a few – was from Oslo, Norway. He was lovely as a man could be, given that they all have an unruly amount of testosterone wreaking havoc. But Bjorn was a gentle man, as soft and refined as the sweaters and slacks he wore, his head a pretty silver, blue eyes thoughtful. He brought me gifts of beautiful Norwegian sweaters, ordered room service. We would have dinner while he made me laugh with quiet humor, his manner modest. He was so very kind I longed for a house with a white picket fence, if only he would agree to be my older Prince Charming, never mind his three children and wife awaiting him in Oslo. There were occasions our visits didn't culminate in physical ignition. Sometimes we'd just talk an hour or two, but even when sex was served, it was never unendurable, usually quick and simple. He was the best kind of client.

There was also handsome Michael, whose blonde head hailed highlights a surfer would envy, with eyes blue green as the sea. He had a strong jaw that I fell a little in love with, was tall, broad-shouldered, his hands generally cradling a drink.

Michael drank a lot. Which I didn't notice much until one day he met me at KING-TV where I had begun interning in the newsroom through the University of Washington. The newsroom felt like a comfortable fit. My job was to edit the Associated Press and United Press International news stories that came over the wire. I liked reshaping the paragraphs, cutting excess. Too late I realized that I had divulged too much personal information to handsome Michael, probably because of his extreme good looks. Probably I had been in a dreamy state when I'd told him I was an intern in the KING-TV newsroom every Sunday because one day, after my shift, as I walked from the KING-TV building, I was stopped dead in my tracks by the sight of Michael, idling by the curb in his white Porsche. The sunroof was open and I could see Michael's blonde head turned in my direction, his eyes glazed. He smiled. "Michelle! Hey Michelle, can I see you?"

"Oh my god, what are you doing here?"

"I wanted to see you." He grinned like he thought he was giving me a gift. "Michelle, can I take you to dinner?"

"Quit calling me Michelle," I hissed, looking around to make sure nobody was within hearing range. "Oh my god. I can't believe you came here. Okay, I'll meet you at your boat, but you can't come here again." I learned my lesson. Watch what you tell your clients otherwise they may crash into your so-called normal life.

Barry was a long-haul trucker who lived with his wife on Orcas Island, a pretty tourist haven filled with artists, two hours from Seattle, but stayed

Jolette

weekly at a humble Seattle motel due to his trucking schedule. By my first appointment with Barry, he had already been through all the girls at the agency. Over the next five years, I visited him weekly. He'd open the door to his small motel room and we'd talk. I'd cater to his sexual needs, then leave. As time went on, he started expecting more, was getting emotionally involved, wanted to nuzzle, wanted to kiss way too much.

Periodically he wanted to marry me, or at least run off with me. If he whined too much about being with me forever, it got annoying, but that's what could happen with regulars. They were too much work. They would start assuming they were actually a friend, or, god forbid, a boyfriend, and even though I saw them more often than my friends, they remained clients. They paid for sex. They paid for company. I judged them much as I was judged by society at large. They were a rung below me.

11

Minneapolis, 1974

The past has a smell. For me it was the smell of the creek behind our house where I played as a child. The creek with beavers, their foamy lodges, algae thick near the creek's bank as soil slipped into the water's universe of microscopic organisms. Every time I'm near a creek, molecules of that smell travel up my nostrils into memory banks, nudging open doors and I am always taken back.

Jolette

One cold dismal Minnesota morning, and what other kind was there, I dragged myself from the warm cave of my bed to get ready for school — my new alternative school, designed for kids who weren't pegged for conventional curriculum. After being expelled a year earlier from Anoka High School when I was in tenth grade, I fit that category.

I'd quickly thrown on clothes, was in the kitchen peering into the refrigerator, when my mother entered, the sound of her slippers shuffling along the kitchen floor, inflating the room with apprehension. I ignored her as per our unspoken agreement, then came the sound of her distinctly hostile monotone voice. "Did you get your period yet?" She raised her head to throw her words at me, her hair was short, thin and limp against her skull, her slight frame wrapped in pajamas, a thick bathrobe enveloped her. She scowled. Always a reliable source of disapproval, she accented her question with accusation. I was caught off guard.

"No," I answered, matching her hostility.

"Are you pregnant?" her voice was as contemptuous as her monotone allowed. My mother had an obvious monotone. It was as though she didn't open her lips to speak, the words slipped out small, tense, mad. She was always so mad. "What kind of mood is mom in?" would be the first thing I asked one of my two younger brothers when I came home from school. Ricky and Mitchell were three and five years younger than me and were subject to a less hostile version of my mother. She reserved most of her hate for me.

"Bad," was the leading response. I would roll my eyes, try to get to my room without being noticed. "I don't know," I answered. "I'll find out in a few days."

"You better not be pregnant, girl." She shuffled out of the kitchen, a snarling countenance.

I gulped down my cold cereal, raced from the house, but before I reached the car a rush of fluid propelled from my stomach and sprayed the icy street. Morning sickness, I found out a few days later. I was sixteen and pregnant.

Teenage pregnancy in 1974 was an unsavory affair, especially in Midwest suburbia where homogeneity was king, patriarchy ruled, followed by a wife, two children, two cars, and that proverbial white picket fence. Even if the patriarch was dominated by the matriarch, as in my family, the nuclear family was best kept sanitary, no deviance from the norm. Might as well have a blimp in the sky towing a banner reading PENIS AND VAGINA if your teenage daughter was pregnant. My parents couldn't shoo me away fast enough. Fear of judgment from the surrounding community dominated my parents' response. They gave two knee-jerk options — abortion or go away.

"I'm not having an abortion," I said. I had already decided. I would not abort. I wanted to experience pregnancy. How could I have known at sixteen that this might be my only chance? But it was as if I knew. And I wasn't cutting short this life inside which had just started. I just wasn't.

"You're too young to have a baby," said my mother.

"An abortion is not a bad thing," said my father.

Normally quarrelsome, my parents' unfamiliar harmony was disturbing, making my stomach queasier than morning sickness. Together, through Lutheran Social Services, they located a foster home where I was hastily dropped, far from their home, forbidden to come to their house, or my father's dental office or to contact Ricky or Mitchell, my younger brothers who didn't know why I'd suddenly disappeared.

My new foster family was Christian, thick with nice and do-good desire, which compelled them to open their doors, provide sanctuary for those who had strayed. I walked in the front door, apprehensive and unwilling, and looked at their faces. The tall, thin, baldish father who seemed kind, the dark-haired, pretty mother, and their two children, a daughter a few years younger than me, a twelve-year-old boy, were all soft-spoken, politely subdued. The mother led me upstairs to my new bedroom. My cowboy boots clunked loudly against each step, my "question authority" bell bottom jeans did not provoke any visible reaction. They were too well behaved to be obvious, but I could feel the assessment, the kids unsure, the parents unsure too but steadfast. The mother softly said that supper was at five, closing the door behind her. I threw myself down on the bed, ready to cry. I wanted nothing to do with these very nice people. Their quiet, nice home felt more disturbing than the thick undercurrent of rage I was familiar with in my parents house.

Mary, my best friend in kindergarten, and I were on a raft going down a river. It was flimsy, thin logs loosely tied together, the river's current unusually fast and strong, becoming stronger and faster by the second. Suddenly I realized we were about to be swept over a waterfall. "Jump out, jump out," I called to Mary as I started to jump off the raft, then woke up. Did I make it? I didn't know. My eyes struggled to focus. My mind raced to place the unfamiliar room, then I remembered. I was in a new home.

"Would you like some breakfast?" the pretty-faced mother asked me when I clunked down the stairs.

"No thank you." I hadn't joined them for supper the night before. They'd left me alone except for one uncertain evening knock on my door. "Come in," I'd called out. The thin father opened the door, "Everything okay?" his eyes earnest.

"Yea, I'm okay."

"We're happy to have you here," he'd said.

"Thank you."

"Your bus to school will pick you up just down on the corner. You'll have to transfer but it will take you pretty close," pretty-faced mother said. "You should really have some breakfast."

"Just a piece of toast is good, thank you."

I hitchhiked to school. It took twice as long as normal to get to Colfax and Lake Street where my alternative high school — a three-story dirty white concrete chunk with windows forlorn as the winter — humbly resided. Far removed from my parents' neighborhood, the building remained impassive to the muddy snow being hurled onto the sidewalk by rude passing cars, the words Work Opportunity Center was printed above a weathered front doorway. Nothing had changed since the last time I'd been there, only the week before, but with my life so drastically altered it was odd to find it unperturbed. Instead of a comforting familiarity it only underscored the vast difference between last week when I'd lived at home, such as it was, and this week, cast in foreign surroundings. I felt uneasy as ice cream under a hot sun.

Devon was in my art class. "That's fucked up you got sent away," she sympathized, her hands attached to a clump of clay on the potter's wheel, her foot working the pedal that turned the wheel, her hands nimble, the slightest pressure raising the clay to a towering height, a careless thought bringing collapse.

"I'm not staying there. I'm not," I complained. "I mean, the people are nice but I don't care. I just can't do it. It's way out in the sticks."

"Where can you go?"

"I don't know. I'll find something."

"Are you going to keep the baby?"

"I don't know."

Mary and I were in a car. I was driving an out-of-control car that roared toward the edge of a cliff. I hit the brakes. They didn't work. I screamed, "Jump out! Jump out!" as I pushed open the car door. I woke up. It was another nightmare. I'd had one every night since moving into the foster home. They were always the same. Mary and I going over a cliff or plunging waterfall or our airplane crashing, and I always called "Jump out! Jump out!" never knowing if we made it or not.

Day five at the foster home I found a nanny job listed in the classifieds. On Mt. Curve Avenue, close to the Guthrie Theater and downtown. Familiar, desired territory. Perfect. I dialed the number. A woman answered, her voice matter-of-fact, nothing super friendly. I said I'd like to apply for the job, that I was sixteen and pregnant. I held my breath. She invited me over.

The Guthrie Theater was founded by a group of thespians in 1963 who were "disenchanted with the commercial demands of Broadway." That's what a newspaper article said. The group included Jessica Tandy, George Grizzard, and Hume Cronin. Opening with *Hamlet,* the theater quickly became an epicenter for theater and music. Within its intimate embrace, I'd already seen Loudon Wainwright III, Bonnie Raitt, and Duke Ellington. The prospect of proximity to such grandeur thrilled me and I couldn't have been more excited as I hitchhiked to the neighborhood where the Guthrie reigned supreme among an entourage of affluent homes.

I walked down the block of plump stately homes, the windows like idle eyes that kept watch as I searched for 759 Mt. Curve Ave. A light layer of snow on the rooftops gave the houses a semblance of cakes with frosting. It was picturesque and lovely, my breath visible, the winter chill stinging my face as I located the home of Mrs. Grady.

It was a big house. Grand home might be a more suitable description, given the evident pedigree. The front door opened in response to my nervous knock, a woman met my eyes and the words no-nonsense rushed into my brain. I hastily entered, the way everyone coming in from the cold hastily enters a warm house, and smiled.

"Hi, I'm Jolette."

The woman wore a serious expression. Her return smile didn't warm the somber cast of her eyes. Her hair was short, brown, curly, her eyes blue. She wore a soft gray dress belted around a comfortable waistline. An aura of confidence encased her. Hard to tell but maybe she was in her forties. "I'm Mrs. Grady. You can leave your snowy things here. Let's go talk in the living room."

I scrambled out of my boots, mittens, bulky coat, and followed her retreating form. The entrance was formidably spacious. I felt like I was entering a museum. At once my eyes riveted to the life-sized statue of a nude woman standing in a corner. "Oh wow, that's neat," escaped my lips.

Mrs. Grady murmured, "Oh, yes, everyone likes her."

I followed her brisk step into an immense living room, empty but for several L-shaped couches, a large chair, an enormous shin-level table. She positioned herself on the couch, sat back, slightly shifting to take on the task at hand, her eyes thoughtful. I sat on the edge of the opposite couch, hands dutifully folded on my lap, knees together.

"Are you in high school?" The interview had begun.

"Yes, it's really close by. It's called the Work Opportunity Center and I go from ten to two." I took in the mammoth living room walls covered with sizable abstract paintings, which I tried to like. Mrs. Grady's eyes followed mine. "My ex-husband is an artist. Those are his."

"I really like them." I didn't.

"Yes, he's quite good. So, are you experiencing any morning sickness and are you able to do light housework?"

"Sure I can do housework. No, not much morning sickness anymore I don't think."

"When are you due?"

"April sometime."

"What do your parents say about you getting a job as a nanny?"

"They put me in a foster home that's too far away for me. It's hard for me to get to my high school. They don't know yet that I'm applying with you."

She paused for a moment. "Well, alright. Why don't you make sure it's okay with them first and then move your things in as soon as you can. I'll show you your bedroom."

"Really? I'm hired?"

"Yes, let's give it a try," Mrs. Grady nodded.

Unbelievably, within a short period of time, I found out I had a baby evolving inside of me, was sent to a foster home, which I hated even though the family was nice, but now was going to move into a handsome mansion with a huge statue in the living room just down the street from the famous Guthrie theater and close to downtown, my favorite romping grounds.

The nightmares stopped once I moved into the Grady house. My bedroom was a shoebox, down the hall from Luke's room, a six-year-old boy who would become my best friend during that gestational time, his head a sprig of blond curls, blue eyes discerning, bright. We watched early morning cartoons together, me yawning, trying to sit cross-legged on the floor but could barely do it with my growing big belly. I poked a finger into my swollen ankles, rested my hands on my protruding stomach, semi-slept until it was time for me to fix breakfast. We would idly chat. "I get tired of all the snow," I said. "Don't you?"

"Yes, but it brings spring," he said.

"Huh. I like the way you think," I said.

"I like the way I think too," he said.

"Smarty pants."

Lenny, along with my old life, faded. I wasn't smoking, doing drugs, and didn't want to go out at night. My belly was inflating daily. It was a struggle to get to school each day even though it was only fifteen hitchhiking minutes away. I was just too tired. Being pregnant, housecleaning, taking care of kids, was enough for one day. Along with Luke, I would oversee Tellie, the ten-year-old daughter with chubby cheeks and sassy mouth, who was a little harder to get along with since she was smarter than everyone else in the world. My job was to make breakfast, dinners and do light housekeeping during the day including ironing the bed sheets, which didn't seem that light to me. I had never ever heard of ironing sheets before, but there I was in the basement with an ironing board and iron trying to press wrinkles out of huge swaths of sheets, an impossible task, causing a swell of tears to break loose.

It was after one of the ironing episodes that I called my mom asking for reprieve. Couldn't I please come home?

I cried to no avail. The answer remained no. Not that my parents completely ignored me. We'd meet for a cordial lunch or dinner. They'd tell me what my younger brothers were up to. Ee'd leave the restaurant and they'd drive back home and I'd return to the Grady house. Picking the kids up from school, making dinner, vacuuming, dusting, morning cartoons, weekend marathons of watching the kids, boisterous friends in tow. Sometimes in the early dark of a wintry evening I would pull on my boots, wrap in the requisite layers, and set out to take a walk around the block. The snow's crunch under my boots, my breathing amplified under a thick scarf were the only sounds in the otherwise still night. I trudged through the snow, peering through well-lit windows into the cozy warmth of homes where life appeared content, safe, and much further than just a sidewalk away.

12

Minneapolis, 1974

There are ships sailing to many ports, but not a single one goes where life is not painful.
Fernando Pessoa, 1888-1935, Portuguese poet, writer, philosopher.

My stomach stretched into a taut prominence. I felt movement inside, placed my hand against what felt like a small foot, the miracle of a new life. I dropped out of high school. I was too tired. I'd finish later. My lower back hurt constantly. Tennis balls under my spine at night allowed me to sleep. The days blended, slipped off to wherever the past goes.

Mrs. Grady liked jazz, art, theater, politics, fundraisers, committees. Her agenda was packed. Most evenings her close friend Darren would stop by. They'd have a few glasses of wine before the advent of their evening. I was unsure of Darren's status. Short, rail thin, frail, he maneuvered with a serious limp, requiring the constant service of a cane.

Starkly contrasted, Mrs. Grady was robust, her demeanor that of a captain. She dressed frequently in blue, which enhanced the blue of her eyes, pretty against her dark hair. She reddened her lips and though she was attractive, it was her composure which drew people. Extremely self-assured, her forthright nature had been in place for many years it seemed. She wore an expression most often thoughtful, serious, intelligent. She was highly energetic and consumed with current affairs. This, combined with her wealth and ready stance, made her a tad intimidating for the regular plebeian. She was on a multitude of committees, on this board and that, had lived in Rome for eighteen years, been an assistant to Audrey Hepburn, which she never even mentioned – I found that out years later — and married a rather well-known abstract artist. She had been content, at least it sounded that way, and had loved her home in Rome where she birthed two children.

Then her husband, the scoundrel, had an affair with the children's nanny and her world screeched to a mad halt. She divorced him as fast as she could, and returned to Minnesota of all dreary places, to be near her family.

Sometimes I assumed insight into her person and felt compassion though she never showed any evidence of needing comforting. Her manner, often brusque, was always fair with me. In retrospect I suspect she invited me into her home not so much because I was capable of doing housework and taking care of children, but instead because I too had been abandoned.

Mrs. Grady broke her ankle in the spring, a misfortune of wrongful placement when stepping off an icy curb, and she and Darren were now both reliant on crutches. Not that this prevented their gallivanting to the theater, concerts, art shows, political fundraisers, events familiar to those pillowed by affluence. The snow, a resolute crust, hard and glittering, was softening under the sun's closer trajectory.

By April the days were lengthening. Spring arrived and, as if Glinda the Good Witch of the South had waved her magic wand, sprinkling the land with warmth, the grass nudged up, buds blossomed, birds started choirs, hope crawled from winter's recesses.

April 19 brought a dreamy blue sky filled with clean white clouds. I stood in the Grady front yard, eyes closed, face tilted towards the sun, when a sudden twinge rippled through my abdomen and, as though experienced with a history of childbirths, I recognized immediately that I was in labor. This doesn't hurt at all, I thought. I can do this. I wore a soft smile through the day, musing over nature's gentle guidance, until late afternoon when the sun gathered all her gracious nudges and slipped away to the other side of the planet, leaving me to the mercy of the night shift, a menacing band of savages who delighted in trying to rip me open with thunderbolts of pain and merciless contractions. There was nowhere to hide. I curled up and cowered. "It really hurts now," I whimpered to Mrs. Grady.

"Do you want to go to the hospital?"

"Yes."

Mrs. Grady, unwieldy on crutches, managed to drive me to the hospital while I contorted. I waddled ahead of Mrs. Grady who was held back by her crutches, and found an annoyed nurse behind the counter who looked like she hadn't smiled in forty years. "I'm having contractions. They hurt a lot."

"Alright. Just a minute," she grumbled and I fell back into a chair as Mrs. Grady slowly pushed through the hospital doors to join me. I couldn't assist Mrs. Grady. I could only hold my stomach while grimacing through yet another malicious twisting of my tender insides. I looked at Mrs. Grady who slid into a chair beside me. She sighed, exasperated as she tried to place the crutches beside her. They kept slipping and she finally let them fall on the floor.

"Do these get much worse?" I asked her.

She knit her brows. "Yes, I'm afraid so."

"Oh, no. Really?"

Just then the sullen nurse came, pushing a wheelchair in my direction.

"I can walk," I told her.

"Just get in the wheelchair," she said grumpily. I looked at Mrs. Grady who raised an eyebrow. "Okay, thank you," I said sweetly. I heard Mrs. Grady laugh as I was wheeled away.

"You have to go home and come back later," grump nurse said after I was probed by the doctor.

"What? Why?"

"You're not dilated to two centimeters yet."

"You're kidding. These hurt. I must be close to having the baby by now."

"No, you're not. Come back later. We can't admit you unless you're two centimeters."

Mrs. Grady and I stumbled back to the car. Back to the house. I called Lenny.

"I can't just sit here having contractions all night. Will you go to a movie with me?"

"Yes, let's go. What do you want to see?"

"The Great Gatsby."

Robert Redford and Mia Farrow were distractingly beautiful on the big screen with their luminous blue eyes, skin glistening with a lustrous sheen meant to portray the sweaty heat of a 1920s summer in Long Island where their tormented characters twisted and longed for each other in this ill-fated love story. I gazed at their magnified gorgeousness, twisting myself under labor's ruthless progression. Clutching my extended stomach, I would miss most of F. Scott Fitzgerald's tale of love remiss. When the movie ended, Lenny found me huddled over in the bathroom.

"I wonder if that crappy hospital will let me in yet," I said. Lenny took me by the arm, helped me to the car. "It fucking hurts, Len."

"I know."

"You're always gonna be my friend, Len, aren't you?"

"Yes, forever."

"Push!" demanded an irritated nurse. "You should feel like pushing now. Don't you have an overwhelming need to push?"

"No," I said feebly. It was around midnight when I'd finally been admitted into the hospital. I quickly dismissed my earlier notion of refusing any drugs. "Give me everything," I said to the non-smiling nurse. All of the nurses wore a scowl.

Jolette

"Why are the nurses so mean?" I asked Lenny who sat with me while I lay laboring.

"Probably because you're young. You know, teenage pregnancy. Fucking bitches."

Lenny sat by my side until early the next morning when I was wheeled into the delivery room, my eyes fastened to her face until the swinging doors closed. She wasn't allowed in.

The delivery room could have been used for meat storage. It was freezing. A huge clock on the wall glared at me. My legs were spread wide and strapped down tightly into the stirrups. I was a bug pinned to a board. Between my kneecaps swirled a world of activity. The doctor and several nurses were holding a conference in front of my poor panting vagina, the chaos not enough to distract me from the pain of being severed in half. I tried to push but it wasn't enough to convince the new life inside of me to venture forth. "Push! Just push!" the nurse kept repeating. She seemed mad at me. Evidently my not knowing how to push was really getting on her nerves.

Then my daughter began to emerge, her head making its trusting introduction. I strained to see her, but the nurses were in the way. There was a whisk of movement and I glimpsed her being placed in an incubator on the opposite side of the room.

"What's going on?" I asked, craning my neck, trying to see. "Is she alright?"

No one answered. My legs were still tied down. I couldn't move. I stared at the clock, its sharp hands refusing to budge, elongating the unbearable present. "Is she alright?" I tried calling to the nurses who were clustered over her. A nurse came over.

"She's a little jaundiced and she has amniotic fluid in her lungs. Probably because you didn't push her out fast enough."

I hated that nurse. "What's jaundiced?"

"Yellow. She's yellow."

"Yellow? Oh god. Why is she yellow? Can I get untied yet?"

Jolette

"No. You have to be stitched up."

Episiotomies were standard in 1975, needed or not, a slash between the vagina and rectum to expand the vaginal opening, then after delivery, sewn up, which wins silver in most excruciating painful experience ever, second only to labor, which of course takes gold. Needles piercing an exquisitely tender part of the body, the perineum, which should never be subjected to the light of day much less being sliced open then patched up with a needle and thread.

An arrogant doctor insisted there was no pain, though I thought the electric chair might hurt less. Anguished, I stared at the imperious face of the clock. I don't think I can stand this anymore, I thought. I'm going to explode or implode. I felt a crumbling inside. I'm imploding, I thought, I'm imploding. I couldn't move my strapped down legs. An internal avalanche stilled me, causing a wave to move through me, making my lips suddenly burst with an anguished sound, causing my shoulders and head to sway as I tried to hold on. Then, from across the room, I caught a glimpse of dark hair on top of a little head, my daughter was being taken away.

"Her name is Naomi Pearl," I managed to call out.

13

Minneapolis, 1974

Life goes on, I know not why.
        Gertrude Stein, American novelist, poet, playwright, 1874-1946.

Lutheran Social Services sat on Park Boulevard in Minneapolis. It was a pretty boulevard, easy and wide under a canopy of Dutch elm tree leaves. The sky, a perturbed frustration of grays with furrowed clouds, matched my mood. My mother and father — perfunctory, seemingly removed — and I entered the brick building where a judge would strip away my parental rights. Naomi Pearl was also in the building, in the nursery. I was not allowed to see her.

"I stand by whatever decision you make," Lenny had staunchly declared some months earlier. "I'll help you raise Naomi."

"Thanks, Len," I'd said. I already knew though. I'd already decided. "But I'm going to be hitchhiking across country, living in lots of different places. I don't think a little baby would be okay with that and I don't think I'd make a very good mother."

Naomi was a physical replica of her birth father, Albee. My first love. I was fourteen. He was sixteen, just kids on the outside, but inside there was a deep recognition between us, some kind of old love that appeared like a brilliant sun and would survive through everything, even death, for he died young and I still love him today.

Albee looked at the world through hazel eyes, sometimes they turned a pretty green. He was friendly, fun, troubled the way a lot of sixteen-year-olds are troubled. Maybe a little more. He lived in a turbulent household, it seemed, for his mother tried to shoot herself in the head, but the bullet just glanced the side of her skull and she survived. His brown hair hung straight and long but couldn't quite offset the super jock image made by his favorite baseball jacket that he refused to abandon. He stood out like a sore thumb swerved around by those in patched jean jackets emblazoned with peace signs, flowered flowing smocks, and ripped jeans at the West Bank in the University district where slouching figures huddled on corners selling yellow sunshine, orange sunshine, purple haze, blotter acid, electric Kool-Aid, or micro-dot, all names ascribed to the small LSD tablets that exploded the mind in a mire of hallucinations.

Maude and I scored orange sunshine on one of those corners the night we hitchhiked to a Deep Purple concert and ran into Albee with his friends. They were two years ahead of us in high school, and nodded from their superior perch as high school seniors when we caught sight of each other in the mob packed in front of the stage. Later they gave us a ride home and the night would end with the beginning of our relationship – me and Albee, sitting cross-legged, facing each other in the middle of a quiet suburban street, talking. We were both tripping. LSD was taken like M&M's in those days, the 70s. I navigated it like I was in a river. You had to go with the flow. You couldn't fight it. Otherwise you might have trouble.

One night, when Maude and I were tripping, we were running through the field near the railroad tracks, where on weekends kids converged and made a big bonfire, tipping bottles of booze into their wet, sassy mouths, smoking pot, which seems to be the timeless prescription for trying to have fun. Maude and I were laughing and running when suddenly she screamed. I turned to see her face contorted, her leg drawn up. "Something bit me! Something bit me!" she cried. "Are there snakes out here? Poisonous snakes?"

Jolette

When you're on acid, reality shape shifts. Between the hallucinations and the cascade of nonlinear thinking, it was difficult to discern reality. We teetered on the edge of wondering if her life was ending in a minute, after being bit by maybe a poisonous snake. For we had no idea if poisonous snakes lived in the fields of suburban Minneapolis, in the flatlands of Minnesota. Finally, we ran into some kid, who assured us that there were no snakes and we were left laughing. But, you see, that's how fast life changes on acid. In a split second.

LSD could be a real bummer. But I never had a bad trip. I always liked it. I think taking acid once a week for a year helped form my thinking in a good way. It helped me realize what was important in life. Feelings were important. Purpose, integrity, and love were important. Not money and materialism and stuff like that.

The night I sat with Albee in the middle of the street, we talked until the sun came up. I let him know how the world worked. "It's all a flow. You have to be able to just let go and not try to hold on. That's the mistake, trying to hold on," I said, and he nodded. "Far out," he said.

For two years we were together. Then I became pregnant. His family had moved to Tucson a few months earlier. He went with them. When I wrote him a letter, telling him I was pregnant, he never wrote back. He never called. His grandmother lived in Minneapolis and had become my friend. She was mad at Albee and called him a coward. I knew he was just afraid. I knew he loved me. But he was just a fucked up kid. And he wasn't strong. I was the strong one.

He overdosed on heroin when he was thirty-one. He was dead before his life had really started. We had stayed close friends. Not the kind of close friends who see each other, but the kind who talk over the phone once every few years. The last time I heard from him was in the middle of the night. The phone rang. He was in Phoenix, high. At a phone booth. He said he wanted to hear my voice. "Hang in there, girl. I love you." "I love you too, Albee," I said. Two months later he was dead. Overdosed on a speedball, a lethal mix of cocaine and heroin.

Naomi Pearl was in the nursery somewhere in the building, I ran down the hallway searching. No one tried to stop me. I found the nursery and opened the door. She was in the center of the room, swaddled, eyes closed, breathing light and steady. I tried to memorize her face, placed a hand on her blanket, felt the warmth of her small body. I stood still for a minute and said the only thing I could wish for her.

"I hope you have a good life, Naomi Pearl."

14

Seattle, 1981

Whenever she imagined her child, grown-up without interference from a judgmental world, she imagined its male and female halves as complementing each other, and as being secretly, almost magically powerful.
         Kathleen Winter, b.1960, Canadian writer.

Lisa was eighteen. She was new to Elite. We were meeting at a client's house in Kirkland, a well-upholstered suburb, smug and fat on the shores of Lake Washington. A small dark car was curbside when I pulled up. A brunette head behind the wheel turned my way, a young woman smiled. I locked my car, smiled back. Lisa had the legs of a gazelle launching her up to about five-foot nine-inches. She was slender, wavy dark hair floating over her shoulders, her face so young, she looked thirteen. Her brown eyes held hesitation.

"Lisa?"

"Hi. Michelle?"

"Is this your first call?" I asked.

"Yes," she nodded.

"Ever?"

She nodded.

"Okay, well, it will be fine. I guess this guy is a football player," I said as we walked up to the well-manicured home.

"He is?" Lisa asked. "Seahawks?"

"I don't know. I don't pay attention to football." I knocked and the door opened quickly. Dan was huge, six-foot-five-ish, maybe in his early thirties, dark hair above a perhaps handsome face. It was hard to tell, a smear of lipstick painted his mouth, green eyeshadow caked his eyelids. What must have been an extra extra-large slip curtained his enormous torso and one of his gigantic legs had been shaved. The other had not. "Dan?" I smiled.

"Oh, hello girls. Come in, come in. I don't want the neighbors to see," he fussed, pulling us inside.

"You look pretty," I said.

"Do I? You don't think this eyeshadow is a bit much?"

"No, I like it, but I think you need some mascara. I'm Michelle, Dan. This is Lisa."

"Oh, hi. You girls are cute. I want you to help me dress up nice. Call me Danny, okay?"

"Okay Danny. Could we just take a look at your ID first please? Carol probably told you to have it ready?"

"Oh sure, sure. I guess you have to be careful. You never know who might call you. Here." Danny handed me his driver's license. I glanced at the name, address, and expiration. "Always check the info, especially the expiration," I said to Lisa. "Make sure you really look at it." Lisa nodded.

"Lisa's new," I told Danny.

"You are? Oh, that's sweet. You are so cute, Lisa. Help me put on this bra."

"Sure, okay." Lisa set down her purse, moved into her role. "Okay, turn around. This is a pretty color. Let's see if it fits you. "

"Danny, can I use your phone? I need to let the agency know we're here."

"Sure, it's on the table over there."

"Elite massage," Carol's voice sweet as a peppermint stick.

"Hi, it's Michelle. Lisa and I are checking in at Dan's house."

Jolette

"Okay. Everything alright?"

"Yep, fine. I'll call you in an hour."

Lisa and Danny were giggling when I turned back to the living room. Clothes were laid out all over the couch, Lisa was trying to put mascara on Danny's lashes. "Hold still, okay?" Lisa was saying. "Now don't blink." Danny stared straight ahead, eyes wide, obediently not blinking while Lisa applied mascara.

"There you go," Lisa said.

"That looks beautiful," I said. "All you needed was some mascara. You look great."

"Do I? Girls, I want you to wrap my cock in nylons, only I don't want you to call it my cock. Call it my pussy."

"Sure, where are your nylons Danny? I want to wrap the nylons over your pussy." I said.

Danny groaned, touched himself, an erect penis visible under the slip. "Are you playing with your pussy?" I asked. "I think you should wait until I get the nylons."

"Oh, I don't think I can wait," Danny said, groaned again, touching himself. Lisa glanced at me. "Let's get the nylons, Lisa, and play with Danny's pussy."

"No, no, wait a minute," Danny said. "Wait because what I really want to do…" deep breath, dramatic pause, "What I really want to do is dress up and go for a walk. Right down my street. Oh, you girls are inspiring me. What dress should I wear?"

"What dresses do you have?" I asked. "Do you have a blue one? That would be pretty on you."

"Should I walk down the street? That's what I really want to do." Danny turned to me.

"I'm not sure if you really should or not. That's up to you," I said.

"Well, I want to wear my red dress."

"Okay. Do you want to try it on for us first?"

"Yes I do!" Danny left the room. I turned to Lisa.

"When Danny gets back, let's use his nylons and make him feel really good," I said loud enough for him to hear.

"Yes, let's make him feel really good," Lisa said, following my cue. "Is he really going to walk down the street?" she whispered.

"I don't know," I whispered back, then called out, "Danny, did you find your red dress?"

"Well, I've got a bunch of dresses," he said returning, arms filled with dresses, face flushed. He dropped them on the couch, holding onto a red dress. "What do you think? Do you like it?"

"I love it. Let's see how it looks on," I said and he pulled the frilly dress over his head, squirmed to squeeze into it, pulling it over his thick torso, yanking it down over his massive thighs.

"Very pretty," I said. "Look in the mirror and see if you like it."
"Oh! No, no! I don't like it at all! It doesn't fit right. I'm too fat," he said.

"You're not fat at all," I said. "You're perfect. Gorgeous."

"You're not fat," Lisa chimed. "You look great! What dress do you want to try next?"

"The blue one. Didn't you say the blue one would look good?" He turned to me, his thickly painted face held consternation.

"It would match your eyes. It would be pretty," I said, picking up the dress, holding it against him. "Yes! I think this is the one. It will look nice." I tried to reassure him.

"Oh, I don't know," he frowned at the mirror.

"Try the blue one. You'll like it better," I said.

He squirmed out of the tight red dress, miraculously it didn't rip. Then he pulled the blue dress over his massive body. His eyes brightened when he looked in the mirror. "Oh! I do like this one better!"

"That's much better," I nodded in agreement, then brushed up against him. His penis was erect. "What's this?" I teased.

"No, no, not yet. I still have to walk down the street," Danny protested. "I'll wear the blue dress."

"Okay. Maybe you want to walk down a different street?" I asked.

"No, I want to walk down my street." He giggled, paused. "I think."

"Well, let's get your nylons on, okay?" I said. "Lisa, did you see where the nylons are? Danny, we should put your nylons on. Want us to help you put them on?"

"That would be so nice, girls. Yes, please." He sat on the couch, Lisa handed me the nylons.

"Those aren't going to fit," Lisa said.

"We're going to make them fit," I said, smiling at Danny. "I love the feel of nylons don't you?" I wrapped the nylon around my hand and ran my hand up his leg. "Doesn't that feel good?" I asked.

"Yes," he murmured and lay back on the couch. I brought my hand up to his penis, lightly stroked it.

"Oh god, not yet," he murmured. "Not yet."

"It's okay. Hold on a second. Hold on." I stopped brushing the nylon against his penis for only a moment then firmly grasped his shaft, providing friction — up, down, up, down.

"Oh god. Oh god." His hips thrust forward and a small bit of come spurt up. He jacked off a lot. I could tell by the small amount of come. It landed on his slip.

I gave a moment, then murmured, "That was nice."

He appeared slightly dazed, adjusted himself, and sat up. "Yes, that was really nice."

"Want me to wash off your slip, Danny?"

"No, I'll just throw it in the washer. Okay, thank you girls. That was good." His voice almost imperceptibly deepened in register.

"Okay. Well, I'm just going to use your bathroom for a minute, okay?" I went and washed my hands. Lisa trailed behind me, doing the same.

"Here, girls, this is for you." Danny opened a drawer filled with large bills. He grabbed a handful. "That was good. Thank you." Danny held out the money.

Well, it was nice meeting you, Danny," I said.

"Yes, nice meeting you," echoed Lisa.

"Thank you girls."

"You're welcome," we said.

"I'm glad he didn't walk down the street." Lisa leaned into me as we walked down the sidewalk to our cars.

"I am too," I said. "I wasn't sure for a minute there. You did good." I looked at Lisa.

She smiled. "It was kinda fun."

15

Minneapolis, 1975

Listen for the call of your destiny, and when it comes, release your plans and follow.
    Mollie Marti, American psychologist, lawyer, coach, author.

There was no normal after Naomi Pearl was born, after I had signed papers relinquishing parental rights, after she was adopted by her new family. Postpartum depression wasn't a mainstream phrase yet, but it flattened me anyway. Life acted as if nothing had changed, as if there hadn't been a significant event, as if everything were normal though I was not. I couldn't budge the numb feeling that squashed me like a boulder. I could only go through the motions of daily living, survival instinct the only thing intact, an instinct deeply hardwired that paid little heed to the broken heart or staggering mind.

I graduated from high school with credits mostly from art class. Mrs. Malmlov ran the art room. Her assistant Babs had long dark hair and wore turquoise rings she'd ease off her fingers, set aside when she'd work the potter's wheel, foot pumping the pedal below. It wasn't unusual to find a group of students circled around, watching. She had a deft sleight of hand, the clay swirled, shapeshifting until final fruition. Babs could center clay faster than anyone. Centering was difficult. Not everyone could do it, which spoke to life itself I suppose.

Jolette

I would miss the art room. I would also miss my social studies class where Mr. Roberts, a devoted socialist, held court, and where Rusty, a pretty, quiet redhead, had spent some of her last days. A poem of hers about death — uncannily written just prior to her murder — was published in the *Minneapolis Star and Tribune* after some serial killer motherfucker picked her up when she was hitchhiking to school and smashed her head in with a hammer.

Kathy Schultz, nicknamed Rusty, had been hitchhiking to school one September morning as did many kids who attended the Work Opportunity Center. That morning Harvey Carignan, a serial rapist and killer, picked her up, most certainly presented her with the prospect of driving with him up to northern Minnesota to get his second car. He probably said he just needed someone to drive it back and he would pay her. That was his ruse. Rusty's body was found in a cornfield in northern Minnesota, her head shattered from the blunt force of a hammer. We were all stunned. Mr. Roberts had a hard time recovering, his tears refusing to dry. Death. Capturing a schoolmate. Taking her far away. With the grim allure of the unknown.

I sat at a bus stop by our school, looking for the green Chevy Capri the killer had been spotted driving. I didn't know what else to do. My eyes squinted, searching passing cars, looking for the deranged man who had taken the life of our schoolmate, unable to stop thinking about Rusty, her quiet pretty face, how bewildered and betrayed she must have felt before ushered into death by such brutality. A target because she was a young woman, tantamount to being a rabbit in a thicket of coyotes.

Carignan was arrested within a few weeks. Authorities suspected numerous rapes, assaults, and murders were committed by the repulsive man with beady eyes and a severe facial tic, but he was convicted of only two murders – Rusty's and another young woman's — and was sentenced to life at the Minnesota Correctional Facility, where he remains to this day.

Jolette

For ninety dollars a month I had the key to a small studio apartment close to Mrs. Grady's house. She brought me groceries one day, her blue eyes sweeping the small room, murmuring approval. Under the only window, a slivered rectangle that admitted whatever light managed to squeeze in under gray skies, was a polished hardwood floor, where my mattress lay hidden under blankets and pillows, a stack of books within easy reach, and a bedside lamp.

The only other piece of furniture was a spinet piano, beautiful in repose. Renting the piano was my gift to myself and, though not played often, I admired it daily. In earlier years, from seven to thirteen, I would rise in the freezing stab of morning, scramble into clothes, set the timer for one hour, and begin the 7 a.m. ritual of piano practice. Bach, Beethoven, Mozart, and Debussy animated the chilly home where we burrowed deep under blankets through frigid nights. The house unable to withstand the freeze that slipped in easily, like a master thief. I warmed as I played Claude Debussy's Arabesque No 1. My blood memorized the notes, created permanent neural pathways extending through my fingers, etched the melody so deeply that any hint of its sound far into the future would invoke Miss Rogers, my piano instructor with the beautiful hands, with one brown eye, one green. I was struck shy in her presence. She placed a warm hand on my shoulder, called me Jolettie, gently coaching, turning my heart soft. Occasionally I left her gifts of chocolate on the piano bench as I quietly slipped from the room after a lesson, and worked hard to please her, studying the scrawls she made on my sheet music.

"Don't rush!!!! FEEL the notes! Move your body INTO the keys! FEEL the notes!"

I inhaled her words, letting them shape my thoughts. Would carry them with me far down future paths where they would find a destination. FEEL! I leaned into her much as I leaned into the keys of the piano. Forever living with the goal of FEELING, as she had once instructed. Leaving her and the piano only when, years later, I was drawn away by beckoning forces.

Mrs. Grady rested a hand on my beautiful spinet before turning to leave. "Come by and visit the children soon, would you? They miss you. Would you like to join us for dinner Saturday?"

"Yes, sure! I miss the kids." I did miss the kids, but was done working as a nanny. It was time to get back into the bigger world.

A waitress job at a coffee shop inside The Curtis Hotel, downtown Minneapolis, provided access to free food. A slow period in the middle of my shift allowed escape out the cafeteria's back door, which opened to the hotel's interior. I roamed the halls exploring. An auditorium held an impressive grand piano on a stage begging to be played. I had to sink my fingers into the keys, press the pedals, play Bach's *Solfeggietto*, Beethoven's *Fur Elise*, *Debussy's* Deux Arabesques, my fingers giving a recital to the vacant auditorium. It seemed fitting somehow that I should be playing to emptiness, filling the room with crescendos and decrescendos. I finished, lifted my fingers from the keys, turned to face the audience of gaping seats, the piano's voice lingering only a moment, then the room returned to silence, so void of life I had to escape and raced down the aisle, pushed out the doors to continue exploring.

There was a beautiful Asian rug at the far end of the hotel lobby. A plush carpet, deep with light greens and soft pinks. No one noticed me in my waitress uniform staring down at the most gorgeous rug I'd ever seen. No one noticed me at all, which I noticed, which planted an idea. Darcy was an amiable kid who worked in the cafeteria, bussing tables. He had a car. Bonny was a waitress with the innocence of a delicate doe. She'd graduated from my alternative high school around the same time as me. She'd aced centering clay on the potter's wheel, which granted her esteem in my book and though she was doe-like pure, she seemed friendly enough to assist with some harmless deviance. I raced back into the coffee shop, calling excitedly, "Come here, come here, come here," to Bonny who was being held captive by a long-winded counter customer.

"Hi, I'm taking Bonnie." I flashed a smile at the older gentleman who was undoubtedly dismayed that I was pulling beautiful Bonny from him.

Jolette

"Come here, I have to show you something," I said.

"What?" she laughed, letting herself be pulled. "Oh gosh, can we leave like this?" she asked as I pulled her through the back door.

"Yes, we can. Where do you think I go every day?" I dragged her through the hallways, then pointed. "Look at that rug over there. Isn't it neat," I asked, both of us breathless.

She nodded, her long blonde hair shimmering. She wrinkled her nose, pushed her glasses up, and looked at me. "It's super pretty."

"I want it, Bonny. Will you help me get it?"

Bonny laughed.

"I'm serious. I know how we can do it."

The coffee shop quieted between three and four each afternoon. Bonny and Darcy were willing conspirators, so at 3 p.m. Bonny and I left through the back door, into the hotel's interior, wound round the halls until the beautiful light green and pink rug was before us. It was huge. We assumed serious expressions and proceeded to roll the rug up, our faces pointed down towards our work. No one questioned us. No one noticed us. After some struggle — it was really large and heavy — we had it rolled up, then, glancing at each other, we proceeded to lift each end and walk out of the lobby. I was dying to laugh but had to squelch it. We still had work ahead of us.

We exited through the hotel's back door. Darcy was there with his car, engine running, back door open. I slid in with the bulk of the rug. Bonny heaved the rest of it in, then she ran back to the coffee shop. Darcy and I sped off, the beautiful rug on top of me in the back seat. It took ten long minutes to drive to my studio, where we lugged the rug to my small room, dropped it, and raced back to The Curtis Hotel. The cafeteria was just beginning to fill as Darcy raced into the kitchen and I flew back to the counter. I glanced at Bonny. She was poised with a pen, taking an order, her pretty face flushed. She glanced at me and smiled, looking so angelic you could almost see her halo.

Jolette

That evening I unrolled the beautiful rug and my room was a vision. My bed, books, polished piano, and gorgeous rug. Perfect.

I started taking classes at the University of Minnesota and the days fell into place, passing by the way they do. Funny how days work, they seem so much the same but you will never get any of them back which makes them seem sort of special even though they weren't. You only get more new days which many people don't know what to do with. They long for the old days.

Jolette

16

Minneapolis, 1975

Life isn't about finding yourself. Life is about creating yourself.
George Bernard Shaw, 1856-1950, Irish playwright.

My future husband wore rose-tinted glasses that straddled his nose, a large amethyst ring hugging his little finger. Straight brown hair framed his face, which was largely hidden under a wild, untamed beard. His eyes were blue, somehow not pretty. His name was Marion and he was in my political science class at the University of Minnesota. Marion was bright, self-assured, and mildly provocative, the most vocal student in class. My ears picked up whenever he spoke.

"What do you think about the fall of Saigon?" I asked him one day after class.

"The whole Vietnam war is a travesty for a myriad of reasons. There are a lot of moving parts. Supposedly we got involved to stop the spread of Communism but basically we just slaughtered thousands of innocent civilians, abandoned hundreds of children over there who were fathered by our guys in the military. And the fall of Saigon?" He blinked at me, his forefinger pushed up his glasses. "Well, that was pure betrayal. The civilians were abandoned, betrayed, and left to be killed. They got fucked," he said. "I was over there."

"You were?"

"Yea, not in combat. Just at a desk, getting high like ninety percent of the guys serving."

Marion looked at me with his not very pretty blue eyes, through his rose-tinted glasses, and asked for my number. We went out for dinner. I ordered a salad, which was always a mistake on the first date. There is just no way of getting a fork load of greens into the mouth smoothly. They do not tuck nicely into a bite size. They frolic, cavort, shoot out unexpectedly, escaping through the lips, down the chin. I looked down at the greens on my plate. They dared me to try. Since I was so focused on my challenging plate of leaves, it wasn't until after dinner when Marion and I settled into a couple of big comfy chairs in his dorm room at the University of Minnesota that I got to really gauge him and was unexpectedly spellbound by his recitation of China's history. His words fell into place so well.

"He's so succinct," I said later to Lenny.

"What the hell is succinct?"

"He's just so good with words."

"Well, whatever floats your boat," Lenny said. "As long as he's good to you that's all I care about."

Turned out Marion's own history proved mesmerizing as well, for only a year earlier he'd biked up to the ticket counter at the Metropolitan Sports Stadium in Bloomington, Minnesota, on Harmon Killebrew day, brandishing a gun and demanding money. We were still ensconced in the big chairs in his UM room, the history of China finished, when he began to tell his story. He ran his hand through his hair.

"Wait. What? You robbed the Metropolitan Sports Stadium?" I asked.

He nodded.

"But why? What happened?"

"I got caught because my lookout failed me. He took off when the police showed up. He didn't warn me." Marion, a white boy from the suburbs, was handcuffed, thrown in jail. He received a slap on the wrist — one year's probation — and was sent to college, where he was ordered to live at the half-way house on the UM campus, appointed the job of house counselor.

"What? And now you're a counselor here? Really?"

"Yea."

"But why did you do that? I don't get it." Armed robbery. My interest heightened. And then I was unsure, teetering on judgment.

"I was going to give the money to my mom. I was tired of her waitressing and working so hard for all of us and my dad is such an asshole, he doesn't even help. So, I was going to mail her the money anonymously." Marion's mother was divorced. She had ten kids to feed, and waitressed at Embers restaurant for a pittance, barely making ends meet. "The shrink said I have a Robin Hood complex," Marion said, pleased.

"Oh," I thought for a moment. "You used a gun?"

"Yea, but it wasn't loaded."

"But the people you pulled it on didn't know that."

"No, they didn't."

"I don't think that's right, pulling a gun on people. That's going to stay with them forever."

"I know." Marion shrugged uncertainly. "I just wanted to help my mom."

I concluded he was bold and brave and a month later asked him to marry me. His eyes widened at the suggestion. He pushed his glasses up with a forefinger to think.

Had it not been for the US Army, I would have never proposed marriage.

The Army's recruitment centers in the 1970s populated regions much as Starbucks does today. The "I Want You" poster with a skinny, menacing Uncle Sam, his tall blue-striped and white-starred top hat, his bony pointing finger, was as familiar as the blue in the sky. I happened to pass a recruitment office one sunny Minnesota day, when a thought – *I'll bet the Army would get me out of Minnesota* – made me pause. A recruitment officer's eyes lit up as I approached his desk.

The U.S. Army admitted women into its hallowed realm only in traditional roles such as cooks, nurses, and seamstresses back in the 1700s during the Revolutionary War. Some women, however, were so motivated to serve in a combat role, they disguised themselves as men and it is estimated that during the Civil War over 400 women disguised as men fought in the Union and Confederate armies.

In 1942, President Roosevelt established the Women's Army Corps, which increased military job opportunities for women, albeit unequal job opportunities. It wasn't until 2016 that women were granted the right to choose any military occupational specialty desired, including ground combat. But in 1975, discrimination was still embraced by the U.S. Army. Women were second-class citizens.

"So you'd send me somewhere else besides Minnesota?" I asked the immaculate, shorn-haired recruitment officer.

"Yes, absolutely you will leave Minnesota and you'll see the world, live in another country if you want."

"And once I sign, I'm really going. Nothing can get in the way, right?"

"Once you sign, you're in the Army and you're leaving Minnesota for a long time," he said.

I scrawled my name on the dotted line fast before I changed my mind.

"Now let's see what kind of training we can sign you up for." He snatched the signed paper like it was a pot of gold. I followed him to a computer where he pushed a few keys, and offered three options. "Let's see, there's factory training, laundry training, and truck driving school. Which one do you want?"

"Factory, laundry, or truck driving? That's it?" I looked over to the next computer where a guy my age was seated, another cloned Army recruiter beside him, and couldn't help but overhear "medical training" as one of his options. "How come he gets to be a doctor and I only get these choices," I asked the recruitment guy who'd foamed at the mouth to get my signature and now smacked his lips.

"Well, nobody said the Army didn't discriminate. Heh heh."

"That's not fair," I ventured.

"Nobody ever said the Army was fair." He let out a chortle, seemed to find himself amusing. I sighed and chose truck driving school.

"You'll go to basic training at Fort McClellan, Alabama, get trained and be transferred to Germany for two years."

Basic training, which would lead to my new glamorous truck-driving Army life, wouldn't begin for two months. I had time to take a few classes at UM, long enough to encounter the succinct bearded felon who was now seated beside me.

"If we were married you could come and live with me in Germany. The Army would pay for it," I said. "Do you wanna get married?" I looked into his not very pretty blue eyes.

He thought for a moment, then looked at me. "Yea, okay."

Our legal union took place at city hall, a few friends and family in attendance. Marion wore bright yellow slacks, a red and white checkered cowboy shirt and his huge amethyst ring, loud and purple, an exclamation on the entire mismatch. I submitted to a pale pink dress, heels, a sprig of baby breath in my hair. My parents stood by slightly confused, my brothers took a bar of soap to Marion's car, scrawling Just Married! Marion drank too much, his eyes glazed. We ended the day with a party at his apartment, now our apartment. I found him staring lustfully at his slender fair-haired female neighbors, swaggering with a bottle of beer clutched in his hand, the future's forecast.

"Congratulations Marion," they chirped.

"Yep, I'm a taken man," he stupidly slurred, his bleary eyes suggesting otherwise.

I was married. Two weeks later I was in basic training at Fort McClellan, Alabama.

17

Fort McClellan, Alabama 1976

A yellow bird with a yellow bill, he came upon my windowsill, I coaxed him in with crumbs of bread and then I smashed his fucking head.
Army cadence

I was sweating. Humidity, thick and sticky as syrup, drenched the Alabama countryside, making the air hard to breathe. Pretty rolling hills and apple orchards decorated the landscape but on the bus that carried about twenty of us fresh recruits from the airport to Fort McClellan, where we would begin basic training, no one noticed the scenery. We were caught up in the forward motion of the bus, craning our necks to better see where our life was headed. Pouring sweat, we complained about the heat, but were exuberant, chattering, laughing, until the bus veered into the wide entrance of the military base. Then were suddenly silent, each of us wondering what we were in for.

Fort McClellan stretched over 46,000 acres of Alabama's green rolling hills and housed the US Army Military School and US Army Chemical School, known for such pleasantries as napalm, Agent Orange, and nerve gas testing, all of which were dispensed in the Vietnam War, poisoning people and environments in both Alabama and Vietnam. In 1952, the Women's Army Corps was founded at Fort McClellan and was kept segregated from all men with the exception of a few male drill sergeants. I knew none of this.

I didn't know that the grounds were already contaminated with low levels of radiation particles, compliments of the chemical school. Nor did anyone know that the Fort would be shut down in 1999, nine years after the Environmental Protection Agency declared the area to be one of the country's most toxic sites in need of clean-up. As our bus pulled to a stop and the doors flew open and we were met with loud shouts and commands, all I knew was that basic training had just begun.

There were probably one hundred fresh-faced girls arriving at the same time. We scrambled off buses to loud voices shouting commands. "LINE UP! LINE UP! LINE UP!" We flew into a loose formation, a big-mouthed woman bellowing that she was the commanding officer. Then we were shuffled into the barracks. "PICK A BED. PICK A BED. PICK ANY BED, BUT THAT WILL BE YOUR BED AND YOU WILL BE HELD RESPONSIBLE FOR THAT BED!" a drill sergeant's voice followed us into the barracks, which offered long rows of bare mattresses on beds elbowed with lockers, blankets, and sheets folded on top. I raced to the first unoccupied bed. A girl I'd been talking to on the bus grabbed the bed next to me. Stephanie was from some small town in Illinois. She was an affable smiling girl, regular as could be. I liked her. Stephanie said her sister had been through basic training the year before, so she already had an idea of what to expect.

"They don't let you sleep," Stephanie said, as we shoved our backpacks into our new lockers. "We won't get any sleep cuz we're gonna be up half the night ironing our uniforms, even though the men get to send their clothes out to be ironed. We have to iron ours, and my sister said everybody sleeps on the floor so they don't have to make their bed in the morning."

"You're kidding. Shit."

Jolette

"Yea, and they get you up at five and then we march three miles before breakfast. What's your job gonna be?" Stephanie asked.

"Truck driver in Germany. What about you?"

"Factory work in Germany. I'm just doing this for the benefits."

"I'm doing this for my country," boomed a big voice from a big girl passing by who'd overheard us. "There's only one good reason to sign up and that's to protect our country." Heads swiveled our direction. "I don't know why anyone else is here, but I'm proud to be here. I want to serve my country and I hope every single person here does too."

I turned towards my bed, rolled my eyes. Stephanie's face remained expressionless, but I could tell she wanted to roll her eyes too.

We were issued uniforms, a green wraparound skirt covering green shorts, a crisp hard-to-iron light green blouse, a canoe-shaped cap, white socks, and black shoes that were big clunkers. Name tags pierced our shirt's left breast. Elizabeth Carter was from Kentucky. Short hair, bangs swept to one side, her style was butch. She was strong with voice and eye contact, wore a bold grin, frequently with hands on her hips.

"Don't ever call me Beth or Liz. Call me Carter," she said to everyone.

There was something about her I liked. I smiled at her. She smiled back.

Maria was pretty, coquettish, Italian, from New Jersey, and slim. Picture her with a sweet smile, head tilted to the side, long lashes, short blonde waves over her lovely head. She seemed so soft I wondered how she would handle this tough terrain. Bernice, the girl who'd joined to protect our country, was wide-hipped and loud, plain as a doorknob and friendly as a bossy cow. By the third day she was screaming at us like she was the drill sergeant. "GET READY TO LINE UP! GET READY TO LINE UP!"

"Shut up Bernice," one girl finally had the nerve to say, which brought a sashayed walk from Miss Bossy Cow over to the girl's thin form. The girl's face twitched, visibly unnerved by the mass now in front of her. Bernice opened her cavernous mouth. "The Sergeant is coming in two minutes. SO I'M TELLING YOU NOW, GET READY TO LINE UP! YOU GOTTA PROBLEM WITH THAT? NOW LINE UP!"

The thin girl, her name was Darlene, and was athletic – you could tell by her agility and toned muscles – lowered her eyes, mumbled something acquiescing, turned away. Miss Bossy Cow turned around, "LINE UP! HOW MANY TIMES DO I HAVE TO SAY IT? LINE UP! SERGE IS COMING IN TWO MINUTES!" I was glad Bernice's bed was far from mine.

The Army's pyramid structure was comprised of squad, platoon, company, and battalion, brigade, or regiment. Six to ten soldiers made up a squad. Three to four squads made a platoon. Three to four platoons made a company, and three to five companies made a battalion. Three to five battalions made a brigade.

Stephanie and I were in Delta Company. There was Alpha, Bravo, Charlie, and Delta. Besides keeping a wrinkle-free bed, uniforms were ironed daily; shoes polished nightly. Our main drill sergeant bore resemblance to a braying donkey. She had a way of sneaking up behind a recruit, stretching her neck forward, letting loose an ungodly bellow, and enjoying the frightened jump of the designated target. Everyone scrambled to adapt. Some of the girls seemed stronger, some more flustered, everyone tumbling like so many clothes in a dryer.

The Army segregated male and female recruits. Any notion of gender equality was a jeered topic. We were all under the surveillance of the military police, the MP's, who drove around in jeeps like little emperors. Our drill sergeants warned us to steer clear of them and any errant male recruits. "Stay away from all of them," our only male drill sergeant said. "The MP's will give you a hard time. You can't trust em, and make sure you are never alone. Make sure you are always with someone. If you stray from our compound, and you had best not, but if you do, IF YOU DO, you had better take a friend with you. The men are nearby and they WILL RAPE YOU if they find you alone."

That scared all of us.

The ground was covered with a layer of dust, easily stirred during daily running and marching drills. It always found its way into my mouth, drying my throat as I dutifully mumbled, "Run me now, run me now, run me some more, hey." Cough.

We marched multiple times daily, the sun as brutal and relentless as the drill sergeants. "MOVE IT MOVE IT MOVE IT." I kept pace, droning, "Run me now, run me now run me some more, hey."

The drill sergeant suddenly popped up. "I can't HEAR YOU," she screamed into my face.

"Run me now, run me now, run me now hey," I pushed out. "LOUDER, I CAN'T HEAR YOU!"

"RUN ME NOW RUN ME NOW RUN ME NOW HEY," I screamed.

The drill sergeant veered away, starting a new cadence, "I GOT A MAN IN OLD MILWAUKEE, WE MAKE LOVE BY WALKY TALKIE."

We all repeated, "I got a man in old Milwaukee, we make love by walkie talkie." Then we slowed to a march. "HUT. HUT. YOUR LEFT FOOT. HUT." This went on for several hours.

Carter found me later sitting on my bed. We had ten minutes before we had to be in formation outside. "Hey! What are you doing? You better get moving," she said, grinning as usual as she sauntered by.

"I hate this," I said.

"I know. Everybody does," she said.

"No, I mean I really really hate this," I said, on the verge of tears.

She looked at my face and sat down beside me, serious. "I know, but you can do it," she said.

"I know I CAN do it but I don't WANNA do it."

"Come on, why did you join in the first place?" she asked.

"To get out of Minnesota," I mumbled.

"Why didn't you just DRIVE out of Minnesota?"

"I know. That would have been easier. Shit."

"Listen, just get through these six weeks, you can do it. Come on," she poked me in the stomach like I was a kindergartener, and I couldn't help it, I giggled. "Come on, get up off your butt. Let's go," she grinned, and I did feel better and followed her to line up.

We marched five miles that afternoon and I learned a new song – *I got a man, his name is Bill, he won't love me but his brother will.*

We marched until I couldn't feel my feet. The drill sergeant never shut her mouth. "HUT HUT HUT, LEAN BACK, LEFT FOOT, LEFT FOOT, LEFT FOOT, HUT."

Five miles was a long time to listen to "left foot, hut," and I couldn't stop it from playing through the back of my brain when Stephanie and I went to the mess hall later.

"I don't wanna do this anymore," I told Stephanie.

"Well, they're not gonna let you out, if that's what you're thinking," she said.

"I think I'm gonna talk to one of the commanding officers and tell them I made a big mistake."

Stephanie snorted. "Good luck with that. My sister said you have to practically commit suicide to get out."

We sat with Carter and Louise, a tall, bronzed pretty girl from Florida who looked weepy.

"Louise wants to get out," Carter told us as we dropped our trays on the table, shooting me a look.

"You do?" I looked at Louise.

"I can't do it. I'm tired. I don't feel good." She looked at me with reddened eyes.

"She's just homesick, that's all," Carter said to us and then to Louise. "Don't be such a baby, you can do it." Carter, who was cute as shit, looked at me, smiled, and said pointedly, "This is where we get tough, that's all."

I turned to Louise. "I hate it too. I want out too."

"You do?" Louise's voice was tiny.

Jolette

"Oh you guys are just wimps," Carter said.

"Maybe," I said. "I don't care. I don't like it. It's a bunch of bullshit. They just make you go through a bunch of crap just to get a shitty job. I don't even wanna be a truck driver." I looked at Carter. "You're so tough and strong. Of course it's not a problem for you."

"It's all in your head," she said. "If you think you can't do it, well then, you probably can't."

"I could do it, but I'm not gonna," I said.

Carter grinned. "Oh really? What are you gonna do?"

"I don't know. Maybe just tell them and see if they'll let me out."

The girls laughed. Carter looked at me, shook her head.

We were up way before the sun the next day. As usual. Our drill sergeant, the braying donkey, stood near the bathrooms, blatting away at some recruits to get moving.

"Hi," I interrupted, not caring that she looked like she was going to blow a gasket, staring at me like I had three eyes. "Um, who do I talk to if I made a mistake and I don't wanna be here?"

She stared for a moment, then gave a crooked mean little smile, looked off into the distance, and said in an over-casual voice. "Just talk to the commanding officer."

"Okay. Where is the commanding officer?"

She nodded towards a hallway and grinned. "Office at the end." I'd never seen such a smirky grin in my life.

I slid down the hallway, peeked into a room where a woman sat behind a desk, head bent over papers.

"Um hello, Excuse me?" I said.

Her head shot up, her voice a bullet. "Name."

"Um Jolette."

"No, it's not," she barked.

"What? Yes, it is. I mean I think… "

Jolette

"It's Private Mitchell. Isn't that your name, Private?" She cut me off.

"Oh, yes. Yes, Private Mitchell."

"What do you want, Private Mitchell," her voice a machine-gun.

"Well, I made a big mistake coming here. I can see that this is not the place for me. It's a big mistake and I want to go home now. I'd like to leave."

She seemed to be suddenly smiling, although I couldn't really see the smile, I could just feel it. She paused, then spit out, "You don't want us, we don't want you." I think she thought my feelings would be hurt or something because she looked surprised when I smiled, "Great. Okay, thank you. Should I just go somewhere else now or how does this work?"

She hesitated, then said, "It takes a few days for the paperwork." Her head bent back over her desk.

"Okay, thank you, commanding officer," I sent her a smile that was ignored and slipped back to the barracks.

"They're not letting you out," Stephanie said.

"She said they would. She said just a couple of days."

"Don't be dumb. You have to threaten suicide. They won't do anything. You'll see."

It was 7 p.m. Time to polish our shoes. A group of us sat outside, cloth, polish, black clunky shoes in our hands. Carter had a guitar. Everyone was excited, chattering, singing with Carter. I felt miscast, didn't fit in, and was subdued by the time we disbanded at curfew, 8 p.m. Carter fell into step beside me.

"Whatsa matter, baby girl?" she said. I liked being called baby girl by her.

"I don't fit in here. It's just not for me."

"Come here," she said and pulled me down the hallway where the washers and dryers were. No one was around for a change. "I don't want you to get out," she said.

"You want me to stay so you can watch me suffer."

"You know what, Jolette? Louise asked me who I'd wanna be with if I could pick someone from our company."

"Oh, yea? Huh."

"I said I'd pick you."

"Oh," I said, a warm feeling came up my neck, through my scalp, over my face.

"Haha. You're blushing," she said.

"I don't blush," I almost inaudibly protested, my lips not working quite right. Now I was against the wall and Carter leaned next to me. "You just seem so open-minded and not judgmental, ya know. And yeah, you do too blush." She moved in close. I felt hot, sweaty. I turned my face towards Carter, she put her mouth on mine, pushed into me and I pushed back but I could feel her teeth. They were sharp. They hurt my lips. I didn't want to pull away because I liked her and I didn't want to be rude and this was my first kiss with a girl, but I was going to have to pull back before my lips started bleeding. Then we heard voices and she pulled off. My lips breathed a sigh of relief. Some recruits were coming to wash clothes.

"Hey, punk, you washing clothes this late?" Carter was back to her boisterous self, talking to the recruits. We gave each other a look before I slipped back to my bed. I got under the thin, flimsy covers and thought about the kiss. I wasn't sure what it meant. I didn't think it meant that I liked women now. It was just Carter. She had something about her, and the kiss, even though it hurt, was okay. I'd do it again.

"I'm going to kill myself." Once I decided I wanted out, there was no going back. I had to make it happen. I found another commanding officer. There seemed to be as many commanding officers as there were mosquitos at dusk, which is to say a ton. "I just don't think I can handle it anymore." This one was also a chaplain.

The commanding officer chaplain sat behind his desk, unimpressed. "What's your company?"

Jolette

"Delta and I just don't think I can do this anymore. I feel like I want to kill myself."

"Give it another week."

"I don't think I can make it another week. This is too much for me. I can't sleep. I can't function."

"Go back to your barracks."

"I told you," Stephanie said. "They're not letting you out."

Relay races were scheduled for that afternoon. All the companies would be there, including the multitude of commanding officers looking identical as penguins lurching about on migratory breeding grounds. For the first relay race a drill sergeant chalked two circles on the ground some distance apart, Alpha against Bravo against Charlie against Delta. One girl ran, picked up the eraser, brought it back, handed it to the next girl who ran, put the eraser in the circle, and ran back. Next girl, same thing, repeat. Third grade stuff. It was my turn. A girl shoved the eraser at me, I ran, dropped it into the circle. It hit the chalked line. I began to run back, and heard a drill sergeant thunder, "DISQUALIFIED!"

"Oh shit, I hit the stupid line," I mumbled to myself.

"WHAT'S THAT, PRIVATE? WHAT'S THAT YOU JUST SAID?" the drill sergeant screamed.

"I said I KNOW! I KNOW I HIT THE STUPID LINE!" I whirled around to look straight at the drill sergeant. I never liked being yelled at.

He shot over like I was about to toss a grenade. His huge hand grabbed my arm. "You're not running this platoon, private. Who do you think you are? YOU'RE NOT RUNNING THIS PLATOON!"

"I never said I was. Hey, let go of me!" His meaty fingers pressed my arm. I filled with anger; it spewed out of me like a shooting geyser.

"LET GO OF MY ARM! LET GO! FUCK YOU. FUCK YOU ALL."

Adrenalin gave me strength. I yanked my arm free, turned and ran hard towards the trees, charging into the woods, branches scratching at me, my heart furious, breathing so hard it took a while to realize no one was following. I stopped and panted. Ripped off my wraparound skirt, threw it to the ground, tried to dramatically rip my name tag off my shirt, but it wouldn't rip, so I had to settle for just unclipping it and throwing it as far as I could. I looked around. I was in the middle of a woodsy field. I started walking. The field was endless, my breathing calmed, then the faint sound of an engine. In the distance a jeep was headed my way.

"Hey!" a voice yelled.

I could see two men in the jeep. I began to run in the opposite direction. The drill sergeant's warning replayed. The men were not to be trusted; women had been raped. I tore through the bush, the jeep raced after me. An abrupt fence brought me to a halt. On the other side was a highway. I took that fence like a seasoned athlete, charged across the highway, not even pausing when a vehicle pulled over, a uniformed man jumped out, shouting. "Get back here! You get back here!"

I made it across the highway, ran straight up a green hill into a community of trees who buffered me with a quiet calm surround. They seemed to whisper,"there, there." I dropped to the ground, pushed my back against a strong trunk, inhaled, and looked around. The trees were still but strong. I could feel them. I drank in their quiet strength. The air was thick and muggy. After a while of sitting, I started feeling sleepy. Alabama was even more humid than Minnesota. By the time the MP's found me, some hours later, I was sticky with sweat but relaxed, docile, polite. They were polite too. They didn't rape me, just drove me back to the base where I was assigned to Flunky Troop.

"Did the MPs do anything to you? Did they?" several drill sergeants asked, eyes keen, excited. When I shook my head no, they were disappointed. "They didn't? They didn't do anything?"

"No, they were nice." They disbanded, deflated, without any tales of horror done by the MPs and I was taken to my new bunk in Flunky Troop.

Flunky Troop was one step away from being discharged. It would be an honorable discharge. I wasn't considered AWOL since I wasn't gone twenty-four hours. Paperwork would require at least a week, until then me

Jolette

and the six others in Flunky Troop were assigned garbage pick-up. We emptied garbage cans, picked up litter. Oddly enough, Bernice the bossy cow, was in Flunky Troop too. Someone told me she couldn't cut it physically. She had some kind of health issues.

The days inched by. I received a few letters from Marion. He signed his letters "Love, Marion," which made me miss him. Looked like we wouldn't be moving to Germany after all.

I only got to see Carter one last time. She came around one late afternoon. We were done picking up trash for the day and had some downtime.

"Hey," she said, coming into the Flunky Troop building.

"Hey!" I was happy to see her.

"I only got a minute," she said. So, are you getting out?"

"Yea, next week I think."

"Ah man, I wish you wouldn't have left. You know, we could have…." She left off.

"Yea, I know. I'm sorry," I said.

"Me too," she said. "I gotta go but I just wanted to tell you I really like you."

"I like you too," I was eager to say it. She grinned and then was gone. I only saw her one more time, the next day when our old troop went marching by carrying the flag. We were emptying some garbage cans when we caught sight of the troop, the flag waving. We all stopped to watch. Bernice immediately put her hand over her heart, then glanced at the rest of us. "Put your hand on your heart! Stand at attention!" She was such a bossy thing, the girls were intimidated mostly by her heft, and they obeyed. Everyone except me. She glared at me. "Get your hand over your heart. Show some respect."

I wrinkled my forehead. "No. I don't feel like it."

"Get your hand over your heart. Now!"

I don't know what the hell happened to make me submit to Bernice, of all people, after all I'd been through. But I did. I put my hand over my heart while the troop marched by, the flag triumphant, held high, and I caught the profile of Carter, marching by in the dusty heat, her light brown hair shimmering under the sun, and I wondered where her life would lead, was sorry I didn't get to have her press her sharp teeth against my lips again. In the meantime, I remained angry with myself for allowing bossy cow Bernice to order me around. I vowed not to let anything like that happen ever again.

18

Minneapolis, 1976

There ain't no answer. There ain't gonna be any answer. There never has been an answer. There's your answer.
                        Gertrude Stein, American novelist, poet, playwright, 1874-1946.

My Army career was terminated before even beginning. I returned to Minneapolis five long weeks after leaving and was fleetingly happy to be back in the place I loved to hate. Minneapolis was like quicksand, clasping my ankles, never letting me escape, the city most often sitting under a cap of bleak gray skies, inhabited by sad, old buildings with small, cringing windows, offering a view of cloudy skies and pouring rain or the still, skeletal terrain of winter. Even later, after escaping the clutches of the Midwest, I would still feel that melancholy. The dreary land I thought I'd escaped had managed to seep under my skin, would travel with me, depression a constant shadow. I tried to shake it, but it was far easier to remain depressed, the strain of striving for a higher state of mind too strenuous. The depression a rut so deep, even if you climbed up, you'd only teeter, like a bug in a sink, then fall back. It seemed to me a lot of people were depressed. Happiness was a faraway land. I wasn't sure what happiness meant anyway. I wasn't sure it was what I wanted. What did I want? I suppose I wanted to at least like life. To feel interested, stimulated. Yes, I'd settle for stimulation. That's what I wanted. To be stimulated in my life. Yes.

My return from Fort McClellan in July was a leap from one humid region to another, cool relief only a longing, at least two months away. I went straight into the sweaty arms of Marion, regaled him with tales of my military mishap, minus Carter. He laughed.

We moved into an apartment on a pretty tree-lined avenue, both of us back taking classes at the University of Minnesota. We assumed the role of wife and husband, ignoring that our very reason for such a union had been eradicated. It was easier to stay married. He called me his wife, which made me uncertain. It was such a relegating term, implying notions I wasn't sure I had allegiance with. Like the husband always drives. The husband has the ultimate authority. The husband is head of the family, his last name the preferred choice. Even when you knew those things shouldn't be true, it was beaten into you, the subtext of life's daily fabric. Never underestimate the power of these elements. They get to everyone.

We started saying I love you, the words nice to say, comforting as a warm bath that was not too hot, not too cold, but just right. We took evening walks together, Marion's rose-tinted glasses, his unkempt beard, his hand warm and strong clasping mine. We murmured of the day's events, pointed out yards we liked, stopped to chat with neighbors.

I started waitressing at Rudolph's Bar-B-Que on Lyndale Avenue, which was a new restaurant only two blocks from our apartment, on an especially lively corner. Across the street sat Club 26, a popular bar where people spilled from its doors at all hours. Adjacent was a food co-op, the little store filled with barrels of grains and nuts. It was all very homey with volunteers stocking shelves, the air thick with community spirit. The sidewalks — cracked and broken from protesting tree roots — were filled with people strolling or grouped at bus stops, climbing onto city buses which blew dark smoke, arriving at hurried intervals. I was witness to these events from the large restaurant window that gave full view, and as I wiped down the condiments, poured together bottles of used ketchup, and bent to

Jolette

lower plates and fill coffee cups, my gaze would return to life outside, where freedom reigned. As I walked a deepening path from the kitchen to tables to the coffee station, I felt invisible chains tighten and so it was with slight relief the repercussions of a visit from Marion one quiet evening at Rudolph's.

I put Marion in my section, of course, and recommended the restaurant's signature dish, a rack of pork ribs (the pig, a highly intelligent, sentient being, but that awareness hadn't yet made its way into my consciousness)with coleslaw and french fries. Marion dug zealously into his meal. Afterwards, I encouraged his departure without payment only to be promptly confronted by the owner, a stick of a man with a flop of curly dark hair. I didn't deny giving Marion a free meal, and was surprised to be abruptly fired.

"But it was just for my *husband*," I protested, enunciating the word husband like a badge announcing conformity. The word to be used when convenient. It mattered not. I was fired.

With some relief, I untied my apron, left Rudolph's, walked down the soft, darkened street, the trees strong and silent on either side, their boughs stretching overhead forming lacy parasols. Minneapolis was pretty. I wanted to leave but maybe when I got old, like around 40, I'd come back and settle down.

Who could have guessed that the owner of Rudolph's and I would meet again, some fifteen years later, 3,000 miles away, when I was a massage therapist in the hills of Topanga, California, working at a spa retreat where guests spent big dollars for a daily regimen of 400 calories and seven hours of exercise. The guests also received daily massages and was where I, a trained massage therapist by then, spent the day pushing my palms and fingers into the tight muscles of exhausted bodies. One early morning a guest appeared who rang familiar. He was from Minneapolis. He got on the massage table and closed his eyes. Then I recognized him.

"Oh!" I exclaimed. "I know you! I used to work for you! At Rudolph's restaurant. You fired me!" I laughed and his eyes opened, startled. He looked at me without recognition, but as I refreshed his memory, he became increasingly uncomfortable and his thigh muscles– the quadricep femoris muscles which are a group of four muscles covering the femur or thigh bone, working together to allow leg extension and hip flexion, and are responsible for walking, running, rotating hips and other useful items - suddenly became very tense. During the remaining 45 minutes of his massage, he never did relax.

It seemed odd that we should meet again in such an unlikely circumstance and I wondered if it was meant to be for some reason. Or was it random? It's nice to think that there is a universal power adoringly watching us face challenges, giving gentle guidance, knowing what lessons we each must learn for some reason. But probably it's just random. Us on a rocky planet. Stars and debris colliding, causing reverberations, our little selves finding significance in the symmetry or asymmetry of the landing pieces. I found a quote by Gertrude Stein and though not satisfying, it did seem fitting. "There ain't no answer. There ain't gonna be any answer. There never has been an answer. There's your answer."

19

Minneapolis, 1976

Growing up is losing some illusions, in order to acquire others.
Virginia Woolf, 1882-1941, English author.

Marion and I curled up at night. He sat in his overstuffed chair, his book, James Michener's novel *Alaska,* open in front of him.

"Read to me please," I said, pulling a chair closer to him so I could stretch my legs out, rest my feet in his lap.

He idly rubbed my foot and read. *"Alaska would always call forth the best in a small handful of daring men and women, but those who did not relish the contest or who refused to obey harsh rules which governed it would find the bitterly cold land repellent and would flee it if they could retreat before it killed them."* I should have realized then, with Marion's obsessed immersion into Michener's *Alaska,* how swiftly he would depart when his older brother, who had moved to southeastern Alaska years earlier, crooked a finger in Marion's direction. "Come on up for the summer or longer, bro. Check out Alaska," wrote older brother, and whoosh like a speeding train, Marion became distracted, gave an absent-minded kiss goodbye, and headed out the door.

I wrung my hands like a widow. "When will you be back?"

"At the end of September probably. I'll write," he said and vanished, casting me aside like a pair of worn shoes, leaving the apartment hollow and me shoveling my latest pacifier, tubs of orange sherbet, into my mouth as I sat on our couch staring out at gray skies, tree branches tapping on the windows. Loneliness blew in, as if it had been at the door, just waiting for the chance to enter.

My parents tried to cheer me up after Marion left for Alaska, taking me to dinner at a friendly new restaurant on Lake and Hennepin, a desirable locale, adjacent to Lake Calhoun, as it was called then. It was just one of the thousands of lakes that had given Minnesota the title, "Land of Ten Thousand Lakes." A low number, it's really closer to 12,000 and that doesn't include ponds or marshes.

Lake Calhoun was assigned its English name in the 1800s when federal surveyors determined the lake should be renamed after John Calhoun who was the Secretary of War and a strong proponent of slavery. "Slavery is a positive good," said Calhoun. Prior to that arrogance or ignorance, both actually, the lake had been called Bde Maka Ska (Lake White Earth) by the residing Lakota tribe. (Ultimately, the Minnesota Supreme Court would rule decades later, in 2020, in favor of the Lakota name. Bde Maka Ska it is today.)

We were more friendly, my mother, father and I, since I'd moved out of their domain, for while residing under the same roof the environment had simmered. Me, not an obedient child. They, having little to no parental skills. I have sympathy for those who must nourish human growth — who drop a child from a body designed to perpetuate the species. The challenge frequently exceeding ability.

My father had spent a lot of time running around the house, shutting windows as if that would prevent the neighbors from hearing me scream, "Fuck you," in answer to my mother's tirades. As she clawed at me, tried to rip a shirt off my back. The shirt fashioned from a US flag. Or when I left the house with the word FUCK written on my forehead with lipstick. My parents unable to stop me.

My mother was no saint either. For a monotone person who barely moved her lips to speak, she was astonishingly capable of loud roars, always shocking though also routine. She wore an angry mask much of the time, snarling if you dared approach. In my younger years she was daunting, as I got older, I learned to make fast exits and to verbally hit back, utilizing the wonderful word fuck, which had magnificent power to stun. My mother, always in a simmering state, would periodically erupt, her explosions rocking the house. She'd furiously crank the TV and radio to the loudest volume, then storm to the refrigerator where she would whip the door open, slam it shut, whip it open again, its residents falling to the ground like war casualties. Her anger a hurricane blowing the house apart.

I didn't know why she was always so furious. Much of the time, it seemed directed towards me but she was plenty mad at my father too.

One night when I was seven, I was in bed, reading my favorite Nancy Drew detective novel, and my father came in, sat on the bed and asked me about being in Brownies. Did I like it?

Yes, I did.

It was unusual and flattering for my father to engage me in conversation. He said something which made me laugh and then suddenly came a gallop of footsteps racing down the hall and my mother was at the door, screaming "You can both go to hell!" She stormed off as my eyes widened.

My father appeared astounded and speechless. Then he stammered, "I'm sorry," and left.

The next day, my mother looked at me coldly, and said, "The only reason your father talked to you last night was because I told him to. He should talk to you more."

I said nothing but was confused and from that point on, I noticed that every time my father and I talked for any length of time, she got mad. She tried to be a good parent — maybe — but her inner demons wouldn't let her. She was too selfish and jealous. A lot of people are that way, it seems like. My dad was the nice one but he wasn't safe either. I learned to keep my distance from both of them.

I recalled those earlier days of walking home from grade school, gazing up at a wide sky full of soft clouds morphing into an elephant, cat, lion, the wind whimsical, giving gentle puffs, the clouds never staid. Rows of quiet houses lined the road, modest rectangular boxes providing shelter, a sprawl of space between the homes, the plus of suburbia, room to stretch. Childhood included Brownie Troop and Girl Scouts, violin and piano lessons, hopscotch, 500 card rummy games with a steady crew of girlfriends, getting decent grades, not stellar but B's, and reading every night, always reading, sliding into the easy world between book covers. Away from the constant low boil of the house.

When I was eleven, my mother approached me. She was upset, her eyes reddened. "Your father kissed his secretary," she blurted out to me as if I were her confidante. I shrank away, didn't want to hear it. She had been too mean for too long for me to be her friend. I felt sorry for my dad.

A few days later I came home and saw a streak of blood on the kitchen wall. My brother Rick whispered, "The police came. Dad had to go stay at a motel. Mom attacked him, She clawed his arm." I was a little scared but thrilled that the police had come. That there was blood on the wall.

"Is she in her bedroom?" I whispered back and he nodded. The blood elevated the day. I couldn't wait to tell my friends.

My dad returned the next day. Not a word was spoken. We returned to our normal.

"What happened to Jolette over the summer?" my French teacher asked my parents in a teacher-parent conference for eighth grade one fall day after a notable summer. She had been surprised by my new look of bell-bottomed patched jeans, no bra, jaw defiant. I used to stare at Mademoiselle's wrinkled neck as she warbled out, "La table, le crayon, le papier," the flesh of her neck hanging like a flag at half-mast. She walked with a severe limp, her metal knee brace clacking — she had suffered polio as a child — her cane thudding. Thud, clack, thud, clack, up and down the aisles between desks.

"Jolette has changed so much. What happened to her over the summer?" a look of concern on her old face.

Jolette

"We don't know," my parents answered. My mother told me this story many times. "We had to say we didn't know what changed you," my mother would say, leaving a question I refused. I would just laugh and walk away.

I'd started smoking that summer. Cigarettes were fifty cents a pack, I chose Marlboro, bought from cashiers who easily flipped the cigarettes on the counter, dropped the quarters into the cash register.

The cigarettes made me dizzy. It took a long time before I could comfortably inhale and not feel sick. But I immediately liked the look and sure liked lighting up, blowing out the smoke. The statement it made as it dangled between my adolescent fingers. Fingers, a major distinction of the human species, hands, the main source of interaction with our environment, and our long thumb, its opposing force — that little digit was the human body's superior trait.

I was twelve that summer before eighth grade. My cousins had come to visit; three girls, one my age, one a little older, and the oldest I rarely saw because she pasted herself to the grown-ups. But the two around my age, Darlene and Randy, short from Randolyn, and I hung out.

Darlene was twelve, Randy was fourteen, slender, smart, and sassy. Her cigarette laced coolly between ringed fingers, her hair dirty blonde, long and straight, bangs falling right into her eyes, which never bothered her at all. She didn't wear shoes, her tanned feet kicking up dust as we walked to the bowling alley, her bell-bottomed pants hanging low on beautifully sculpted hip bones, which were covered by sun-browned skin that stretched across her flat abdomen. Her shirt tied up under well-developed mammary glands, and when we ran into Jack, a popular kid at school, and his friend, their eyes just about popped out of their heads. We stopped to talk with them for a minute. Jack was mesmerized by Randy, could barely speak. She hardly noticed. We left them standing speechless and went inside the bowling alley to throw some heavy balls down the slippery shiny floor, aiming at the big white pins that just sat waiting to be smashed.

"Darlene, you were supposed to get money from dad," Randy whined, upset she didn't have enough to buy a pop.

"Well, I didn't. Why don't you just ask him yourself for money," Darlene retorted. She was a little chubby. It was easy to see that Randy probably ran the show with her sharp mouth but it didn't mean that Darlene was a total pushover.

"You could have just asked him yourself. I'm not your slave girl."

"You know daddy won't give me money. He doesn't trust me," Randy said, grinning," For some fucking reason."

"Because he knows you're going to just get into trouble," Darlene said and looked at me. "She got in so much trouble last summer. She had so many boys over and daddy caught one of them spending the night."

"He whipped me with his belt for that one," Randy said, taking a drag from a cigarette she'd just lit.

"I don't think they're going to let you smoke in here," I said. "Could I try a cigarette?"

"Sure," Randy said. "Let's go out and have a smoke."

Randy was better than the chocolate-dipped vanilla ice cream cones that my dad used to drive me and my kindergarten best friend Mary to get at Dairy Queen. Mary and I lolling in the back seat of the car, our sandaled feet under skinny kid legs, life made full by a soft serve, raising us to a pinnacle of good feeling, just like Randy did for me now as we walked down a bland Anoka Street smoking cigarettes. I lapped up every move she made, every sound she uttered.

"You should have stayed with Danny. He was really nice," Darlene said to her sister as we walked.

"Danny was a stupid idiot. He was a dumb fuck," Randy said.

"He was not. He was really nice and he liked you a lot."

"Oh, so what, who cares, I know I don't."

"You're not very nice, Rae," Darlene protested.

Jolette

"Yes, I am. I'm really nice. But only sometimes," Randy laughed. I laughed too. I wanted to be just like her.

By the time my cousins left that summer, I'd learned how to smoke, learned a few other things too, like disdain and how to use the word fuck in neat ways.

I started running away at fourteen, climbing out my bedroom window at night, racing down the street to the highway where I'd throw out a thumb, jump into any car that would speed me far away. Abandoning my parent's house and everything in it, the exhilaration rushing through me like a drug. I'd be gone for days, returning when tired, having slept in the back seats of unlocked cars on cold winter nights, a feat almost impossible to endure except when you are young and fresh.

One late freezing night, I was huddled on a cold back seat when the driver's door opened, a man slid in, turned the ignition.

"Um, excuse me, I'm in your car," I squeaked.

He jumped, startled, was driving his car into his garage. He looked at me with sympathy, then invited me into his home with his wife and kids. It was very late. Everyone was sleeping. He tucked me into an empty bed in his kid's room and in the first light of morning, I quietly snuck out, whispering to his two young children who tentatively approached me with big eyes. "Bye, tell your dad I said thank you."

Or Lenny would sneak me into her house at night, and I'd roll under her bed. She'd hand me ice cream sandwiches, and I'd try to get comfortable on her floor, pushing the ice cream into my mouth. Lenny, sneaking me out in the morning, where it was so cold I could see my breath, her fingers to her lips. "Shhh," she whispered."Wait here and I'll get you breakfast."

One time I stayed at an older friend's apartment. But, after a week, I didn't know what to do. I called my mom.

"Hello," she said, monotoned as ever. I didn't say anything. "Hello," she tried again, then, "Jolette?"

I hesitated and said, "Yea."

She paused and in a nicer voice than I'd ever heard, said," Do you want to come home?"

"Okay."

"Okay. Come home, Jolette. We want you to come home." She was nice that time. For a while. I even tried to be normal. I did homework at my desk in my bedroom, just like a regular teenager. But that felt odd and unfamiliar and was short-lived. Like a boomerang, hostilities were restored, family life resumed its familiar unpleasant rhythm.

We were much better once I was out of the house. Once I had moved out permanently. That seemed to be the solution. Since I was the problem. Or so I'd been told.

These days they even seemed concerned, which surprised me. It was nice. My mom and dad and I sat down to look at the menu in the new cozy restaurant on Hennepin with only ten tables. I hung my head."I'm lonely. I miss Marion."

"Well, he should be back in a few months," my mom consoled.

"Maybe. Maybe not," I said. "I don't know what to do."

"Well, Jolette, why don't you just continue with college? Get a job and finish school," dad said.

"Yea, I don't know, dad. I don't really want to stay here. I think I wanna go see him. In Alaska."

"How would you do that? Please don't hitchhike," mom said.

"Okay. Maybe a ride-board. I'll check the one at school."

"You should really finish school so you can get a good job," dad said.

"I know. I know, dad, but there's more important things in life than a good job," I said, trying to hide my exasperation with his ignorance. "I have to go out and experience the world before I worry about stuff like a good job. I need to find something I want to do first."

We ordered apple pie for dessert and my parents gazed at me in what would be our final dinner before I left Minneapolis for good.

20

Seattle, Alaska, 1976

Dancers wanted for the Shamrock Bar in Ketchikan, Alaska. Free transportation to Ketchikan. Call Jerry - Seattle Times, 1976

My feet hit the ground in Seattle on First Avenue right in front of Pike Place Market, on the waterfront of Puget Sound, built in 1907, considered one the oldest public farmers' markets in the US. I jumped out of the car that had delivered me from Minneapolis, a two-day drive with Edward, a serious student I found on the bulletin rideboard at the University of Minnesota. I rattled on to him about Alaska. He was stiff in response. I ran out of steam and slept for long spells, waking to the lull of the car's motion with a queasy stomach, reminded that I had suffered from car sickness all my life and this adventure would be no exception. The car was mostly silent. Edward never played the radio unless I asked. Then the car filled with static until we gave up and turned the radio off.

New lands spread like giant welcoming mats beyond the car's windows. Through the flat plains of North Dakota until the Welcome to Montana sign in letters bold and red next to a rendering of mountains. Just the image of a mountain shot an excited thrill through me. The gateway to the West. Through Montana and then to Idaho, the Rocky Mountain State, also the Potato State, which yields about one-third of all potatoes grown nationwide, if I remembered right from grade school where it was deemed important to memorize each state and its agricultural abilities.

Jolette

Edward was going to Seattle to attend the University of Washington. He would study law, he said. Edward was very straight. Straight, a term describing those in rigid conformity to society's directives.

"Never straight, always forward," Maude and I would say to each other anytime someone uttered the word straight, then we would peal into laughter, raise a fist, consider ourselves rebels.

Waving goodbye to Edward's studious face — was that a small smile I witnessed before turning to take in the grandeur of Pike Place Market – I wasn't sure but gave an extra wave to the stalwart student before turning to embrace the view, my nostrils immediately assailed by a strong pungency. Fish. I looked to the market's tables of hundreds of dead fish staring up from icy beds, then was hit with a whiff of salted air fresh off the ocean.

The ocean, spread before me, was big and broad, its surface complacent, but so immense you knew there was powerful potential deep within, with a predator's ability to lunge. It seemed like life itself, which could sit quiet for a long time, then just a flick of its finger and the world crumbled, leaving you floundering for a life raft. I ran my gaze across the idle frolic of waves, the ocean only a relaxed giant that day. Sleepy under the sun.

I swung on my backpack and set out to find the YWCA. It was up Seneca Street, a steep grade of a hill that abruptly yanked its occupants from sea level. The best way to take an incline, I knew, was to keep my head down, just concentrate on each individual step. Do not look up because the hill would only appear insurmountable, helpful not one bit. Probably applied to life in general. But that was really too difficult to do in this intoxicating city, full of smells, ocean, and mountain views. My head spun, taking in as much as I could. I was panting by the time I registered at the Y, took a moment to dump my backpack in the small room with only a slip of a bed, ran back outside, plunging down the street, gravity pulling me into a run, all the way into Pioneer Square, a cobblestoned common ground for transients, tourists, and locals. I inhaled the salty ocean air, my senses quickening. This was so much better than Minnesota.

Each morning, I pored through the *Seattle Times* newspaper, searching for ideas to get to Alaska with my very limited funds. How to get to Ketchikan. How to get to Ketchikan.

Marion had taken the ferry up to the salmon capital of the world, the south-eastern-most city in Alaska. He'd slept on the ferry's upper deck amidst a group of kindred travelers. They'd thrown down sleeping bags, slept under the stars. Marion had drifted off while lullabied by someone strumming a guitar, his gaze fixed on the dark recess above, festively lit by around 5,000 stars, which astronomers agree is the number of stars visible to the naked eye of a reasonably sighted person. There are perhaps 9,000 stars visible to the naked eye worldwide. Cut that in half when you look up to your half of the hemisphere, and consider that you are only gazing upon the smallest fraction of existing stars. Also consider that there are 100 to 400 billion stars just in the Milky Way. These hot gaseous balls, kept intact by the force of their own gravity, are primarily made up of hydrogen and helium with a dash of carbon, nitrogen, oxygen, and iron, components which make up every single thing in the Universe including humans, except there's no helium in the human composition.

One morning, a few days later, an ad appeared.

Dancers wanted for the Shamrock Bar in Ketchikan, Alaska. Free transportation to Ketchikan. Call Jerry.

Perfect.

Jerry was a pudgy fellow, maybe thirty or forty or fifty, with greasy combed-back hair. He asked if I had any experience dancing.

"Yes," I lied.

"I need to see your breasts," he said. I knew he was lying too. I opened my shirt, lifted my bra, watched him look. He didn't change his expression much. "Ok," he said, his eyes small and beady, but seemingly harmless. His small office just off First Avenue, held only a messy desk, smudged walls. There was nothing lucrative about Jerry except he was generous enough to take me shopping for the lingerie and shoes he said I'd need for my new dancing job. He purchased my airline ticket and the next day I boarded Alaska Airlines, buckled myself next to the window, and stared down at Washington's diminishing evergreens.

The descent into Ketchikan, only ninety minutes later, was through a thick bank of gray clouds, a threshold from one world to another. The plane lowered, breaking free from the dense gray to a striking clear view of the Pacific Ocean, mammoth and swaggering, and an abundance of trees covering jutting mountains, the patchwork of lush greens beyond measure. Small houses dotted the land, lazy curls of smoke rose from chimneys. Something very raw and world-removed seemed to govern. I felt an immediate cut from the lower forty-eight states.

"You the dancer?" a man standing next to an old bus, wearing knee-high rubber boots and a hardy red jacket, asked as I stepped outside the Ketchikan International Airport, the name bigger than the place.

I nodded, "Yea, I guess so." I'd barely sat down, the sole passenger, before the rickety bus sprang into action, hurled down a road through the densest population of trees I'd ever seen, bringing us to a cluster of small shops, downtown, past a winding creek and a boardwalk that held a row of houses just above the creek's rushing tumble. The boardwalk – Creek Street – was known for Dolly's House, I learned later, a brothel built in the 1800s for lonely pioneers and the financially strapped women who serviced them. Now a highlight on the tourist ticket. Prostitution made acceptable with a wink.

The bus managed to brake its stiffened joints and came to a stop in front of a giant green shamrock painted on the front of a building. The Shamrock Bar. My stomach tightened. I stared for a moment at the bar where I would make my topless dancing debut.

There was a roar coming from inside. I shoved open the door to a small bar filled with baritone voices, loud and raucous, competing with a blaring juke box. The men were plying themselves with drink, trying to fill the hole between scraggly beards and their mustaches. A congestion of small tables crowded close together. Peanut shells covered the floor. The stage was a frugal platform where a slim girl wearing a bikini bottom, heels about ten feet tall, and nothing else, moved to Donna Summer's *Love to Love You Baby*. Her breasts were small with dark nipples. She moved well. Oh shit, I thought nervously. My dancing skills were not great. Plus I wasn't super skinny. I was okay, but not skinny. That was the voice on one shoulder. Luckily the voice on the other shoulder was much stronger. What the fuck. Who gives a shit. Just dance, get paid, and go to Rose Inlet to find Marion.

"Hi! I'm the new dancer," I pushed my way through a couple of burly men to yell at the bartender who was slamming drinks at a frantic pace. "Excuse me, hey, hi, I'm the new dancer!"

"Oh yea?" the bartender yelled back, scanning me like I was produce at a grocery store. "Hey Stewart, we gotta new dancer. Take her upstairs." He grinned, yelling, "What's your name?"

"Jolette."

He went to a chalkboard hanging behind the bar, used pink chalk to write Juliet next to DAY DANCER. Juliet was the only name in that category. There were six names after NIGHT DANCERS. BAR HOURS 9AM TO 4AM.

"I'm the only daytime dancer?" I asked the bartender. I didn't correct the spelling.

"Yup, the stage will be all yours."

"Oh god," I mumbled and followed Stewart, a young skinny kid, to the back of the bar where a narrow staircase led up to a darkened attic.

"This is where all the dancers sleep." Stewart, who looked about twelve, smiled at me.

"Okay. Uh thanks."

The ceiling was low. I had to bend over. About eight cots were scattered about, piled with sparkling lingerie, nylons, and shoes with gigantic heels. This was supposedly where I would sleep, a laughable notion, I learned, as the blaring music was never silenced.

Jolette

The other six dancers knew I was a newbie at first glance. They were friendly in a nonchalant way. "I don't even know how to dance," I groaned to one of the girls.

"Don't worry. Nobody cares," a thin, red-headed, green-eyed girl named Christy said. "Just flash some titty and make your tips."

There was no sleeping the night before my topless debut. I tossed and turned on the small cot, the music blaring. At 9 a.m. I stepped on stage, wearing heels like stilts that I could barely walk in, much less dance. I faced the audience, a small group of men watching me the way you'd observe a minor car crash, neutral with no investment. I snapped my fingers, basically walked in place to Thelma Houston's *Don't Leave Me This Way*. Nobody had to tell me. I knew I was lousy. On the third song – Christy told me to wait til song three – I pulled at my lingerie top, got it off, leaving my black lace bra underneath. By the fourth song, I had already tried a couple of times to smoothly unclasp my bra but finally just had to stand in place, my fingers clumsy, slow, trying to unhook the thing.

"Need help with that?" A voice from one of the three tables. I laughed, a nervous sound, got the bra off, threw it in the corner, and shifted around in what was supposed to pass for dancing with at least a half-dozen eyes glued to my breasts. Someone opened the door, a cool morning breeze blew in against my skin. It felt good. I relaxed. It didn't seem like a big deal at all to be topless.

"You know what? They have a new dancer at the AquaMarine Club. She's some Asian girl and she smokes cigarettes with her twat," Christy said later when I went upstairs to collapse on my little cot for a ten-minute break.

"How are we supposed to compete with that?" She lit a cigarette, blew out smoke. From her mouth. We were strictly topless at the Shamrock, no complete nudity.

"Ew, that's gross," I said.

"Yea, well gross or not, it's packing 'em in. She's making a fucking lot of money."

It was on my second day when I noticed two red sores on my chin. By the time night rolled around they'd multiplied and were oozing yellow pus. Someone gave me band-aids. I pasted them over my chin, but more sores were forming and white flakes of skin were flaking off like snow. Eyes were now glued to my face more than any other body part. I was the dancer whose skin was falling off her face.

"Impetigo," a doctor at the Ketchikan medical clinic said, and prescribed antibiotics. Impetigo is a contagious bacterial skin infection, commonly striking travelers, he told me. I invested in antibiotics and stuck a few band-aids next to my nose. The sores were getting big. I continued to take the stage, band-aids shining under the single spotlight.

I met Roger, an easygoing young guy. He thought it was terrible that I could never get any sleep up in the Shamrock attic and offered his bed as a quiet place to rest. Avoiding my bandages, we consummated my quiet place to rest, sex as natural as a handshake. In the morning he gave me $50. "I want to help you," he said.

I rushed to buy a seaplane ticket to Hydaburg, which was one step closer to Rose Inlet and Marion, and ditched the Shamrock, saying a quick good-bye to Christy who still had two more weeks dancing at the Shamrock before her next dancing job who-knows-where.

It was early morning when I boarded a small seaplane to Hydaburg, excited as a kite on a windy day.

21

Seattle, 1981

Travel is more than seeing of sights; it is a change that goes on, deep and permanent, in the ideas of living.
   Miriam Beard, American historian, archivist, activist. 1876-1958.

"Let us go then, you and I, when the evening is spread out against the sky." Jeffrey's voice, patient, gentle, reflected his persona very well.

Jeffrey was my neighbor, his apartment one floor below. Picture him standing, legs together a little too tightly, hands hanging in front of him, one over the other, oddly placed near his crotch but that was just awkwardness. He generated no sexual heat. He smiled, lips pressed together, never any teeth. He asked for no special attention.

"Will you read to me?" I'd asked him and he readily agreed for he was an agreeable sort, and he loved literature. That was where his stance became more comfortable.

"Like a patient etherized upon a table; let us go, through half-deserted streets, the restless one night cheap hotels and stardust restaurants with oyster shells."

"I love that," I interrupted, reclined on a couch, eyes fastened on the ceiling, seeing half-deserted streets. The key to understanding poetry, in this case T.S.Eliot's *Love song of J. Alfred Prufrock,* was to listen, abandon preconceived notions, allow fresh concepts. Really hard to do with a brain that is hardwired to resist change, thrives on preconceived notions, and, like our bodies, resides in a state of inertia to preserve homeostasis, a state considered necessary to maintain normal body temperature and other items that ensures survival. The brain oversees electrical wiring, coordinating the needs of a cumbersome body, integrating relevant and irrelevant data, all while submerged in tons of fat. There is a lot of fat in the brain. To attempt transcendent thinking is asking a lot of an organ that has so much to do. No wonder it was so hard to get past the mundane, the main ingredient of daily life.

"In the room the women come and go talking of Michelangelo."

"What does that mean?" I interrupted again and Jeffrey forgave me because that was his nature. He was compliant, hesitant. Too hesitant to ever make a pass at me, which was good because I was not interested. He was too meek. He was a good listener, but that meekness had an odor. I could smell it. The furthest he dared venture was to tell me I had a pretty collar bone.

"I like your collar bone. It's so pretty," he said.

"Thank you. What does it mean?" I asked. "The women come and go talking of Michelangelo."

"Well T.S. Eliot is open to interpretation, but I think it refers to perhaps the shallow nature of inflated discussions while life delivers a series of struggles, as depicted in the other lines. Maybe it's a reflection of modern superficial society in those times."

"Hmm. Okay. Will you keep reading?" I asked, looking back at the ceiling as he began to read again but this time my mind wandered. I was distracted, now more interested in thinking about myself. I'd been thinking of leaving Seattle lately. He finished, looked at me.

"That was so nice. Thank you. Have you written any poems lately?" I asked, listening to his answer absently because again I was more interested in thinking about me. I was thinking about traveling. Maybe I'd go to Europe. Maybe go live in Europe. I liked that idea.

Jolette

There was a pause. I'd missed the last beat of his response. I covered with a nod, "I'd like to read some of your poetry." Then a non-apologetic shift. "You know what Jeffrey?"

"What Jolette?" He smiled, indulged me, and I allowed myself indulgence. There was no heat between us, and I was not nervous at all with him, the way I was with some men I was attracted to. I don't know why my body created so much fluster when I was attracted to someone. I had no problem at all with clients, was smooth as glass. What the hell.

"I think it's time for me to get a European education. I think I need to move to London or Paris. I think I'm going to go."

"What about school? Don't you only have a few quarters before you graduate?"

"Yes, but so what. I can do it later. I'm feeling like I need to go now. I'm getting depressed being in Seattle. I feel confined in school and I'm tired of being around those students. I have nothing in common with them. Nothing. I'm going to leave in a month. I'm getting a ticket to London."

"Really? You are? I'll miss you," his voice plaintive. Plaintive made my skin crawl. I ignored him. "Can you read some more T.S. Eliot?"

I bought a one-way ticket to London, was leaving in ten days. The girls gave me a going away dinner. We were at an Italian restaurant in the University District. Nadine, Liz, Lisa, Helen, Carol, and Trudy were all there with reddened lips, legs freshly browned from suntan booths.

"Girl, I don't know why you gotta go so far away." Nadine had just gotten new hair. It was parted in the middle, straight, long, charcoal black. Her eyes were lined thickly, lashes plump, I thought of Cleopatra.

"Love the do, Nadine," I said.

"Well, you should, I paid enough for it, I know that." She swiveled in her chair and called out to a waiter, "Baby, can we get some drinks over here?"

"Yea, we need some drinks here," Trudy reinforced, looking like she'd already had a bottle of wine, cheeks rosy, eyes super bright, animated a notch above normal. The girls were feeling rowdy. They loved their alcohol. I was the only teetotaler.

"Michelle, how long will you be gone, honey?" Helen asked, maternal as always.

"Yea, Michelle, how long are you going for?" Lisa asked. It had been a year since we went on her first call together. She was a hard worker, a graphic artist by day, escort by night, was leaving the business soon I knew. Was just saving enough to put a down payment on a house. Smart girl.

"I don't know. Maybe I'll live in London or Paris for a year or two."

"But what about Augustus? What about your new man, honey?" Helen asked.

That was the thing. I had met someone. It all stemmed from the vantage point of my third-floor apartment window, widespread, giving an easy visual to the scampering of pedestrians below on University Avenue. One morning, on a groggy walk from my bedroom to the kitchen, a glance out my large window brought a glimpse of a dark-haired, broad-chested fellow who had just parked a blue Chevy curbside. I stopped dead in my tracks, stared down, liked very much what I saw.

He was extremely masculine, overflowing with testosterone, palpable all the way up into my apartment. Dark hair, light blue t-shirt stretched over a healthy set of chest and abdominal muscles, jeans, tennis shoes.

I started looking for him every morning and was rewarded. He parked in the same spot, around the same time, 9:30 to 10 a.m. every day. Most days he had a female in tow, frequently a petite redhead, but there were a few brunettes, at least one blonde. The man never seemed to be alone. He and whatever female was accompanying him that day, would amble down University Avenue, and enter the Grand Delusion Coffee Shop. I put him on my list of men I was interested in, undaunted by his feminine coterie. Because, though insecure down to the bone, I was also extremely confident at the same time. It didn't make sense.

Jolette

One ordinary work night I was headed home a little earlier than usual. The night was still young as I drove through the University District where people were milling on the sidewalks, friendly lights illuminating just enough to grant a warm glow. It was the kind of evening where it seemed fitting that something special would occur.

The Grand Delusion Coffee Shop was open. The languid evening invited outside lounging. My eyes skimmed the small crowd then caught the profile of the dark-haired man through the window. He was at the counter, taking coffee orders. I immediately swung my car into a parking spot, jumped from the car, strolled through the coffee shop's entrance. There was a line in front of the counter. Yes, it was him, taking orders, turning to handily steam and froth liquids, churning out lattes and cappuccinos from the espresso machine. Close up he was even better, his eyes a deep brown almost black. They managed to stir me even from the back of the line. Then he smiled and something about that smile sent a bunch of oxytocin to the pleasure center of my brain, undoubtedly accompanied by dopamine, estrogen, and adrenaline. By the time I got to the counter my cheeks were flushed.

"Hi, what can I get you?" His eyes were finally on me and though, unbeknownst to him, I had already had a flood of emotion due to his presence, I was surprisingly able to maintain composure.

"Is there anything with chocolate in it?"

"How about a hot chocolate or a mocha coffee? Have you ever tried a mocha coffee?" he asked.

"No, that sounds good. Okay."

He turned to the espresso machine, my eyes resting on his well-defined shoulder muscles. When he turned my way I smiled and said, "Nice night out tonight isn't it."

"Yes," he responded with that smile. "The only thing that would make it better is a bottle of wine, but we don't have any here."

"Do you want me to go get you some?" I asked. "I could just run over to the market and get you a bottle."

"Really?"

"Sure," I said. "What kind of wine do you want?"

"Ah, how about a cabernet sauvignon. Here let me give you some money."

"I'm Augustus," he said when I brought him his wine at the Grand Delusion.

"I'm Jolette. Here you go." I handed him the bottle, a little out of breath ostensibly from rushing to the market but really from heart palpitations.

"Have a glass of wine with me. Let's go outside. Rick, I'm taking ten," he called to a short man with big glasses.

"Yeah, sure, Augustus," the short man said.

I followed him. The air was enchanted or maybe it was just me flooded with endorphins.

"You work here?" I asked.

"I co-own," he said, handed me a small glass of wine. I didn't drink wine. It made me sleepy, gave me a headache, but I couldn't say no. My lips took in the smallest sip of wine ever taken in the history of wine sipping. I lifted my eyes, yes, I really liked his face. He smiled and my body released more oxytocin striking my brain's pleasure centers again, ding ding ding, just like a pinball machine, sensation raised like the crescendo of a choir.

Then he began talking about his ex-girlfriend and I instantly shot back to earth. Not where I wanted to be, but at least it leveled me out. He was distressed over the woman who'd just left him. I couldn't tell if he was more anguished because she was gone, or because she'd been the one to leave. Nobody had ever left him before, he mourned. I placed a sympathetic expression on my face, nodded a tremendous amount while he agonized. He finally asked for my number.

I was a little ill each time he picked me up, nervous as a cat on a high wire. After two months of dating during which time we'd had plenty of sex — robust, acrobatic, lacking in intimacy but who cared – I decided to tell him I was a call girl, having a notion about the value of honesty in important relationships, wanting him in that category. Ultimately, I wanted to see his smile for the rest of my life. If I could have attached myself to him surgically, I would have.

Normally, my disclosure that I worked as a call girl to someone I was dating was employed only when I wanted to break up with the guy. Under the pretense of confiding because, "I thought you had a right to know." This big reveal guaranteed stunned expressions, a flustered few words, then either immediate rejection — "I don't think I can handle that,"or an interim of a few days during which it was being thought over. Followed shortly by rejection. The technique easy as warm butter spread on bread.

My disclosure to Augustus would be different. An attempt to build a relationship. With honesty.

It was one of those rare Seattle days, sunny with a warm breeze. Augustus and I were going to the Green Lake Café for lunch. He pulled his car next to the lake, a blue sparkle of promise attended by flocks of joggers and bicyclists. Though nervous about the impending big reveal, my heart was elevated, my steps light. It was difficult to stay anchored firmly to the ground when near him.

"There's something I want to tell you," I started as we walked side by side, me feeling that being by his side was where I was meant to be, what would we name our children.

"Yes?" his head came close to mine. I looked into his dark eyes, felt like I was going to fall in.

"I think I need to tell you what I do for work."

"Okay, I thought you worked telephones somewhere."

"No, I don't do telephones. That's just what I tell people."

Just then a female voice penetrated our sphere. "Augustus!" It was the petite redhead whom I'd seen climbing out of his blue Chevy many early mornings. She'd just come from the café.

"Hi! You just go for lunch?" he called.

She stopped in front of us, pretty blue eyes, long red hair, no freckles. "Yea, try the onion pate, it's delicious."

It bothered me that I didn't know what pate was.

"Judy this is Jolette. Jolette, Judy."

"Hi," I smiled hesitantly.

She dubiously smiled back, dual assessments made. Her eyes flew back to Augustus. "You going to the gym later?"

"Oh, probably," he said.

"Okay, see you," she smiled and I didn't actually see her raise her leg and spray, but I swear she marked him before sashaying off.

He turned his head towards me, "Now where we were?"

"Oh, I was just going to tell you what I really do for work. I hope it won't bother you or anything. I mean, I'd like to keep seeing you," I stumbled, my momentum usurped by Judy's untimely intrusion.

He tilted his head. "I'm positive there is nothing you can tell me which is going to make me not want to see you."

My throat gulped, which I tried to hide. "Um, well, what I really do is um I'm a call girl. I work for an escort agency."

He paused, a look of surprise on his face. "Really?"

"Yea, no kidding. How do you feel about that?"

"Huh," he thought briefly. "That's interesting. So, you get paid to have sex?"

"Well, yes."

"Can I apply for the job?" he laughed.

I laughed uncertainly. "Um, seriously, how do you feel?"

"Well," he paused." I'm flattered that you sleep with me for free."

"Oh," I said. "Really? Is that it?"

"Should there be more?"

"No, not really. I mean it's just a job, strictly business."

"Okay," he said in the most good-natured tone I'd ever heard. He took my hand, we walked into the Green Lake Café, and didn't order onion pate.

When I said I was going to London, was going to travel through Europe, he asked if he could join me. "Sure, if you want. That would be nice." I managed to moderate my tone while my heart suffered a sudden case of fibrillation. He said he would join me in London three weeks after I left, turning what would have been an ending into a beginning and even though I was obsessed with this man, could think of nothing else, still, no matter what, I was going to Europe because, honestly, there are just some things one should do.

"I'm crazy about him," I said to the girls.

"Girl, you crazy, period," Nadine had to mouth off.

"I think I'm madly in love."

Liz cooed. Lisa and Carol smiled. Trudy rolled her eyes.

"Oh honey, that's wonderful. I'm happy for you," Helen gave the sweetest smile.

"He flirts with other women though. I don't get it," I said.

"Oh shit, here we go." Trudy took a big gulp of wine, turned to check out the restaurant, her radar up for available men. She'd already heard my complaints.

"He stares at other women when he's with me," I said, turning to Helen, whose support could always be counted on. "I mean, we're having dinner and I'm all mesmerized by him and I look up and he's got his eyes on the woman at the next table and she's smiling at him." I raised my voice with some indignation.

"Baby, that's just a man thing. It doesn't mean anything," Helen comforted.

"I hate it."

"Of course you do, honey. Just ignore it. Just act like you don't even notice," Helen solaced.

"Oh, bullshit to that," Nadine said, "I say you look him in the eye and say, Who you here with anyway? You here with the girl at that table? No, you are not. You are here with me. Now please act like it and quit disrespectin me."

"Or maybe you could just have a talk with him," Liz said. "You know, ask him could you talk about something that's important to you?"

"Or maybe you could just stab him, hahaha," Trudy snorted, grinned. "That's what she's gonna end up doing anyway. He's gonna drive you crazy with that." She pointed the last sentence at me, then swiveled, "Let's get another bottle of wine."

"Well, honey, I'm sure that once you get more serious with him, he'll only have eyes for you," Helen said. "Now baby, we are going to miss you. You get Europe out of your system and then come back to us. We love you."

22

London, 1981

Penises are essentially the same worldwide.
Jolette

I flew into Heathrow Airport on October 8, 1981, the date etched into my mind because Egypt's president Anwar Sadat was assassinated while I was 30,000 feet above the world. It was only after emerging from the Tube in London's Victoria Station, that my eyes caught the screaming newspaper headlines, "EGYPT'S SADAT ASSASSINATED!"

Oh no, I thought, and scrambled to read the story. Anwar Sadat had been assassinated in Cairo the day before. Oh, no. He'd been attending a military victory parade, was sitting in the stands when a squadron of soldiers suddenly detached from a truck in the parade, and raced towards him. Sadat had stood, saluted, mistakenly taking the approaching soldiers as part of the celebration. He was saluting the soldiers when they gunned him down. Oh no. I liked Sadat. He was brave, elegant, the first Arab leader to sign a peace accord with Israel. Gunned down. Oh no. My mind faltered. Maybe this was only real in London. Maybe it wasn't real in the rest of the world.

Dazed with jet lag and shocked by the news of Sadat's assassination, I tightly cinched the belt of my backpack, which squat heavily on my back, and walked out of Victoria Station. The streets were damp under light rain, throngs of people moving rapidly with purpose, each intent as an ant following a pheromone scented trail promising reward.

I flipped open my *Visiting Europe on $5 a Day* book to the page I had marked. The YWCA was within walking distance and though I'd only left Seattle a day earlier, life in the U.S. already seemed a solar system away.

The YWCA was a dry respite from London's wet chill. I signed in at the front desk, was sent to a room with a handful of bunk beds, most unoccupied. I chose one near the wall and was unpacking when suddenly a thunderous boom split the air and the room shook. I stood stunned, then ran to the lobby.

"What was that?" I cried to the first woman I saw, who stood stock still, her eyebrows raised.

"Musta been a bomb. Musta been close," she said.

"Yes, that was really close," said another woman.

"That was two blocks over," called a woman from the next room. "They bombed a building two blocks from here."

I already knew that in the 1970s, London suffered a slew of terrorist bombings inflicted by the Irish Republican Army (IRA), a militant faction in pursuit of independence for Northern Ireland from English control. I had read about the hostilities between Ireland and England that stemmed from hundreds of years of Anglo-Normans invading Ireland. The Irish people writhing for centuries under England's determined control. In 1919 the IRA was created and over the years the group committed bombings and assassinations in an effort to free Northern Ireland. The 1970s saw an energized IRA, intent on disrupting the economics of England by bombing commercial establishments in London and killing British soldiers.

It was one thing to read about it for a class at the University of Washington, another thing entirely to stand only a few blocks from a real bombing. I found out that, when I arrived, bombings were a regular occurrence, this one close enough to raise eyebrows and momentarily pause activity. Then life resumed, for bombings had apparently become the new normal. I was startled and unsure for a few moments, then took my cue from the women around me who had returned to normal, and went back to unpacking.

Augustus was due in a few weeks. In the meantime, I set my sights on Fleet Street, aka newspaper row, three miles away. I had fallen in love with journalism only a few years earlier, had fallen under the spell of the printed word as a young reader, and for years had steadily searched books for just one inspirational sentence which could be mine forever. The allure of the printed word almost as mesmerizing as my infatuation with Augustus. Almost but not quite.

I took the Tube, exited Blackfriars Station, walked down the famed Fleet Street, home of London's newspapers, stopped in front of a commanding upswept building, my neck bent back to look up at the lettering on the buildings front: The Daily Telegraph. I felt like I was in the presence of greatness, and was hushed as I walked under the front doors arch and approached a man seated behind the sole desk in the lobby. "Hello," I smiled meekly. "I'm a journalism student from the United States and I just wondered if I could please have a tour of the building?"

"You are American?" the man asked. He seemed pleased.

"Yes," I said.

He stood, shook my hand. "Welcome to The Daily Telegraph. My name is Frederick. Allow me to get someone to assist you."

"Oh, thank you," I said.

He nodded his head, bent to the phone, pressed a button. "Norman, there's a young woman, an American journalist here who's requesting a tour of the building."

"I'm a student, a journalism student," I corrected. He nodded again, smiled, "Yes right, very good. Well, then, one of our reporters will be here momentarily."

I surveyed the vacuous lobby, its ambience sober. I was excited, mildly intimidated. Funny the esteem granted to the published word. The authority granted to penned scrawls or a typed page lifted onto a newspaper, magazine, or book. The words put into uniform, pressed onto pages, status automatically elevated. I'd been witness to such a transformation, seen it with my own stories when writing for college papers, amazed at the facelift achieved by mere mass production.

Footsteps made me turn. A man approached, offered a vague smile. "Hullo, I'm Norman," he said. I'm a reporter with the Telegraph. You'd like to see the newsroom?"

"Yes, I said, "I'd love to see the newsroom."

"You're a reporter in the States?"

"No, no, I'm a journalism student. I've just written for campus papers."

We turned to walk to the newsroom. I was gliding along beside the reporter, who then told me he had once dated an American long ago – Janis Joplin.

"Really, Janis Joplin? Neat."

He'd met her during an interview. He told me this before we reached the newsroom, which was good because there was a sudden increase in volume, a machine-gun staccato of typewriter keys clattering. Fingers madly racing to meet deadlines. The slinging of carriages that sat atop the typewriter, sending a zinging then a slamming sound through the air. We entered the newsroom, were devoured by the din. Square desks populated a large fluorescent-lit room. Each desk clutched a suit-attired man. Held him captive while he labored over a black, old-fashioned typewriter.

The reporter said something, but there was no way I could hear him. "What?"

He raised his voice. "This is where all of the stories are written. Right now they're on deadline for tonight's last issue."

"Do any women work here?"

"They're in the fashion department. I'll take you there." He whisked me down a hallway to a quieter, less populated room. "Bernice, this is Jolette. She's an American journalist and is taking a tour today."

Jolette

"Student, I'm a journalism student, hi." I offered my hand to Bernice, a large woman who wore a well-sprayed coif resembling a car hood ornament. She offered a slight white hand, limp in my grasp, blinked her eyes at me, lifted the corners of her mouth, almost cracking the solid paste of makeup which smoothed her face like plaster.

"This is the fashion department," she proudly announced.

"Oh!" I exclaimed for her. "How many women work here?"

"We have three full-time women working in this department," she stated. "Would you like to see where we lay out the design?"

"Yes, please."

"Come and get me when you're finished here," Janis Joplin reporter said. "I'll take you to the presses."

"Okay, thank you," I said, taking another look at the reporter. He was tall, slender, with a nose so thin it was a wonder oxygen could get through. His hair was longish; his eyes behind a pair of glasses were moist. He wasn't appealing but he'd dated Janis Joplin, was a reporter for The Daily Telegraph. That was enough to allow some enhancement.

I turned to follow Bernice. She wore a dark blue dress that fell below her knees. Her hips were wide, which spoke of many hours sitting, typing perhaps, plying herself with sugar for energy, I suspected. I spent an hour with Bernice. She was generous once she got going, and seemed to relish the attention. "The men won't hire women for the news department because they think women won't want to go out, get wet in all the rain, you know, and the hours are long and irregular, so most women wouldn't be interested in all that."

"Really? That seems ridiculous, but I mean, do you think that's true?" I asked.

"I suppose it's about true for anyone, women and men alike, but I'll bet they'd be plenty of women who wouldn't mind at all taking on the old newsroom. I wouldn't mind it myself. Where are you from in America?"

"Seattle, Washington."

"Oh, near the White House then?"

Jolette

"No, Seattle is in Washington State. Where there are a lot of trees."

Being American was a good thing at The Daily Telegraph. I was introduced time again as the American, received stares I imagined celebrities were subjected to. It didn't take long before I expected admiration just for being born in America although it would be short-lived. I'd get the opposite when I went to a pub later with Janis Joplin reporter.

"Could I have a 7up?" I asked the waitress at the Grasshopper Green, a pub favored by Janis Joplin reporter.

"Lemon-lime?" she asked.

"Yes, sure."

"A lager," Janis Joplin reporter ordered. He was amiable in a non-smiling, intense manner. He'd guided me through the clamorous press room where gigantic paper sheets were unrolled into letterpresses, machines shrieking like patients in an insane asylum.

"This paper is called newsprint. It goes through the letterpress," the quiet Joplin reporter had to make an effort to be heard. It seemed an unnatural act. When he'd asked if I'd like to go to the pub I immediately nodded. I wanted to hear more about Janis.

"Where did you meet her?" I asked, sipping my lemon-lime, strong on the lime.

"In 1969 she was playing the Albert Hall. I covered the story and met her backstage."

"What's the Albert Hall?"

"You don't know the Albert Hall?"

"No. It's an arena?"

"It's just the most famous stage in the world," the reporter said, the allure of his British accent softening earlier judgment. I pushed my stool closer. The Royal Albert Hall is where all the big artists play. It seats over five thousand people."

"Over five thousand? Jeeze."

Jolette

"Yes, and the night Janis played was brilliant. She was so happy because she sold the show out and she got everyone up and dancing in the aisles for her entire show. That never happened before at the Albert."

"What was she like in person?"

"She was a sweet girl really. Very good sense of humor and friendly. A nice girl."

"Excuse me, are you American?" a man from the next table said.

"Ah yes," I smiled, ready to give an autograph.

"Your country is very arrogant really."

"Oh."

"You should tell your President that America is not the center of the Universe," the man said, a woman next to him laughed.

"I don't actually know the President," I mumbled.

"Mate, that's enough," said the reporter and the man turned back to his table, more laughter erupting.

"So, the English do or don't like Americans?" I attempted recovery from the tumble off my throne.

"Some do, some don't. Americans have a bad reputation. Is this your first trip abroad?"

"Yes."

"Depending on where you go, they'll either love you or hate you."

"Where will they hate me?"

"France most likely."

I was back at the YWCA early that evening. I'd shaken hands with the reporter. We'd parted, no suggestion of dalliance from him. I'd been anticipating that I'd be accepting or rejecting his advances and voila there were none. So much for my assumptions. Arrogant American.

There was a crowd of women gathered in front of the television, the screen a smallish black and white, the room quiet, the women intent on watching a murder mystery. I stopped only a moment then went back to my bunk bed. Nobody else was there. I laid down, closed my eyes, willed the next three weeks to go by quickly.

23

Alaska, 1976

How can I miss you when you won't go away?
I keep telling you day after day
But you won't listen, you always stay and stay
How can I miss you when you won't go away?
     John Prine, songwriter, musician, singer, 1946 - 2020.

During the last Ice Age, an incomprehensible chunk of time ranging from 110,000 to 12,000 years ago, sea levels were extremely low. Most water had transmuted into gigantic swaths of ice. One such swath, about 1,000 feet wide and 620 miles long, was called the Bering Land Bridge because it stretched from Siberia to Alaska and was probably the route taken by Native Americans into the Northern Continent from Asia or someplace around there. The Haida tribe most likely migrated along this path, first settling on a Canadian island, later traveling further to the Prince of Wales Island in Alaska, calling their new settlement Hydaburg. Survival was ensured by a bountiful sea and verdant forests, still the dominant features, as evidenced when my seaplane lowered to the ocean's surface, next to several large fishing seiners, a collection of skiffs, and a lone dock.

We came to a gliding stop. The pilot cut the engine, jumped onto the dock, tied us to the cleats, turned to help me from the plane. The sudden quiet was deafening. It took a moment for my ears to empty of sound, ad-

Jolette

just to the utter quiet. I jumped onto the dock and looked around. I could feel time relaxing, unwinding, for life had just considerably slowed.

I turned to the ruddy-faced friendly pilot. "How do I get to Rose Inlet from here? I just ask someone for a boat ride?"

"You can hitch a ride. Someone's always going out," he said. "Probably someone fishing will take you to Rose Inlet. It's a couple of hours that way," he pointed, all directions identical, ocean, mountains, a yield of trees.

"How do I hitch a ride?"

"Just ask the fishermen. They'll be down here. You'll see."

He tucked back into his mechanical bird. The small plane lifted, its sound swallowed by the sky, leaving only the soft slap of ocean waves against fishing boats. Then I was alone on the quiet dock and the stillness curled around me, curious and sniffing. Within ten minutes a handful of locals spilled down to the dock, curious and sniffing too.

"Where you… from? Lower forty-eight?" an older man asked as he approached with several young boys whose silky dark heads reached my kneecaps. They brightly eyed me, smiled. I smiled back.

"Oh hi. Yes the lower forty-eight. I'm from Minnesota, but I just came up from Seattle."

"Ah…Seattle."

"Yes, Seattle." I could feel my body's metronome reduced by half.

"Where you…headed?"

"I'm trying to get to Rose Inlet. My husband's there."

"Oh."

"Yes."

"Rose Inlet."

"Yes."

"What's his name?"

"Marion, do you know him?"

"Yea."

150

"Oh!"

"Yea, they...come here...for supplies. Him 'n his brother. Bout three...weeks ago already."

"Oh, well yes, that's where I'm trying to go. Do you know of anyone going that direction?"

"Yea. Murray."

"Okay."

"He's ...going fishin'. He'll...take you."

"Oh good. Where is he?"

"He'll be down."

"Ok," I said. "Um, are these your boys?"

"Gran kids."

"Oh." I smiled a lot, then plopped down on the dock next to my backpack. "It's very beautiful here," I said.

"Yep."

Hydaburg's population was around 200. The Alaska Native Claims Settlement Act in 1971 awarded $962 million and forty-five million acres to compensate Alaskan Native Americans for lands and rights wrongfully taken from them. That meant the cozy Hydaburg community had received a ton of money. A bunch went towards creating schools, a medical clinic, and a jail, but teachers had to be imported up from the lower forty-eight. There were no doctors or nurses, no sheriff or police, leaving the clinic and jail utterly empty. One of the locals told me later. "Dem buildings...are...empty."

The locals dropped their words at a snail's pace, the cadence contagious — like many unattractive habits — and it didn't take long before I was doing the same.

Murray showed up a short while later. His slow gait was directed straight at me. He'd already heard I needed a ride, I knew. A smile creased his friendly face.

"You goin'....to Rose...Inlet?" he asked.

"Yes,... are you...Murray?"

"Yea, I...can take...you."

Murray had to be at least forty, wrinkles congregated at the corner of his eyes. He looked like he smiled a lot. He was full Haida, he would tell me later. He looked at me. "You need... boots." He indicated his own pair of rubber boots that climbed to his knees. I looked down at my tennis shoes, their thin fabric no match for the muscular drench of the sea, slippery docks, and, southeastern Alaska's signature, relentless rain.

Murray's boat was a thirty-six-foot salmon troller, *Eloisa* painted on its sides. I climbed in. He started the engine – an eardrum-shattering roar – sending gas fumes my direction, inhibiting conversation. I sat in the back of the boat, the stern, while Murray steered *Eloisa* towards Rose Inlet. My eyes rested on the endless ocean, islands, trees. A few unhurried hours later - me dazed with so much wilderness, the boat's steady rock and the gaseous fumes threatening a revival of my stomach contents - we approached Rose Inlet. But just as we approached the inlet's tip, Murray turned to me. "...Goin...to...fish awhile...first."

I had to restrain a scream as he turned from the inlet's entrance, resigned myself to sitting, watching Murray attach bait to fishing lines, the boat cut to trolling speed, four lines in the water, we sputtered one direction and back again. This continued for several lifetimes. My eyes grew heavy, I fell asleep.

I smelled gas. My eyelids fluttered. There was a rocking motion I couldn't place, oh the boat. Murray was pulling in fish, poor gasping flopping fish who'd made a big mistake in the water below, now paying the ultimate price. I sat up, inhaling fresh air laced with gasoline, looked to the horizon, the ocean was doing a back-crawl to the end of the earth.

"You wanna...go Rose...Inlet now?" Murray grinned.

"Yes, yes, yes!" I jumped up, twirled to look back at the inlet, which would lead me to Marion. I couldn't wait to see him.

Jolette

Rose Inlet had been a fishing cannery in the early 1900s, just one of at least a hundred canneries built in southeastern Alaskan inlets and ports. The cannery itself was long gone. As the *Eloisa* made its way past the tip of the inlet, I could see what was left, only a small house, jettisoned far above the ocean on top of a steep hill, a wisp of smoke coming from the chimney.

Below, at sea level, were five people, one of them sure to be Marion. They appeared excited, were waving. Visits were a rarity, I could easily guess. I waved back. As we got closer, I could make out Marion, his glasses, hair ponytailed, and I was sure he could see me. I grinned and waved even more. His smile vanished. Was that a look of apprehension? A funny feeling jig-jagged through me. I hadn't considered that he wouldn't want me here. I grinned anyway.

We pulled up to the dock. All the boys were eager to help Murray tie up the boat, greeting him happily. I opened my arms to Marion. He gave a limp hug, his eyes slipping off in another direction. He introduced me to the guys, Danny, Leonard, Jim, and Marion's brother Gerry, who pleasantly smiled but I thought I saw him shoot a glance at Marion. I felt like I'd suddenly ingested a pile of cement, my insides heavy with the unmistakable rejection.

"I missed you," I tried. "I wanted to see you."

"Yeah, well here I am," Marion turned to Murray, "Hey, man, how's it going?" By the time Murray left, I thought maybe I should have stuck with Murray for his return trip to Hydaburg for the message was loud and clear – I'd crashed a boy's club.

A torrent of rain struck the little house far up on the hill that night. I lay beside Marion in bed as the rain hit the roof like a machine gun. He automatically responded to my hesitant overtures, remained distant even while we engaged in the ultimate act of love as some people liked to call the insertion of the penis into the vaginal opening. And though I'd just traveled over 2,000 miles to be with Marion, we were unmistakably a million miles apart.

Jolette

"What's wrong?" I tried to ask the next morning, but he avoided me.

"What do ya mean, nothings wrong."

Hot tea, bread and jam provided breakfast on my first day. As I chewed the stale bread, I realized that I had become invisible, for none of the guys noted me, especially Marion. They were gung-ho to go crabbing even during the torrential downpour. They joked, laughed, guffawed, spit, fart, belched. As loud and as much as possible. All befitting a rural boy's club.

Marion put a big pot of water on the wood stove. It would take about three hours for the water to boil. My job would be to stay and watch the water.

"You want me to watch water boil?" I asked.

"Yea, just make sure it's okay." Marion departed with not even a glance as they noisily clamored down the steep steps to the dock below. I looked around. Scattered fishing magazines, ashtrays spilling over, pipes, rolling papers, bags of tobacco, pot, and empty beer bottles. One ragged couch and a big chair, both looking a hundred years-old. Seemed doubtful they had the strength to hold up the vigorous masculine forms of the current residents.

I made a slight effort to tidy the kitchen and flipped through fishing magazines. By the time the water had begun to boil, I heard voices, feet clumping up steps, and the boys charged into the house. Marion darted to the boiling water, threw a flailing crab into its scalding midst.

I screamed, then cried out, "What are you doing?"

The boys, suddenly silent, turned to look at me. "Why did you do that?" I screamed into the silence.

"Well, shit, Jolette, that's what you do with crabs," shrugged Marion. The boys let out small laughs.

Crabs don't have vocal cords, but they have two nerve centers and feel pain. If they could scream it would shred the air while being boiled alive. I didn't actually know that then, but to see a living creature thrown into boiling water was unmistakably brutal. There was just no way not to notice the cruelty. In Minnesota there wasn't much seafood, my knowledge on this commonplace method of killing sea life was nil.

"Well, thats terrible. That's fucking horrible." I returned to the bedroom, slammed the door hard, furious for the poor crab, furious at Marion, furious at being rejected. I stayed in the bedroom the rest of the night, ignoring Marion when he opened the door and invited me to eat. Later that evening when he came to bed, I looked at him, disgruntled. "Did you miss me at all?" I asked.

He met my gaze. "How can I miss you if you won't go away?" Laughter broke out in the living room. They could hear everything. Anger filled me as I recognized the words from a John Prine song.

"I'm leaving just as soon as I can," I said. "When can I get out of this fucking place?"

"In a week we go to Hydaburg for supplies," he coolly responded.

The next morning the sun was slightly flirting. I shoved a piece of stale bread in my mouth and went outside for a walk. Except there was nowhere to walk. The dense forest plastered itself against the house on three sides. You'd need a machete to take two steps. The fourth side was the front yard, an open patch where a bathtub sat, surrounded by a panoramic vista. Marion came up behind me. "Hey," he said, tentative.

"What?" I asked coldly, trying to stab him with the word.

"I'm sorry. It's just I'm in the middle of this thing here and I didn't expect you."

"I know you didn't. I thought you might be happy to see me."

"Yea, well, I'm sorry but this is like a guy's thing," he said, then brightened. "You wanna take a bath? Look, I'm getting a bath started for you."

The clawed feet of the bathtub launched it up just enough so that Marion had been able to start a small bonfire beneath it. "You get the water from the rainwater barrel on top of the roof and then wait til it heats up and look at that view! Here let me show you."

We walked to the back of the house where a ladder and a bucket waited. "Just take the bucket up to the roof, fill it with water from the rain barrel and go put it in the bathtub. By the time you're finished you'll be ready for a bath. It's really great," he smiled, the first genuine smile I'd seen from him. I sighed, took the bucket and climbed the ladder. An hour later I never wanted to see a bucket ever again. I climbed into the tub's lukewarm water and sat, looking out at the jagged mountains, the ocean where sometimes a dolphin or whale surfaced. The sky a gorgeous topaz blue. The scenery magnificent. I couldn't wait to leave.

Jolette

24

Rose Inlet, Alaska and Tucson, Arizona 1977

...A journalist's job was to bring news, to be eyes for their conscience.
Martha Gellhorn, American novelist, journalist, war correspondent, 1908-1998.

It was a long week of being ignored in the small house on top of the hill, the rain my only steady companion. I ate stale bread and found a few Western novels in the far reaches of a dusty shelf to burrow into while the boys drank beer, slaughtered fish and other sea creatures, and sat around at night, playing guitar, telling stories, singing. I guess you could call it singing.

I had plenty of time to mull over where I wanted to go next and decided on Tucson. It was an easy decision since a few years earlier, Bonnie, my old high school, rug stealing friend, and I had driven to Tucson in a 1969 Chevy, a high school graduation gift from my parents, to visit her older sister, Cindy, a gorgeous non-apologetic nudist. After our three-day drive from the pancake terrain of the Midwest to the magnificent thrust of the Rocky Mountains, we finally arrived at a small house, the door opened by Cindy who was a goddess, tall, lean, and tan with bright blue eyes and blonde hair pulled up into a silky bun on top of her head, tendrils framing her face. Her pubic hair was a swatch of blonde fuzz, her legs long.

"Bonnie!" she cried and gathered her younger sister in her arms, then turned my way and wrapped her long, brown arms around me too, making me inhale her patchouli oil. I liked her and Tucson immediately, the embrace of both pleasant. The hippie vibe of Tucson inviting.

Tucson would be a perfect place to winter.

At the end of the week Marion, his brother Gerry and I got into a small skiff and set out for Hydaburg. A three-hour ride. They were picking up supplies, and I was thankfully leaving. I settled in the bow of the boat and stared out at the blue-green fathomless waters. The engine was loud, and though I heard Marion call to me a few times - overtures he had chosen to forgo the entire week when he'd barely talked to me - I ignored him. The dock at Hydaburg was as exciting as a red carpet in Hollywood when it finally came into view. Finally I'd be able to escape. We pulled up to the dock and I jumped off the skiff. My seaplane was already waiting. I waved to the pilot and turned to get my backpack. Marion was right behind me, helped me put my backpack on and then tried to envelope me in a hug. I allowed brief contact, then pulled away.

"Are you going to write to me?" he asked, suddenly earnest.

"Oh, wow. Are you pretending you give a shit?"

"Well, I do give a shit. But, you know, you came up uninvited."

"I know. I should be executed."

"I'm sorry."

I tried on one of Lenny's favorites. "Sorry don't really cut it." Then I looked at him, his face sad, and sighed. "But yea, okay. I'll write."

"Okay, and I'll come to Tucson when I leave Rose Inlet."

"Oh, alright."

Jolette

I was happy to leave the boys club and climb into the small seaplane which would take me to the Ketchikan Airport where I would fly into Seattle, then climb onto a Greyhound for the two-day bus ride to Arizona. I couldn't wait to be back on the road. The refuge of the road and freedom from all unpleasantries was exhilarating. Just like it was when I first started running away from home.

Tucson, also known as the Old Pueblo, was circled by mountains and the surrounding area held an abundance of cacti, over fifty-one species. The most prolific was the Saguaro, which could grow to over eighty-two feet with up to twenty-five arms, living 150 to 200 years.

I located an apartment on Sixth Street where a piano sat with its bench in the lobby. The building was sparsely populated, only four units and two were empty. I moved into a small room, unloaded my backpack, looked around, and opened my door to the lobby where I met my new neighbor, a specimen favored with an overflow of good genes, his long blond hair prettier than any in a shampoo commercial, with smart blue eyes and a physique vibrating with exuberance.

"Hi, I'm Jolette. I just moved in," I said.

"I'm Tom." Tom walked me around the building, pointed at the backyard, showed me his room, which featured a large pyramid under which he meditated and slept. "If you need anything, let me know," he said.

I contently fell asleep that night in Tucson, its black velvet sky embedded with sparkling jewels, and woke to a bright morning sky, the day already luxurious with warmth. I stretched, got dressed, and opened my door to see Tom plunking out a few notes on the piano. Before I could say hello, the front door of the building was pushed open by a slender, dark-haired woman. Tom looked towards the front door, his face broke into a welcoming smile, the woman shyly smiled in return, and, with arms long and thin, offered him a bowl of bright red strawberries.

I took a picture of that moment. Tucked the image deep into my memory banks. The tender woman bringing strawberries to the beautiful man, her arms long and thin. A moment so exquisite, I wanted to always remember it. I took the mental picture, then quietly shut my door.

I was alone in my new, very still room. I looked around and felt suddenly lonely. The feeling attached like an unwanted sweater. I didn't mind being alone, but there are wafts of loneliness floating around just waiting to attach to anyone who feels uncertain. Once it attached, you had to get active, you had to shift your focus, otherwise it would sit on you until you suffocated, which would only make escaping its clutches ten times more difficult. You couldn't sit and wallow no matter how tempting.

I opened my door to a now empty lobby and walked down my new street. It was quiet, flanked by modest adobe homes in dirt yards with prickly cactus. Stark in contrast to the lush rich green of southeastern Alaska. It was too brown and dry. I didn't love it, but maybe I could learn to. Maybe someday when things were different, when my life really started, maybe I would love the desert then. I put it on my to-do list. Learn to love the desert.

My to-do list for life, so far, included three things. Be bilingual; just one language was a restriction. Join the Peace Corps, not sure when. One item waffled. Marriage to a man, with the addition of children, which would make me complete and allow me to live happily ever after. This notion propagated from infancy. It was a nice fantasy, except it wielded too much power, the idea planted so deep it tended to interfere with productive functioning. Though it would be nice to have someone out there Just For Me. Who would cherish, adore, and support me. Forever. I couldn't wait to meet whoever it was. (I knew it wasn't Marion. That was for sure.)

In the meantime, it seemed that since people came and went, it would be better to have something in your life which no one could take away, something that you could bring with you no matter where you went, that was yours, always. It would have to be something you kept safe inside like knowledge, or a skill for a job you loved. My third item on my list — a work I loved. A work I could love and cherish and carry with me forever.

My fourth goal would be to learn to love the desert.

Jolette

My father, much to his chagrin, had unwittingly informed much of my behavior and ideas. ("I should have never told you that I hitchhiked cross country when I was fourteen," he would lament in later years, since at exactly age fourteen I did the same.) He was a living example of a good reason to find work you loved. He hated being a dentist. Never addressing the topic outright, he would only frequently mumble, under his breath, "I hate my job." And not just uttered once or twice but uttered for years, for his entire life until retirement. Even after retirement he still had nightmares that he was working as a dentist, waking in a distressed state.

"You have to do a job every day? All day long? Forever?" I asked my father in younger years.

"Yes, everyone does. When you're old, you can stop."

"But you have to do something all day long that you don't like, every day?"

"You get two days a week off."

"I'm not gonna do that."

"You have to. Everyone does. Whether they like it or not. If you're lucky you might find something you like."

I signed up for classes at Pima Community College, located on the east side of Tucson where cluttered yards shared broken fences and chickens wandered in groups, clucking down the sidewalks as if going to a bus stop. Where billboards were splashed with big letters – MUY BUENO! — alongside a can of Coca-Cola. I climbed off the bus in front of the school and looked for my classrooms. Political science, English, and fencing. Journalism was my elective.

Ralph Chavez, the journalism instructor, was short, his skin a tan sheen, his hair thick and dark, slicked back from a pleasant face that frequently lit with a high-wattage smile. He brought his hands together, as if in prayer, as he addressed us. "This is Journalism 101. This is where you will learn to write so you can tell stories about our community. This is where you will learn to interview people and to write the who, what, where, when, why and how of a story. Those are the building blocks — who, what, where, when, why and how," Mr. Chavez repeated. "Memorize them."

I was immediately stirred.

"This is where you will write about life. You will learn how to share information with your community. The world depends on good journalism and ethical, unbiased reporting," he continued.

Perhaps his voice's resonance, rhythm, relaxed full tone, and pacing – all key elements in voice appeal – further opened the message center in my brain, for I found I was more than receptive. I was taking a direct hit. Journalism. I couldn't wait to start.

My first byline appeared in the Aztec Campus News at Pima Community College the next week. I wrote about the neighborhood Montessori elementary school.

The philosophy of having children self-direct their activities had been developed in the early 1900s by an Italian physician and educator, Maria Montessori. It seemed the most important story in the world and for several nights, after classes, I sat at my lone table, in my small room, pen in hand, head bent, fervently writing, rewriting, littering the floor with crunched-up papers filled with crossed-out sentences. The goal was to secure the elusive perfect word, hone the stronger sentence, rid excess to create a cleaner paragraph, a better story.

When I finally raised my head, neck stiff, eyes glazed, I was amazed at the time. For three hours I'd been writing. I knew it then. I was struck with an overwhelming feeling that I was in love. It filled me up. This was IT. I wasn't in love with a person. This was better. It was love for a work. I would become a journalist.

Timothy Leary, the LSD guru and psychologist stood only a few feet from me. Famed for having taught at Harvard in the early 1960s, later becoming involved in researching psychedelic drugs, he now looked at me. His blue eyes shone, he wore a light green shirt, white slacks, his hair was a tousle of white and silver. Surrounding him was a brilliant effervescence which struck me dumb. I had never seen anyone even close to having the strong energy he radiated. My reporter's notebook was flipped open, my hand poised with a pen but I was so intimidated it was hard to convince my voice to speak. I was one of four student journalists who had been invited to interview Leary after his presentation to a packed auditorium at the University of Arizona.

"These Universities paid by taxes and administered by politicians are designed to keep you serenely and productively stupid. Like Mommy's arms," he said to us, the four interviewers. His eyes had landed on me. I tried to think of a question but was utterly starstruck, and failed. Another student asked him what he thought the future would bring. Leary thought the future would include living in outer space, which would be cheaper and more efficient. "A few thousand miles up there's limitless energy and natural resources. In twenty to forty years there will be space worlds for bisexual vegetarians. Various space worlds will be devised to suit each particular type of person," Leary said while I furiously scribbled everything he uttered, marveling at his closeness, pasting the resulting article into my scrapbook to be treasured forever, however long that was.

I interviewed the Governor of Arizona, Raul Castro, by telephone, and Mitch Miller, well-known conductor of "Sing Along with Mitch" TV fame. I watched Mitch Miller in the school's auditorium as he rehearsed with his band one afternoon, getting ready for the evening's performance. Afterwards he came to the edge of the stage to be interviewed, declaring that college students only thought about sex, I scribbled it down and wrote up the story, thinking he was the one who probably only thought about sex.

I interviewed everyone I could think of including my neighbor's daughter, Susie, a bright-eyed, precocious seven-year-old, who would declare that, "Even ugly people had feelings," and that we should be kind to each other.

Jolette

Everyone had something to say. Everyone had a story. I wrote nonstop. I liked interviewing but when I found The Face of War, by Martha Gellhorn in the college library, my aspirations elevated.

Martha Gellhorn was a war correspondent and in her sixty-year career, she would report on every major world conflict from the Spanish Civil War (1936-1939), to WWII (1939-1945), the Vietnam War (1955-1975) the Arab-Israeli conflicts in the 1960s and 1970s, the El Salvadoran conflict in the 1980s and finally, at age 81 - AGE 81! - she reported on the 1989 U.S. invasion of Panama.

When WWII broke out, no female journalist had yet been granted the questionable privilege of reporting from the frontlines of battle. Gellhorn made a written request to the military for approval to access combat locations and was denied. Unwilling to entertain defeat, Gellhorn snuck aboard a battleship headed toward Omaha Beach, one of the five main beaches of the Normandy Invasion on D Day, June 6, 1944. She stowed away in a ship's bathroom and disguised herself as a stretcher carrier, carrying the torn bodies from the battlefield, sloshing through the reddened waters in the dark. She was the only female journalist present on D Day and would later lose her correspondent's credentials due to her unauthorized endeavor.

Goosebumps rose on my arms. I leaned into the book about Gellhorn. I felt my blood surge, her fearless pursuits and startling achievements instilled in me reverential admiration I had not yet felt for anyone. I looked around my small room, not seeing a small room. I was seeing my path of becoming a foreign correspondent. A war correspondent. I wanted to be like Gellhorn, brave and daring. I wanted to go where others wouldn't dare. To get the truth. To get information and bring it back to share with the world. I wasn't afraid of danger. I liked it.

In the meantime, I wasn't on the front lines anywhere. I was just at Pima Community College. Passion and purpose fueled my mind and spirit, but it wasn't food and it sure wasn't money.

Jolette

I had been living in Tucson for a month and my BEOG (Basic Educational Opportunity Grant) money was almost gone. I had to finally submit to a waitress job, graveyard shift, at a clattering restaurant, the uniform a knee-length, orange skirt and button-up white shirt. I was plunked down at a counter where I spent nights filling insatiable coffee cups and balancing hot plates on pained forearms. The sun's first tentacles of light signaled release from the carb-inhaling, coffee-slurping customers, and I would race to catch the bus to school. By the time classes were finished, I had only a few hours to sleep before I was back pouring endless cups of coffee. Blurred with sleep deprivation, I had no time to write and began to despise the job that fed me. It was a godsend when my old high school and rug-stealing friend Bonnie called, and asked if I wanted to go on a trip with a friend of her sister's — the goddess nudist. She said the friend would take me on a' vacation-like two-week trip to Colombia to make $2,000.'

"To Colombia? In South America?" I asked Bonnie.

"Yes, right," she said. "I can't say much more over the phone."

"You think it's okay?" I asked.

"My sister just got back and it was no problem. She made a bunch of money."

"It's probably...."

"Yea."

"Umm...so what would I do?"

"Call my sister's friend, okay? I think she'll just get you a plane ticket to Miami and meet you there. That's what she did with my sister."

"And you think it's okay?"

"I think so, but, you know, I'm not really sure. But my sister did it. It went okay."

I thought it over for a second. Weighed the implications. Seemed to me it was a gift from heaven. A way to make a bunch of money. Plus I would get to see South America. "Okay. Okay, I'll do it. Thanks, Bonnie."

I quit that restaurant fast as your foot hits the gas at a yellow light. I was going to Colombia.

25

Europe, 1981

There is a great deal of unmapped country within us which would have to be taken into account in an explanation of our gusts and storms-
George Eliot, pen-name of Mary Ann Evans, British author, poet, journalist, 1818 – 1880.

Once Augustus showed up, bundled warm in a bright orange parka, ready for a winter in Europe – that dark hair, those dark eyes – I saw nothing else. Only Him, capitol H, my heart skipping around like a crazed butterfly at a nectar smorgasbord. I met him at customs.

I saw him first, threw up my arms. "You're here! You're here!"

He spotted me and grinned. "I bet you wondered if I was really coming."

"I did. I'm so glad you're here!"

His skin was olive. His chest a place where soft hairs made a nest for my head. His back held a hirsute patch where my fingers played, twisting the fine threads, morphing the unsightly into a thing of endearment. He was sleeping the next morning, when I turned to face him, and moved closer. I thought he was the answer.

Jolette

"Good morning," I murmured to Augustus when he opened his eyes. He smiled, pulled me close. I inhaled his scent and, like a held newborn, felt content.

"Do you wanna go have some breakfast?" I murmured. "The food is horrible in London though. If you order orange juice you'll get orange soda."

"Yea, let's go have breakfast and see London," he said. "In a little bit." He pulled me under him and when we joined, ascending together towards his climactic release — my own was too much work — I believed in the story that there is a person meant for everyone. That he was meant for me. From that point on, he remained my focus. All else peripheral.

We decided to hitchhike through England, Scotland, and Wales. We traveled through the fall countryside, the trees a bouquet of rich reds, baby light greens, more mature dark greens, aged yellows, all of it a gorgeous backdrop for the most beautiful smile in the world, my eyes constantly finding reason to attach to my dark-eyed companion. He had only to send me a glance to make me sit up much as a dog to a treat.

We arrived at England's northernmost town, Berwick-upon-Tweed, its medieval wall built in 1558 – two miles long, three feet thick, twenty-two feet high — rebuilt but surrounding the coastal town as it always had, its arched stone bridges built in the 1600s. These historical remnants duly noted before my attention riveted back to Augustus. We moved on to Edinburgh, then to Inverness past Loch Ness, a freshwater lake, home to the notorious Loch Ness monster. Augustus got car sick sitting in the back seat of a small Fiat which whirled us around the lake. Chatting with the driver, I turned my head to look back at Augustus who'd been unusually quiet, his face green, looking miserable.

"Do you need to throw up?" I asked.

He could barely shake his head. Even when he was distorted with nausea my heart swooned. I believe there was nothing he could have done that would have swayed my heart any other direction, even when I'd see him wink at women and stare at their breasts, making me hot with fury, my head wanting to spin like Linda Blair's, to spit demonic curses.

"Why did you wink at that woman?" I'd finally turned to him one afternoon as we walked down a sidewalk to a cafe. My jaw was tight.

He'd sighed, poised on the edge of defensiveness, "I'm just trying to have a little fun with people. Do you see how tense they seem? I'm just trying to be friendly."

Fucking jerk. I loved him.

I didn't question why I thought I loved him so much. The feeling had hit hard and at once. His dark hair and eyes, like polished onyx, were likely the catalyst. He had a vitality I saw clearly. I loved the life that danced from him. He was affable, humorous, intelligent, and articulate, though with a tendency to tell bad jokes with feeble punch lines, a trait I recoiled from but forgave and attempted laughter, though it never sounded sincere. And, as time went by, he surprised me with an unbecoming pedantic tendency when expressing political views which was the only time I would miss Marion, whose verbal ability I continued to admire even when all else faltered. But mostly Augustus was affectionate and playful, grabbing my hand, pulling me close, whispering silly things into my ear, making me laugh and generous with compliments. "You're so beautiful even all the women stare at you."

Augustus had been raised in a small town on Whidbey Island, thirty miles northwest of Seattle by ferry, home of the Whidbey Island Naval Air Station, which was an economic boost to the island's population, largely rural. His mother and father divorced when he was young. Augustus shared a story of his mother committing his father into a mental institution, another one of history's blunders both with mental health issues and the wielding of undeserved power, making it fairly simple for a spouse to commit their spouse to an institution. His mother's female lover then moved in, at which

Jolette

point young Augustus was cast aside. His mother turned towards her new lover instead, filling the boy with resentment and a lifelong irk on the subject of women and the injustice most women go through in a society which treats them as second-class citizens.

The first time he voiced disgruntlement with the notion that women had long been treated unfairly and unequally, I was shocked. Everyone knew women were second-class citizens. It wasn't just my opinion. It was a fact. It was odd that he took issue with this perspective. Strange. He wasn't stupid, but I saw that he was flawed. I noted this and decided never to bring up the subject again.

He grew up financially impoverished and embarrassed because of it. The first time he slipped into a mild funk, bemoaning that he was a loser, displaying self-doubt and loathing, I almost laughed. I almost laughed because I considered this perspective ludicrous as I thought, in spite of the above mentioned idiosyncrasies, that he was the epitome of wonderful. I appointed him the highest status in my heart and when he gave me attention, my world felt complete. I couldn't stop thinking about him. He was like a drug. The only character trait I couldn't reconcile was his constant flirting.

Augustus and I ferried into Amsterdam, stowed our backpacks on a bed and breakfast houseboat, which lounged amongst many houseboats in one of the canals in the city. Then we set out to explore. I'd had a shit fit earlier in the day when I'd woken from a nap on the ferry, Augustus nowhere in sight. I wandered around before finding him on the deck sitting smack against a young woman who was smiling up at him as he jabbered away. Their thighs were pressed together.

"Hi everybody," I said, my voice arctic.

"Oh, ah," the startled young woman stammered. She got to her feet, looked at me wide-eyed, "Ah hallo," and stumbled off.

"Goodbye. Nice talking to you," Augustus called after her slim form.

"You were sitting right next to her!" I exclaimed.

"Yes, I was. Is that against the law?"

"The whole bench was empty, you had your leg right against hers! Why are you constantly flirting with other women?"

"I'm not. I'm just friendly. You're imagining things." He was annoyed. I was flabbergasted, made livid by his roving eye. I was not a very open-minded call girl. He was discovering as much.

A frigid chill staunched the space between us until we disembarked into the progressive city of Amsterdam, a city with evidently more tolerance than me, touting a lenient stance towards consensual prostitution and soft drug use. Several neighborhoods were zoned into Red Light Districts, the most infamous called De Wallen located near the waterfront, boasting a long history of sailors and the sex industry.

With the arrival of oil street lamps in 1669, Amsterdam's darkened streets were brightened just enough to nourish nightlife, rolling out the red carpet for proclivities shunned by daylight. Prostitution had long been a strong presence in the tolerant Netherlands, though there are those who would admonish the idea that Amsterdam condoned or found sex-for-hire desirable, pointing out, instead, that prostitution was easier handled by the city when legal and controlled. The sex workers had to file with the city, were responsible for regular health checks, given a red card to show they had passed the gynecological exam, no STDs found. It was managed, taxes were paid, the state was the pimp, sort of. Around the nineteenth century, brothel owners began using red gas lights, a hard-to-miss signal for potential customers and presto, the Red Light District was born.

Augustus didn't hold a grudge and had only to breathe for me to forgive him. We held hands as we located Prinsengracht 263, home of the Anne Frank House, and entered the museum, which had opened in 1960, a mere sixteen years after the Frank family, the van Pels family and Fritz

Jolette

Pfeffer, had been arrested one summer morning by a horde of Dutch soldiers and an SS officer.

The loyal bookcase that had concealed the entrance to their secret quarters for two years during WWII, looked small, an unlikely item of legendary status. Behind the bookcase, a narrow set of stairs led to the sitting room and Anne's bedroom where her movie star pictures remained on the wall, the very spot where she'd once gazed. Difficult to fathom those years, that particular day on August 4, 1944, when they were pulled from hiding. Difficult to process such events in a mind as small as mine whose main thinking revolved around food and desires rendering temporary satisfactions. Difficult for an inexperienced mind to digest such atrocity.

Augustus and I stood subdued in deference to our surroundings. The rooms were empty of furniture but heavy with solemn air, the weight of the past, the rooms having witnessed the eight lives of those in hiding, each person taking an average of 23,040 breaths per day, the walls absorbing the exhales where perhaps some molecules still lingered. Then, in the following years, the somber exhale of all who'd come to observe the rooms where life had been attempted, hope weakly sustained until finally pulled from its shallow roots on the day they were arrested.

Had it not been for the utterings of a snitch perhaps those eight lives would have survived. Instead, death by the gas chamber, disease, starvation followed, leaving only Anne's father, Otto Frank alive, barely alive, to return to Amsterdam and find the pages of his daughter's diary, leaving him surprised and impressed by the reveals of her inner life during those years of hiding.

July 15th, 1944

...It's utterly impossible for me to build my life on a foundation of chaos, suffering and death. I see the world being slowly transformed into a wilderness. I hear the approaching thunder that, one day, will destroy us

too. I feel the suffering of millions. And yet, when I look up at the sky, I somehow feel that everything will change for the better, that this cruelty too will end, that peace and tranquility will return once more. In the meantime, I must hold on to my ideals. Perhaps the day will come when I'll be able to realize them. – Anne Frank

I walked up behind Augustus, reached into the pocket of his orange parka to find his hand.

"What do you think?" I said into his ear. "It looks so small doesn't it?"

He nodded, his face solemn. "Yea, it does. It's hard to imagine."

"I know. Unbelievable."

We headed back down the stairs. I paused for a moment to look up at the building. "Where's the clock? On the church?"

We found it, the Westerkerk church with the Westertoren bell tower and something unearthed in my chest when I gazed at the face of that clock, heard by so many for so many years, the sound that had reassured Anne Frank at night. The clock, witness to all, with no comment, except an unperturbed chime every quarter-hour.

We walked along a canal, inhaled the cool air, stayed quiet, then from the corner of my eye, I noticed an ad stuck to a pole. "Escorts Available." I copied down the number.

"I'm gonna call this place," I said.

"Really?" Augustus responded. "Why?"

"I'm curious. I want to check it out, see how they work over here. Maybe I can make a little money."

"Really? You're curious?"

"Yea. Since I'm here, I wanna see how they do things over here." Which was true. I was curious. I looked at him. "That doesn't bother you or anything, does it?"

"No, it doesn't. I just hope it's safe."

"Oh. I know. Yea, well if it seems weird of course I'm not going to do anything. I'll just call and see. You're okay with the work, right?"

"Yea, I'm okay with it."

"You would tell me if you weren't?"

"Does your work affect our relationship?"

"No. Not at all. It's strictly business."

"Then I don't have a problem with it."

I looked at his face. I believed him.

I called the number from a phone booth.

"Hallo?" a man's voice, his tenor gentle, but surprising. Women usually answered phones at escort agencies.

"Hi, do you speak English?" I asked.

"Ja, yes."

"I saw your ad and I'm wondering if you're hiring."

"Are you American?"

"Yes. I used to work at an escort agency in Seattle, Washington. Do you know it?"

"Ah Seattle. Yes. I have heard. Why don't you come by and say hallo."

Later that day, with the help of a taxi driver, I found the address given, knocked on the door of what looked like a normal Amsterdam house. A tall, thirty-something slim man with a Nordic blonde head opened the door, his eyes bright blue. He gave a disarming smile. "Jolette?" he asked.

"Yes, hi, you are Jan?"

"Yes, come in, come in."

I stepped into a dimly lit room, much more spacious than the façade suggested. Several elegant sofas and chairs were clustered about. A bar ran the length of a wall, behind it shelves abundantly stocked with liquor.

"Oh, this is a nice place. Is anyone else here?" I asked.

"No, we're not open now but yes everyone finds this to be a very comfortable environment. Would you like a drink?" Jan asked, his voice a lovely lilt.

"Oh no, thank you. What is this place?"

"This is a private men's club," he smiled.

"Oh, ok."

"Are you moving into the city?" he asked.

"Well, no, I'm really just traveling through, but I thought if it's possible, I could work a little.

"Oh yes, alright. Well, there is an appointment this evening at the Hotel Sofitel. Would you like to take it?"

"Yes sure," I said.

"When you're finished, here's the key, just come back and leave the key and the money on the bar. He will pay 200 American dollars."

"Ok. You're giving me the key to just come in?"

"Yes, why not. The house isn't open this evening, no one will be here. Are you comfortable with that arrangement?"

"Yes, sure I can do that. When is this place open?"

"Our club is open Thursday through Sunday. We schedule escorts other days."

"It's a really nice place."

"Yes, it's very comfortable for everyone. There's five very good bedrooms each with a jacuzzi."

"That's so nice. It's legal here right?"

"We're not zoned. That's the Red Light District."

"Oh." I didn't know exactly what that meant, didn't want to make him nervous by asking too many questions. I took the paper with the scribbled info and bid the Dutchman farewell.

Later that evening, I took a cab to The Hotel Sofitel. The front glass door led to a large lobby, I found the restrooms tucked down a hallway. It was dark in the restroom. "Where's the lights?" I said to no one, my eyes minimally adjusted, I could barely scrutinize my face in the mirror, smeared lipstick over my mouth.

"Why is it so dark in the bathroom?" I asked the man at the front desk.

"It's dark so people can't see their veins, so they can't sit in there shooting up," he matter-of-factly stated.

"You mean people were shooting heroin in there? The Sofitel?"

"Yes, that's right. The dark lights inhibit that behavior."

"I can't believe people would shoot up in your restroom."

"Well, not anymore they won't." He cracked a tiny smile.

Jim was from New York. Not my favorite place. Guaranteed a lack of civility. Every New Yorker had the same puffy-chested response when I asked for ID. "Hows about I see *your* ID?" As if this were a clever gem.

Jim's face fell when he opened the door to my knock.

"Hi Jim, I'm Michelle. How are you this evening?"

Jim had more shine than hair on his head. He looked at me in dismay. "Are you American?"

"Yes."

"I wanted a European woman. I wanted a French or Italian girl."

I tried not to hate Jim immediately.

"They don't have any this evening. It's just me."

"Oh."

Jim and I went through the motions, mission accomplished with some disdain on either end. I went back to the house where I'd met the pleasant smiling Dane. No one was around. I walked to the bar, put the fee — Jim gave me two hundred American dollars, I kept one — and key on the counter, then wandered around. There were five bedrooms, large king-sized beds plied with luxuriant bedding, pillows galore, one circular bed, large sunken Jacuzzi bathtubs in each room. I helped myself to an orange juice at the bar, left and hailed a cab.

By the time I got back to our bed and breakfast, Augustus was under blankets. He opened his arms. I crawled into his warmth. It would be several days before he told me of his adventures that very evening. For while I was visiting Jim at the Hotel Sofitel, Augustus had wandered into the Red Light District to visit a lovely who sat in a window, as the women did in that part of Amsterdam where prostitution was zoned legal. Sex workers rented small rooms with windows where they could sit, on display for purchase. When a client approached, a fee was determined, and he was allowed entrance. The window's curtain then pulled snugly shut.

I had given Augustus spending money earlier that day, since I had a lot more money than he did. I'd shoved a fifty dollar bill into his hand. "Here, have a nice night," I'd said. He used it to purchase sexual services from a woman working in the Red Light District. "You used the money I gave you?" I asked.

"Well, yeah. But it was terrible. She kept telling me to hurry up. It was a horrible experience."

"Good. You asshole."

"Why am I an asshole? You were out with another guy. Why couldn't I do the same thing?"

"Because I was working. It's all business. Not pleasure. You jerk."

"Yea, well I'll never really know if that's true, will I?"

"Oh god. Of course it's true. You should know it's true because I say it's true. You should trust me."

"You should trust me too."

"But you want to have sex with everyone. For pleasure."

"So what? What difference does it make? You're the one I love."

"I am?"

"Yes. You are."

"Oh." It's hard to be indignant when the man you are crazy about first declares he loves you. I faltered. "Well. I....I love you too." I mumbled the words. My eyes felt the pressure of tears.

"What did you say? Come here."

I looked at him. "You are such a shit though. But I do love you. I love you lots."

"Good. Just trust me. Don't get so mad about every little thing." He kissed my cheek.

"It's hard not to get mad when I see you wanting other women. How am I supposed to deal with that?"

"But I don't really want them. Just for sex. Nothing serious."

"I don't like it."

"I know. But if I can deal with you working, can't you deal with me flirting a little?"

"You mean fucking around," I said but softened my tone. "I don't know, but okay, I'll try." I said the words but only to appease him. I already knew I was unable to squelch the jealous anger that drove through me like an uprise of livid citizens with torches.

"I mean, you're the one who said you believed in open relationships," he continued.

"I did, didn't I? I meant ideally. Ideally, that would be the way to go because monogamy seems impossible. It seems ridiculous that you can only be with one person sexually. But it's really hard in practice. It's too hard."

"It's not that hard. We just have to trust each other. I love you."

"Alright," I said, even though I knew I couldn't do it. Skinning myself alive would probably be easier. But I said obliging words anyway. "Okay. I'll try. I love you too."

Love is a funny word that wields a lot of power and covers such a broad spectrum. From loving ice cream to loving a child. Being in love with a sexual partner usually means an intense attachment to a desired object. But that is not real love. Even though you think it is. It's just attraction. Strong attraction. But you use the word love and attach importance to this fleeting (even though you think it's permanent) obsession. For me, it would have been more fitting to say, I'm obsessed with you. Dangerously obsessed.

Jolette

25

Athens, Greece, 1981

My thinking tends to be libertarian. That is, I oppose intrusions of the state into the private realm - as in abortion, sodomy, prostitution, pornography, drug use, or suicide, all of which I would strongly defend as matters of free choice in a representative democracy.
Camille Pagilla, b. 1947, American feminist academic, professor, author.

By the time Augustus and I got to Athens, Greece, we were famished for greens, overstuffed with the meat and carbs so prolific through England, France, and Italy. Heaven appeared in the form of a Greek salad, readily available from any of the multiple cafes scattered in the busy metropolis of Athens. The streets were an overflow of food vendors, and cafes, skewers of meat rotating on spits in brightly lit windows, kabobs of vegetables on display, sidewalks congested with hastening crowds, bustling and noisy.

Athens, largely known as the cradle of Western civilization, birthed a democratic system under the leadership of Cleisthenes in 508 BC. It was the first political system created that declared "the people" to have the authority to deliberate and decree legislation. But "the people" really referred to men only. Still, it was the first big step towards democratic leanings.

The Hotel Eva, budget friendly on a car-choked, gregarious street, offered a balcony facing out to the traffic, car horns fussy and abrasive.

"It's so loud," I complained. "This is so noisy."

"I'm so tired nothing will keep me awake," Augustus fell on the bed, looked at me, "unless you want to try."

"Oh, you want me to tell you a bedtime story? Is that what you want?"

"Yea, come here and tell me a story."

"Once upon a time there was a man who was really lucky because he met a dark-haired woman. She was the most wonderful woman he'd ever met."

"That's so true," he murmured as I pressed close.

By far the most important element of our sweaty rubbing and thrusting was that I got to have the full attention of Augustus. At least I thought I did, but who knows what he was really thinking. Maybe he was thinking of the women he'd winked at or suggestively smiled at that day. If I could have crawled into his brain to ensure it was me he was thinking about, I would have. My zealous obsession with Augustus did not preclude other interests, however. For instance, I had much curiosity about the escort business in Athens and at least some interest in Grecian history and Athenian life.

We were in a taxi, headed to the Panathenaic Stadium. I'd shown the taxi driver the pamphlet that stated, *The Panathenaic Stadium is the only stadium in the world built entirely in marble. The stadium was built around 330 BC and was where nude male athletes competed.*

"We want to go there. Do you speak any English?" I leaned forward from the backseat.

"Liddle," he said. I sat back, mulling over what I'd been thinking about, then leaned forward again. "Do you know where the girls work here? What bar?"

He looked puzzled.

"Where do the girls work at night here? You know, the working girls."

He glanced at me, then into his rear-view mirror at Augustus.

"You know, the bar or hotel where the girls work? A hotel maybe? Where the girls at night work?"

Jolette

"Hotel Grande," he said, hesitant.

"Let's go there tonight, wanna?" I asked Augustus.

"Sure." Augustus was wearing a soft gray V-necked sweater. It made him look soft and inviting. I had to reach out and place my hand on his chest, I just had to feel him. Sometimes I was overcome with feelings for him. I wasn't sure it was a good thing. He smiled at me. A sparkle in his dark eyes. I smiled.

"Will you help me approach a client?"

"Ohhhh. I don't know. What do you mean?"

"You just approach casually, make conversation, then ask if he's interested in some company."

"Oh, I don't know."

It was just a whimsical idea, the thought fluttered across my mind. We could be a team. It might be fun. Might bring us closer together, since I couldn't physically cement us together like I wanted.

"Come on, I can make a little money for us, I'll tell you the room number and you can wait for me. You'll be my security guard." Even though I knew already he would be useless as a real security guard. And I wouldn't want him to be. Nothing dangerous.

"I don't know."

"Come on, it'll be easy. We could use a little money."

"Oh god."

"Come on."

The Panathenaic Stadium was a lovely spot to stroll, to gaze half-interested at the spot of ancient history, to consider the world in the half-light of early evening, gloriously gleaming over the marble stadium, fingers entwined with the fingers of the most desirable man anywhere. It was easy at that moment to consider the world exceptional.

The older gentleman stood in front of a boutique window inside the Hotel Grande. I'd seen a million like him. He dressed well, looked soft, nice, easy. "Him," I said to Augustus.

"I can't do this," Augustus murmured.

"Yes, you can. It's not a big deal. Just ask him if he'd like to spend some time with your friend."

"Oh god."

"Go, it's fine."

Augustus walked slow as a sloth towards the gentleman.

I waited across the lobby, sat posed in a chair, and maintained a pleasant expression. A century later Augustus reached the man, I saw them engage, the older man looked my way. Augustus, ill at ease, also looked my way, then walked towards me, face reddened. "He speaks English. I don't know what I said. You need to talk to him."

I smiled and walked towards the man who appeared bemused. "Hello," I offered my hand. "I'm Michelle. How are you this evening?"

"Very well, thank you. And how are you and your, er, friend?" He smiled, took my hand.

"I'm good, thank you. Where are you from?"

"Belgium, and yourself?"

"Seattle, in the United States."

"Yes, I know Seattle."

"It's a nice city," I commented dutifully. "You've been there?"

"Yes, I have. On business," he said. "And are you enjoying Athens?"

"Yes, I love it! My friend and I are traveling through Europe and Greece. I was just working a little bit tonight, trying to make money for our travels."

"Oh I see. How much money do you need for your travels?"

"Two hundred dollars."

"I'd be happy to help you with that."

"Thank you very much. Shall I join you in your room in ten minutes?"

"Yes, that would be very nice. Room 1138."

I walked back to Augustus, who looked tense.

"I'll be in room 1138, okay?"

Jolette

He nodded. "Be careful."

"It will be fine. Don't worry."

An easy hour later, I found Augustus waiting in the lobby.

"Are you alright?" I asked.

"That was awkward as hell but I'm alright. Are you alright?"

"Yes, I'm good, it was easy."

"I was worried and that was awkward. I felt like such a jerk."

"But it worked. We did it and you're not a jerk, except sometimes."

"Shut up."

We played a mean game of backgammon before bed that night at the Hotel Eva. The next day I wanted to go back to the Hotel Grande.

"I'm going back to the Hotel Grande tonight. I wanna see how the girls work the bar. Did you wanna come with?"

"Do you need me to come with?" Augustus was sprawled on the lumpy double bed surrounded by a spread of tourist magazines.

"No, I'm fine alone."

"You sure?"

Yea, I'm fine. I'll only be gone a few hours."

"Okay. Be careful, babe."

The bartender at the Hotel Grande's top floor nightclub set my coke on the bar. I glanced around. There was a swell of brunette heads, clinking glasses, perfumed scents escaping hot bodies, steady chatter. I'd barely surveyed the scene when a tall, dark haired, handsome young guy approached. I didn't like handsome and didn't like young. Guaranteed nothing but trouble.

"Hello. Are you alone?" his English stilted.

"Hi, yes."

"You are English?"

"American."

"You are traveling?" he asked.

"Yes. I've been in Athens about five days. It's a great city."

"You have gone to the Acropolis and Parthenon, of course?"

"Yes, they're beautiful."

"You are traveling alone?"

"No. No, I have a friend I'm traveling with."

"But you are here tonight alone? What is your name?"

"Danielle. Yes, I'm alone. I'm working," I said, friendly smile. "Trying to make a living."

His face remained immobile, but his eyes comprehended. "How much?" he asked.

"Three hundred drachma. Two hundred dollars."

"I will give you seventy-five American dollars," he said.

"No, that won't work for me."

"It is what I can give."

"No, I don't negotiate. Have a good night." I moved to the bar's far end. Handsome guy followed me five minutes later.

"Danielle," he smiled. "I would like to spend some time with you. I will give you seventy-five American dollars."

"That won't work for me."

"But I'd like to spend time with you."

"Not tonight," I smiled, moving away again.

Handsome guy was sticking to me like glue. I couldn't shake him. I'd managed to stay away for about fifteen minutes, was just starting a conversation with an older man when handsome guy sauntered over, put his mouth next to my ear, "Danielle, I want to tell you something. I want to tell you this because I like you. I am with the police department and there is going to be a raid in this bar tonight, soon. I want to tell you this so you can leave. So you don't get into trouble."

I turned, gauging his face.

"You must leave now, Danielle. The police will be here soon."

Jolette

I was almost sure he was lying, but felt a flicker of uncertainty. The only true certainty was his apparent determination to interfere with my evening.

"You must leave, Danielle. They are coming now. I will help you."

"Okay. Well, jeeze, thanks for warning me. I'm going to go. Thank you for telling me."

"Come with me, Danielle. I will walk you out."

"No, that's okay. I'm just going to go back to my hotel."

"But I like you very much Danielle," handsome grasped my arm with a strong hand. "I want you to come with me. We will leave. I will help you. Let us go now."

"Can I see your police identification?" I asked.

He leaned close to my ear. "I will show you when we get outside. I cannot take it out here. I am undercover here."

"Ok, well, I'm just going to leave and go back to my hotel now. I'm not coming here anymore," I said, "Don't worry, you won't see me again. I promise." I tried to free my arm, but his grip tightened.

"You are not safe here. Let me walk you out." He steered, I acquiesced and walked along with him, into the elevator, down into the lobby.

"Okay. Well, I'm good now. I'm going to go back to my hotel now," I said making another unsuccessful attempt to disengage.

"Danielle, I like you very much. Very much." He looked at me. "I will let you leave but you must come with me."

"Thanks for warning me, but that scared me and now I really just want to go back to my hotel," I said, polite.

"No," he said and pulled me through the revolving hotel doors into the dark Athens night.

My sudden scream surprised us both. "Nooooo!! Let me go!! Let me go!!"

He was startled enough so that I could yank my arm free. I raced towards the waiting line of taxis, jumped into the backseat of one, yelling, "Go! Go! Go!"

The taxi driver, slow as molasses, took forever to turn his head towards me.

"Go! Go! Go!" I yelled, indicating wildly with my hands. The driver stared at me, unbelievably non-responsive. He said something in Greek.

"Go! Please just go!"

He shrugged his shoulders, his face non-comprehending, then his gaze shifted past me and I turned to see handsome staring at the taxi plates, speaking into a walkie talkie.

I flew across the taxi seat to the far door, jumped out, raced across a stretch of grass to another taxi much farther away. I didn't dare look behind me, kept my focus straight ahead in a direct line towards the desired taxi. Never look behind when you are being chased and you must get away. Never ever. I jumped into the back seat of the taxi. Two men were in the front seat, their expressions heightened at once.

"Go, please go! There's a man chasing me! Please go! Drive!"

The two men exchanged looks of alarm, spoke in Greek.

"Please just go! Go!" I flattened down on the back seat.

"Two men they follow you?" one managed in English.

"Yes! Yes! Please go!"

The taxi sped off. I lay with my head on the back seat, trying to slow my rapid breathing, trying to calm down, the animated Greek conversation between the two men indistinct in the background. Slowly I sat up. I didn't know if the handsome guy was a police officer or not. Probably not. But why did he have a walkie talkie? Had he reported me to the police? How did it work in Athens?

The taxi turned a corner, then another. The men had not asked me where I wanted to go. It occurred to me they had a destination in mind. I realized, just as the taxi pulled up to a well-lit, official looking building, that they would be taking me to get help. I thought it just as one of the men turned to me and said, "The police. We get help."

"No, no, please. I don't want help. I just want to go to my hotel," I said, but the man moved speedily, was already gone, entering the building. My mind raced and my body froze. It was only a minute before the man returned, alongside him was a police officer. They walked quickly towards me. The taxi door opened, the officer climbed in beside me.

"Hello." The police officer smiled nicely, his brown eyes concerned. "You need help? Two men were chasing you?" His English was surprisingly good.

"No, no, I don't want help. Really. I have a bad headache." I put a dramatic hand to my head. "I just want to go back to my hotel. Please."

"No, you must need help. We want to help you," he said kindly.

"My head really hurts," I grimaced. "I just want to go to my hotel. My head hurts."

The officer was noble in his attempt to assist. He repeated his efforts multiple times, but I maintained a headache, refused help, felt slightly bad for being so non-receptive. He became confused, finally relinquished his virtuous endeavor and left the car. The two men in the front seat also appeared confused. They looked at me.

"Go to the Oroscopo restaurant?" I asked weakly. The men, dismayed with me, turned back to the front seat, murmured a few words, turned a few corners and dropped me at the familiar restaurant. I profusely thanked them. They drove away puzzled. I walked around the corner and down the block to the Hotel Eva. Augustus was on the bed, still immersed in tourist magazines.

"Hi, babe. How was your night? I missed you," he said, smiled. I wanted to crawl into that smile and stay there forever.

26

Sahara Desert, 1981

Hospitality is a right rather than a gift and the duty to supply it is a duty to God.
Prophet Mohammad, merchant, prophet and founder of Islam, 570 AD – 632 AD.

The Sahara Desert, immense as an ocean, flat as glass, unrolled to the very end where the desert met the sky and was over 3.6 million miles in size, the same size as the United States. Enormous. I imagined camel caravans, turbaned riders, well-covered with scarves and robes, plodding their way on some unseen path through this sprawl of gravel, the largest hot desert in the world, dwarfed in size only by the larger cold deserts of the Arctic and Antarctica, which claimed the prestige of greater vastness.

The Sahara's stupendous sand dunes, sometimes reaching up to 1,000 feet, the soft mounds inviting, have taken center stage in most depictions but, in reality, the monumental sand dunes make up only twenty percent of the Sahara. Most of the Sahara Desert is an unglamorous spread of flattened gravel and sand. This was the landscape I gazed at from the train Augustus and I took from Tunis, Tunisia to the border of Morocco.

Jolette

"I bet it's about a five-hour train ride," I had said to Augustus in our small room in Tunis, as we peered at the crumpled African map in our hands. "It doesn't look that far."

We'd flown into Tunis, the capital and largest city in Tunisia, from Greece. The streets of Tunis were under major construction, roads were torn apart, the sidewalks bolstering the weight of people and markets, mosques and cafés where outdoor tables full of fruits, vegetables, couscous, coffees, and teas made life appear appetizing and satiable.

Tunisia is part of the Maghreb region of Africa, which is predominantly Muslim and includes Algeria, Libya, Mauritania, and Tunisia. Not that I had a speck of knowledge about the Arab world. I thought all of Africa was a safari, a wonderland of lions and elephants. I was puzzled with Tunis, the lack of black African people, just brown people who spoke incomprehensible Arabic. Tanzania or Kenya, the countries with the animals I wanted to see, were 4,500 miles away. There were five or six countries to go through to get there and many of these countries were at war and travel there was prohibited. This mandated a circuitous route, which would be made more difficult by a two- to four-week wait per country for visas.

In the meantime, we were in Tunis, a dusty city overrun by humans whose main pastimes were consumption and digging up streets, like most peopled places. This was not a fair assessment of Tunis, of course, whose history was far richer than, say, mine. Its location was enviable, right on the Mediterranean Sea, the perfect spot for liaisons between countries, both friendly and not. On its western border sat Algeria. The southeast was bordered by Libya.

In early Tunisian days, the population was primarily nomadic, life lived from a tent. This was after it had been founded in the ninth century by the Libyans but before France had taken a fancy to colonizing the smallish coastal country from 1881 to 1956. Due to that colonial period, there were two distinct quarters in Tunis – the older, walled Muslim neighborhoods in stark contrast to the more modern European styled edifices.

Tunisia was a soup of Islam rule, Muslim leaders, with fluctuating progressive and conservative stances. In 1979 it became the headquarters of the Palestinian Liberation Army whose goal was to unite the Arab countries and liberate the Palestinians in Israel. I had no clue about any of that, I was just disappointed that there would be no sojourn to Tanzania or Kenya, no safaris, given the complications. Instead, we decided to stay a few days in Tunis, then point ourselves towards Casablanca.

A run-down hotel was our home for a few nights, our room holding a bed and a toilet not more than three feet apart, an unmistakable aroma curling up our nostrils when trying to sleep, but at least there was a toilet.

We happened on a bar our second evening and were engulfed by serious clouds of cigarette smoke when we entered. I coughed while my eyes adjusted to the dim interior. The bar was bursting with men who were packed together as if in an overstuffed suitcase. Finding a spot to sit was difficult. I finally lit on a table with two young men and two empty chairs. When I pointed at the empty chairs and smiled with inquiry at the two young men, they broadly smiled and nodded in response. We joined them and were served a drink called boukhe. We all raised glasses and when I took a small sip of the fig flavored alcohol my tongue immediately shuddered and flew up against the roof of my mouth to flee the reaches of the sugared fluid. I managed to smile, put the drink down and did not pick it up again.

"Do you speak English?" I asked one of the young men whose dark eyes brightened when we sat down. Both men appeared excited to have us sitting with them.

"Ah English?" He shook his head, "Un peu. Je ne parle qu'un peu anglaise mais je parle Francais. Parlez-vous Francais?

"No, I'm sorry, no French, " Augustus smiled and shrugged. We all laughed. I watched Augustus as he tried to make conversation with the young men, who told us they were from Libya. Augustus, handsome and earnest, asked if they liked football. It was a word they understood. "Yes! Yes! Football!"

When Augustus looked over at me and took my hand, I felt our bond deepen. Together we were venturing into new lands.

The next morning, we decided to take a train from Tunis to the Algerian and Moroccan border. From there we would transfer to a bus to Casablanca.

Under a glaring sun, we shuffled onboard the jam-packed locomotive - standing room only - and squeezed into the pack of sweating bodies. Our backpacks increasingly burdensome on our weary backs, had to be carefully swung to the floor.

As I bent, I felt a gush between my legs, felt moistness. Oh god, my period was making a grand entrance. It wasn't due for another week but had chosen this inopportune moment to arrive. I felt another gush. I wasn't ready, had no tampons. I had nothing and knew there was no toilet paper within a three-country radius. I resigned myself to bleeding freely while standing in the lurching train packed with a herd of people.

"I hope this is not more than five hours," I murmured to Augustus who looked tired, hot, heavy-lidded. We stood, glistening with perspiration, and shifted along with everyone else in response to the pitching of the temperamental train. All of us resigned to our uncomfortable fate.

Five hours later the inner thighs of my jeans were blood-soaked. It had to smell, I thought but wasn't sure, hardly cared. Augustus and I were both sweltering and bone tired.

"Oh my god, how long can this be?" I said to Augustus who groaned, "Just shoot me."

Each time we spoke, dark heads turned our way. "English?" someone had asked earlier before we were all fatigued to the point of incoherence.

Suddenly, the smiling face of a man appeared before us, and beckoned us to follow him to a compartment. He opened the door and about ten people, all seated on benches, turned our way. They scooted over and made room for us to sit between them. We smiled gratefully. I swaddled a sweatshirt around my waist to cover my bloody massacre and someone split open an orange, pushed orange slices into our hands. The taste hit the membranes of my mouth with a burst of coolness waking sluggish nerve endings like the blast of a trumpet call at sunrise.

Augustus smiled. I smiled. We were all sweating but smiling. Someone gave us bread, then more oranges, all the while trying to speak English. We settled in and after a spell, a man leaned forward as if to ask me something.

"What is this, what is this wood…wood…?" he began to ask.

"What?" I asked.

"What is this…. woodchuck …what is this?"

"I don't know," I shook my head. "I don't understand."

"What is this woodchuck chuck…?"

"Woodchuck chuck?"

"Yes. What is this?"

"Oh! How much wood would a woodchuck chuck if a woodchuck could chuck wood?"

"Yes! That!"

"Oh! You want to learn that?"

The man nodded and I spent the next half-hour trying to teach the woodchuck rhyme to the man whose first language was Arabic and had maybe five English words at his disposal. Still, we tried. He was an earnest student. We went back and forth numerous times until he got most of it and was satisfied. Then we wound down and fell into a lull. Around that time some of the younger kids were getting restless. One young boy held out his hand to presumably his father who gave him some dinar and he got up.

"Where is he going?" I asked. "Are you going to get food? Drinks? I'm coming with," I said, and turned to Augustus. "I'm going to go get us something at the food counter or whatever it is."

"Ok, well, be careful."

Jolette

The young boy looked at me with the brightest dark brown eyes and I followed him, pushing through one crowded train car to another. There were so many people they began to blur into one horrific glob. Hard to believe we seriously consider ourselves a superior species, with our bulbous torsos and wiggling limbs.

It took at least ten minutes to plunder our way to the food cart, but there it was in all its glory with snacks and sodas for sale. Just as I was about to point and buy, there came loud yelling. So loud it quelled all else. My young friend turned to look at me, at the same time an older man with amazing vocal aplomb came into view. He wore what looked like a conductor's hat and he immediately pinned his eyes on me, yelling.

"What? What's he saying?" I asked the young boy who looked frightened and answered me in Arabic. It didn't sound good whatever it was. I felt like I was being accused of something. I turned and pushed my way back through the train cars with the young boy, the shouting conductor close behind. The young boy and I raced, albeit a slow race since there were so many body parts to get through, towards our train compartment. Still the conductor followed, shouting. We made it to the train compartment, and I sat down next to Augustus, folded my hands on my lap and looked straight ahead, as if by ignoring everything, there would be no problem.

"What's going on? What happened?" Augustus asked.

"Nothing," I said, my eyes straight ahead. The conductor appeared in the doorway.

"What did you do?" Augustus asked.

"Nothing, I didn't do anything."

All eyes were on us. The conductor was excited, yelling, waving his arms.

"He say you go him," my woodchuck friend said.

I shook my head, "I don't wanna go with him."

"You must go him," woodchuck friend insisted.

"Why?" I asked and woodchuck could only shrug.

The conductor stood over us. There is nothing scarier than being angrily yelled at in a language you don't understand.

Augustus stood up and reached for our backpacks. "Come on, let's go."

"Oh god. You sure?" I asked.

"Yes. He's not going to leave us alone. Come on. We have to."

The conductor turned, led us out of the train compartment. All of our new friends looked unsure. I gave a fast wave, then maneuvered my backpack through a slew of people once again, following the conductor who at least wasn't yelling anymore. We walked and walked through multiple cars, and then the aisles cleared. There were fewer people. The conductor stopped. He opened a door to a compartment. It was large and nearly empty except for a family of four sitting together on what appeared to be big, comfortable recliners. Two empty recliners were in front of us, the conductor waved his arm at the chairs and abruptly left.

"Is this first class?" I asked Augustus.

"It sure seems that way," he said.

"Did he just bring us to first class?" I said. "Why did he do that?" We dropped into the recliners, could hardly believe our good fortune.

"Maybe he didn't want us mixing with local people. I don't know," Augustus said.

"That's so strange," I murmured, then got comfortable, and fell asleep.

After a day, I was used to the fits of the elderly locomotive, which could only exert itself for six hours before sputtering to a stop, resting for perhaps an hour or two or three, then moaning back up to its feet, moving in reverse for a disconcerting period of time, then forward again for another six hours. It would take twenty years to reach Morocco at this three steps forward, two steps back rate.

Over the next four days the train emptied out. We wandered, sat in what seemed to be a regular part of the train. A conductor, not the one who had yelled at us, walked down the aisle saying something in French or Arabic or both.

"What did he say do you think?" I asked Augustus.

"Oh right, like I know."

"He said the train is stopping in Algiers. Everybody must get off," a man across the aisle said.

"Oh, thank you. When can we get back on the train?" I asked.

"In the morning."

"We can't stay on the train tonight?"

"No, do you need a place to stay?"

"Yes, can you recommend a hotel?"

"My friends will let you stay with them."

"Oh no, that's okay. We'll just find a hotel or something," I said.

"No, you must stay with my friends. I insist." He pointed to two women sitting up a few rows. They wore dark colored hijabs

"That's okay. Thank you anyway."

"I insist." The man called out to the women. They turned their heads. He spoke to them. They glanced at us and nodded. "You will go with them."

"Ok. Thank you." I looked at Augustus, he shrugged, and we followed the two women out of the train station, down an Algerian street where tenement buildings towered on either side. The women chatted, heads together. Augustus and I trudged behind.

The women stopped in front of a tall building and looked back at us. We couldn't see their mouths, but their eyes were kind and we followed them up staircase after staircase until I thought we must have reached flying altitude. Finally, we arrived at their floor and followed them down a long skinny hall where they opened a door to their apartment. We followed them through the door which opened to a tiny box of a kitchen, a living room with a black and white TV making some noise, a couch, a rug on the floor. There was one teeny bedroom, one bed.

We met the grandmother, and two younger children, a boy about ten, a girl maybe six, and a man, presumably the father and husband. Once inside, the hijabs were discarded revealing bright, pretty faces, one younger, one older. Incomprehensible language whirled around us, Arabic and French.

Dinner was served at the kitchen table, three plates with chicken and potatoes, for me, Augustus and the father. The rest of the family sat on the rug on the floor around a large bowl of chicken soup they all dipped into. For dessert, the father offered me a banana. I ate it. Within ten minutes I had a problem. "Oh oh," I groaned, clutching my stomach. "You have a bathroom?"

The young boy happily led me out of the apartment, down the hallway to a door that opened to a room with a small hole in the floor. He pointed.

"Oh, okay," I said, shutting the door. My despair hit hard and fast. I was going to throw up or have a horrible amount of diarrhea, maybe both, I couldn't tell. I took position, released the poison from within, no toilet paper of course, nothing to do about that, at least I didn't feel like throwing up anymore. I stood looking at the odorous mound, a cow pie sitting on top of what was really a small pipe hole. How did they flush? There was nothing in that room except for the vital hole in the floor, no sink, nothing. I opened the door, the young boy had waited for me, he grinned. He was a cute little thing with curly dark hair and a happy face. I must have looked puzzled because his face became inquisitive.

"I don't know how to flush it," I said, hesitantly pointing behind me. He pushed open the door, saw my fecal sculpture, laughed, picked up a bucket of water I hadn't noticed and poured it over the mound, successfully dissolving it into the hole that I hoped ran through the entire building and into the sewer system, whatever that might be. The high-spirited boy seemed very pleased that he could assist. He laughed happily, and we walked together back to the little apartment.

The father insisted we take the bed that evening. We protested, but were met with kind adamance. I wondered where Grandma would sleep. Augustus and I crawled into the soft double bed, didn't wake until morning when we were served a breakfast of eggs, tomato, onions and bread. We ate at the table with the father. The children, mother, and Grandma sat on the rug.

"We should offer money, shouldn't we?" I whispered to Augustus, who pulled dinars from his wallet which was strongly refused. We exchanged farewell smiles, my eyes lingering a moment on the young boy whose face shone with such vitality.

Augustus and I found our way back to the train. We settled in, relieved to be back on the geriatric locomotive. By the end of the day the train had reached the end of the line. It had been five days on the train, not five hours like I'd thought at the beginning. It seemed more like five years.

We were deposited in a dusty village near an aged and overcrowded bus. This would be our bus to Casablanca. A ten-hour ride.

We managed to get a seat in the overburdened bus, which then pitched forward threatening to topple the roped-down items on the bus's roof. I heard the squawk of a chicken from the back of the bus. There was not a spare inch in the arthritic bus, not even for a second chicken, which seemed barely able to make it down a block much less trek through the Saharan desert.

A strong lurch roused me. The bus had come to a violent stop. I'd fallen off to a fitful semi-sleep. I raised my head from the shoulder of Augustus. The movement was enough to stir the man in the next seat whose dark head rested on my shoulder. I glanced his way. He'd been soundly sleeping it seemed, his eyes open but still turned towards the world of sleep. We hadn't shared a word, only my shoulder. It was this way on the bus that had taken us across the border of Algeria into Morocco.

The bus had stopped next to a lean-to shack. There were a few tables and chairs, maybe twenty goats roaming nearby and a strung-up, long rope draped with drying goat skins.

Augustus was tired. He wordlessly got to his feet. "Let's get something to eat," I murmured. We moved in a tight package, all of us, everyone shuffling, bumbling together like a disjointed centipede. By the time we reached the little shack, which was a restaurant featuring the unfortunate unsuspecting nearby goats, the tables were all taken. We silently stood in the welded crowd, waiting our turn to order. The menu options were bread and goat meat. I glanced at the goats busily pulling at whatever scrub they could find on the desert floor and ordered two plates.

We arrived in Casablanca at 3 a.m., dropped from the inner stew of the bus onto a bare, quiet street, our backpacks trying to kill our tired backs.

"We need a place to sleep," I said. Augustus seemed numb. We had been traveling for four months, the toll becoming evident.

I spotted a taxi, or more accurately he spotted us, pulling over. He had a bit of English at his disposal.

"We need a bed and breakfast, a hotel, somewhere to sleep," I said.

"Hotel, yes."

We shoved ourselves and our backpacks into the backseat and sped off to a five-star hotel on a strip of sand, near the ocean shore. Augustus broke out his credit card. We got a key and fell into a room with the most comfortable bed I'd ever seen in my life. Barely a word was spoken before we were under the covers and slept for at least ten hours straight.

I felt much better when I opened my eyes to a very Western-looking room. There were two beds, a table, and an actual bathroom. We were at a beach on the far end of Casablanca. We lazily wandered the shore. A city of about fifty tents was just a short glance away, strewn with garbage piles and clumps of people.

Augustus took off his shoes, waded into the sea. I sat in the sand. He came over and sat down. "I'm going to have to go back to Seattle now. It's time for me to get back," he said. "I have to get back to the coffee shop."

"Oh." I said, feeling as though I'd just fallen on a sword, "When are you leaving?"

"Well, I thought after a week here, or so, we could go back to London and I'd leave from there. I don't want to leave you here alone."

"But…but…what about our relationship?" I was about a half-inch from bursting into tears.

"I don't know. Are you still going to stay and live in London or Paris?"

We sat in the sand, looking out at the Atlantic, the second largest ocean in the world, the Pacific taking first place.

I hesitated, then said, "I think I might want to go back with you."

"I wish you would."

"Really?"

"Yes, really."

"I mean, then it would be easier, you know, to uh stay in touch and, you know, try to keep a relationship," I sputtered like a dimwit. "I mean, you know, I don't need to be in Seattle. I mean, we could, you know, stay in touch easier if I was somewhere in the United States. Not too close, I mean." What was my problem. I was such a jerk.

"Shhh. Be quiet." He took my hand." Why don't you just come back to Seattle?"

"Er. Um or I could do that. Do you want me to come back to live in Seattle? I mean somewhere in Seattle?"

"Yes I do."

"You sure?"

"Yes already. But do what you want to do."

"Okay then. I might travel around a little bit first, and then, you know, move back to Seattle. Then we would, you know, be in the same city and it would be easier to see you." I sounded like such an idiot.

"Whatever you want, but I'd like to have you close." Augustus smiled, which always lit my world like an explosion of fireworks.

"Ok, then. Okay." I sat, my hand firm in Augustus's, and looked out over the sea, the relaxed simple line of its surface misleading for in its belly lived an unknown number of species, eighty percent of the ocean itself unknown and unexplored, the length of its floor covered with an immense volcanic range, unseen but still spewing magma.

27

Colombia, South America, 1976

I've been telling people for 12 years that if you want to get a nuclear device into the United States, just bring it through the port of Miami disguised as cocaine.
                        Tom Clancy, 1947-2013, American novelist.

"Just call me Diana," the woman said, her voice coming through the dirty telephone pressed against my ear in a graffitied phone booth in Tucson. The woman was my contact. She was in Minneapolis. "And don't worry. You're not going to have to do anything. You can just relax, lay in the sun, have a nice vacation. It will be so easy! We'll have so much fun," she gushed over the phone. I cringed. She had just jinxed us. "I'll meet you in Miami in a week. I can't wait!" she said, sounding more like a Girl Scout troop leader than a drug smuggler.

"Take notes," said Tilly, my new friend from Pima Community College. It was a week later and Tilly, who wore tight jeans well, had a penchant for chewing gum, and was the self-assigned rock n' roll music expert for The Aztec Campus News, was driving me to the Tucson International Airport. Tilly loved to interview rock and roll musicians, reviewed as many concerts as possible. She wore red polish on long nails, and gave blow jobs to her boyfriend in semi-discrete campus locations. She was obsessed with journalism just like I was.

"Take notes?" I said. "Are you kidding? I'm not taking notes. That's evidence."

"Well, just make sure you remember the details," Tilly said. "Be careful but remember the details. It's a story."

"If I don't make it back for some reason, call my husband person, Marion."

"Why do you call him husband person? You're so weird."

"I know. Because he's not like a real husband. I mean we're married, but it's not like a real marriage. Anyway, if I don't come back, you'll let him know where I went, okay?"

"Sure, whatever you say," she shrugged. "Hi, I'm Jolette's friend and she's disappeared in Colombia where she went to smuggle drugs. Just wanted to let you know." Tilly looked at me. "Are you scared?"

"No," I said and I wasn't.

I knew Diana was blonde, knew she'd be waiting at the terminal gate — an ominous term if I'd ever heard one — and that she was flying in from Minneapolis. A one-second scan of the brunette crowd was all it took to spot a platinum head sparkling like a disco ball. I steered that direction, caught her eye. She smiled, waved. I was momentarily startled. Diana was not just pretty, she was head-swiveling stunning with eyes a striking violet, hair silvery-white, soft as satin, curled under her chin, curtaining a sculpted face of perfect proportion. She was maybe twenty-four and I knew, even as a novice, that such gorgeousness wasn't good for a trip like this. The plan was to fly to Cali, Colombia, early the next morning, and return in two weeks with one pound of cocaine ironed down flat as a pancake neatly sewn into the lining of my suitcase. I was the mule.

"Jolette? Hi!" Oblivious, or maybe not, to surrounding stares, her smile widened showing off a dazzle of white teeth. She was giddy as a schoolgirl, happy her mule had arrived. "Let's go get your luggage! Our flight leaves at 4 a.m. so we're just going to stay at the hotel here in the airport.

It's going to be an early flight, but we'll sleep on the way down there," she chattered. "How was your flight?"

Before I could answer she was chattering again. "We can eat at this great restaurant here at the airport. We won't even leave. Let's eat and then try to get a little sleep, okay?"

"Yes, sure."

You're from Minneapolis too aren't you? Bonnie said you were. Her sister is my best friend. She was with me on my last trip. We had such a good time. It was so much fun!"

Jinxed again.

"Yea, I'm from Minneapolis. I know Bonnie from high school," I said. "Do you do this a lot?"

"No, not a lot," she said. I could hear the waffle.

The hotel room wrapped us in comfort. We slid between the sheets of two queen beds. Diana giggled. I giggled too, as if we were having a slumber party. She talked about maybe going swimming in Colombia, did I bring a bathing suit, no I didn't, and before she drifted off, she murmured again, "Don't worry. You won't have to do anything. It will be fun."

I wished she'd quit saying that.

The plane to Cali, a major city of about one million people in southwestern Colombia, rattled like it'd been glued together with Elmer's. Lifting from the ground, the little plane groaned, shifted as if trying to get comfortable. "This is a Colombian plane," Diana answered my startled gasps, then she yawned. "They're rougher than American planes. I'm going to sleep for a while." She settled back, closed her eyes. I gripped the armrest, twisted to peer out the window to make sure the wings were still attached. Suddenly the plane dropped. My heart did the same. I glanced over at Diana. Unbelievably she was asleep. I gripped the armrest for the four-hour roller-coaster ride. By the time the unsteady plane landed I was ready to fall to the ground, plaster myself to it, never to rise.

The Colombian air was warm, musty or musky, maybe both, exciting and alarming, definitely both. Swarms of dark-headed uniformed men were

Jolette

busy as an army of ants on a crumb of bread. We were shuffled through customs where all eyes shot to Diana as if she were an apparition, then we jumped into a taxi that spun us down a wide boulevard flanked by gigantic billboards brimming with Spanish verve and exclamation, bookends for swerving vehicles clearly not prone to linear driving. My eyes swept the panorama until stopped by the sight of soldiers grouped on street corners holding what looked like machine guns. Dressed in military camouflage, the soldiers were stopping and searching cars. People were forced out.

"Que paso?" I asked the taxi driver with my 101 Spanish.

"Doctors kidnap," he responded. A prickle of alarm raced through me. Soldiers and guns.

We veered without interruption through a maze of streets and were delivered to a very modest neighborhood. The taxi stopped in front of a small casa midst a block of row houses, each splashed a different hue — blue, green, yellow, pink. From the doorway appeared a family — two young men, one looked my age, one a little older, a comfortable woman with a kind face who gave a shy smile, in retrospect the most noble kind of woman, the unsung domestic, the undeclared nurturer, the keeper of the light in the window. She held a small boy whose curly dark hair tumbled above lively brown eyes, chubby cheeks lifting with a grin, so adorable I had to laugh out loud, exclaim and fuss over the boy, which made him and his mother happy.

Our suitcases were carried into the little house, taken into the back bedroom — the only bedroom — which held two twin beds. This would be where we slept while guests of the family. Where the family slept while we took over their bedroom would remain unknown. Maybe the couch, or maybe the floor. Two chairs, a couch, and a black and white television stood in a slender front room. Adjoining was the kitchen, which was essentially a patio with a fire pit where the mother and grandmother spent much of their time — probably much of their life. The kitchen was partially absent of a ceiling and roof, allowing easy exit for the smoke's plume, the blue sky witness to infinite preparations of tortillas and arepas, a mix of water, salt, vegetable oil and corn meal, birthed daily on an open skillet.

Jaimie and Eduardo were brothers. Jaimie was my age, wore tight jeans, black boots, leaned against a wall, smoking a cigarette, watching me. The older brother, Eduardo, a cluster of dark curls topping his head and not so cool as his younger brother, gazed at Diana, was a stumbling puppy in her presence, became flushed if she threw a word his direction. The poor flustered boy was also the only one able to speak some English. The father of the family, a taxi driver, was responsible for locating one pound of cocaine for purchase, we had only to wait until he secured a connection, made the purchase, then phase two would begin — the concealment.

"You won't have to think of any of this. Just relax and enjoy yourself," Diana's pronouncement suspect with repetition. We settled into a routine of sorts. A morning plate of tortillas de huevos, then Diana would retreat to the bedroom, to hide her platinum head, and maintain a low profile. I would go for a walk. Sometimes Jaimie would come with me. He spoke no English and I could only manage a few 101 basics. "Hola. Que tal?" "Es muy caliente." "Es muy frio." But with a lot of pointing and exaggerated facial expressions, we conversed. One day Jaimie tapped me on the shoulder, pointed to my purse, mimicked holding it closer, then pointed at people around.

"Oh," I said. "Like this?" I hugged my purse.

He nodded, "Claro."

I understood at once. It had been only a few days earlier when Diana had deigned to take a walk with me, that she had been accosted by a child, maybe nine or ten. The allure of the diamond earrings that Diana, ignorantly or arrogantly, displayed on her lovely earlobes no doubt prompting the young child's quick assault. He jumped up, ripped one of the diamond earrings from her ear, and raced off. The child had to have been well-practiced, for he was deft and efficient. It all happened within a split second, leaving us standing shocked, open-mouthed. Diana screamed, her hand flew to her ear. I rushed to her side. "Oh god, are you okay?"

She was too stunned to answer. Diana's perfection was hardly marred. The boy had gotten the earring without ripping her earlobe, the hole in her ear only bright red and angry. I had a strong urge to laugh. I'm not sure why. The audacity of the child, I suppose. Princess Diana knocked out of her comfortable realm, maybe. Diana was beginning to seem more and more like a princess. She spent an incredible amount of time manicuring her nails, mussing with her hair, preening and grooming, seemingly oblivious or indifferent to the surrounding glare of impoverishment. I hoped the child would get a good chunk of money for the diamond.

"Claro," I nodded back at Jaimie.

Though Jaimie's pheromone messaging was inspiring, it was the company of three-year-old Edo I preferred. His cherubic face made me smile just to look at him. He often wore a short pant suit, revealing plump baby legs, dimpled knees. He liked to climb into my lap, touch my face, softly exploring my cheeks and lips with his stubby little fingers. Placing his small palms on either side of my face, he would lean forward and stare very seriously into my eyes. His mother, nearby one day, happened to glance over and shook her head. "Ah, Edo," she said, and we laughed. She had kind eyes and looked at me occasionally with concern.

On our third day in Cali, Diana revealed that she was wanted by the Colombian federales. She and her fiancé, Timothy, had been arrested three years earlier in Cali on drug charges, she said. They had both been imprisoned. Her fiancé remained in prison. Diana had somehow escaped.

"So, I have to lay low," Diana said to me, as if that were reasonable.

"What? What?" I asked. "You were arrested, you escaped? Oh god, what? Why would you come back?"

"It's okay. Calm down. I just have to be careful," Diana said.

"Oh god. You escaped? How did you escape?"

"I got some help, that's all," she said. "So, I can't visit Timothy in prison. Would you? It would be so great if you'd go visit him. I know he's really lonely."

"Oh god. I can't believe you were arrested here," I flustered.

"It's okay. It's not going to be a problem. I promise. Would you go visit Timothy?"

"Um yea, I guess, alright." Jesus.

"And if anything happens between you two, I mean I don't want to ask you to do anything you don't want to, but it's okay with me if something happens with you two."

"What do you mean?"

"You know, I mean, he hasn't seen a woman for a long time."

I paused.

"I mean, only if you feel like it," Diana said. "Visiting hours are tomorrow at ten to five."

The morning was still young when my taxi pulled up to Villanueva Prison, but the sun was already furious, its heat pummeling the air. The prison spread over a dusty city block, surrounded by a formidable wall necklaced with barbed wire. A bleak barrio skirted its periphery. A dark-haired guard met me, surveyed my passport, allowed me entrance. He turned, pointed across a courtyard towards a door. "Esa puerta."

I crossed a sprawl of dirt, eyes squinting against the sun's blaze, pushed open the heavy door and stepped inside. The darkness caused immediate blindness, the door pulling shut behind me. My hand gripped the door handle as I willed my constricted pupils to dilate more quickly. In the eternity of a minute, my eyes slowly adjusted. Shapes morphed into women, groups of women. Every head riveted my direction, staring at me. The room was still.

"Venga aqui," a woman finally said and beckoned. "Venga aqui."

She gave a tentative smile as I approached, indicating that I should raise my arms. Gingerly, she began to pat my waist, down my legs, more gentle than officious. I realized I was being searched for contraband and noticed that many of the women had their pants pulled down to their knees and were bent over. Cavity search – I would learn the term later. I froze, looked at my woman. She wavered. I didn't breathe, then she politely smiled, and waved me towards another door.

The prison was incredibly informal. I entered a bare room. A slim, dark uniformed man nodded at me to sit on the only chair. I sat down. A moment later Timothy entered. I had to restrain my facial muscles so they didn't reveal my astonishment. He was white as chalk, seemingly bloodless, his form nearly skeletal, his head a refuge for feeble strands of hair that could not provide coverage. It was unfathomable that he was the fiancé of the breathtaking Diana, who was lounging back in the bedroom of the little casa, probably brushing her platinum locks or filing her nails. I smiled, extended my hand.

Timothy was nervous. A light sheen glistened his face. "Thanks for coming," he said, his limp hand coated with clamminess.

A feat of extraordinary will allowed me to keep a smile on my face as my hand was slathered by his wet clasp. He turned, spoke Spanish to the guard, who nodded, remained distant. Timothy walked me down a corridor, towards an area called Patio One where his friend had a cell. "We can sit and talk in my friend's cell. It's better than mine."

The cell blocks in Villanueva were called Patios. Patio One was best, an individual cell with a bed and desk, pure luxury by Villanueva standards, reserved for monied prisoners. Patio One was sharp in contrast to Patio Six where Timothy slept, a spot on the cement floor, covered by a thin blanket, one of many thin blankets lined in a row like gravesites. He'd been relegated to the worst patio because he had attempted to escape, he said, but didn't make it. He'd been shot in the stomach, a nearly fatal wound.

"That's where I almost died. Right there." He pointed to his blanket on the floor.

Doc, Timothy's friend in Patio One, was nicknamed for his pharmaceutical abilities. I wasn't sure what that meant exactly. He offered me a chair when I entered his cell. It wasn't often that an eighteen-year-old American girl came through Villanueva's doors and everyone wanted to meet or at least see me. There were fourteen Americans in the prison, Timothy said. All were in for at least six years or more on drug charges. All of them came to Doc's patio to see me. I sat quietly on the chair in Doc's room, made shy by the extreme attention, as a handful of inmates surged into the tiny cell, eager to say hello and share the spill of white powder on the table. Heads bent to snort. I didn't know much about cocaine. I'd never done it. I'd never even seen it until that moment.

"We can get anything," Timothy explained. "The guards. Do you want some?"

I shook my head. The inmates, now animated, asked why I was in Cali, then fell silent with Timothy's candid response. One finally spoke. "Don't do it. Cali is muy caliente. It's too hot. You'll never make it out of the city."

They all nodded in agreement. "Don't do it. Everyone's getting busted. You'll never make it out."

"Really?" I asked.

"Yea, they're making a lot of busts right now."

"Oh no," I said.

"Don't chance it. It's not worth the risk."

"Oh god. Okay, I won't," I said.

Timothy reached for my hand. This time it wasn't a swamp of sweat, "Let's go for a walk," he said. "We'll see you guys later."

I walked with Timothy back to his penthouse suite on the cement floor. It didn't take a genius to figure out this was the time I would provide the female company he'd been deprived of for three years.

"I don't think I want to do the smuggling thing. Diana's going to be mad," I said to Timothy as we dropped to his blanket on the floor.

"Don't worry about that. You just shouldn't do it. It's not safe for you," he said, laying his frail body on top of mine. I was a little worried I might hurt him since he was so delicate, but he scrambled around with some invigoration. I felt hardly a thing then a burst of wet. Sort of like someone sneezing between my legs. When I said goodbye to Timothy, he looked at me with sad eyes. He would be in Villaneuva for ten more years. I felt bad for him, but mostly I felt frightened for me.

"Will you write to me?" he asked, with the eyes of a drowning man.

"Yes, I'll write to you a lot," I reassured him. Then I was escorted out of the prison's maze, back into the unforgiving glare of the afternoon sun, onto the hot seat of the waiting taxi.

28

Colombia, South America, 1976

In 1976, Pablo Escobar founded the Medellin Cartel, which distributed powder cocaine and established the first smuggling routes into the United States. It's estimated that by the 1980s, Escobar led monthly shipments of 70 to 80 tons of cocaine into the country from Colombia. At the time of his death in 1993, his net worth, $30 billion, made him one of the richest people in the world.

Wikipedia

"How was Timothy?" Diana asked when I returned, walking into the bedroom where she was of course polishing her nails.

"Skinny," I said. "And all of the guys told me not to do it. They said I'd never make it out of Cali." I looked at Diana, her perfect face, gorgeous hair, and started to cry. "I'm scared."

"Don't cry," she said. "They really said that?"

"They said I'd never make it. That it was too hot."

"Okay. Don't cry. Don't cry."

"I can't do it. I'm scared. I can't."

"I know. It's okay. I don't want you to be scared. You don't have to do it. Don't be scared.   You don't have to."

"Okay." I sniffled, curled up on my bed, looking gratefully towards Diana. "Thank you for being so nice."

Jolette

"It's okay. We can't chance it. It's okay." Diana sat on the bed, her body still but her mind racing. I could almost see the circuitry of her thinking.

The morning was warm. I'd woken, dressed, had breakfast, and was ready for the day. Diana handed me $5,000 in large bills — fifty hundred dollar bills. I had a large Q-tip box in my purse. I had emptied out the cotton-tipped sticks, rolled the bills up, stuffed them into the box, then back into my purse, and got into the backseat of the father's taxi. Eduardo sat beside me. The father turned the ignition, and we slid into traffic, en route to purchase one pound of cocaine.

The timing was ironic. Ten minutes after Diana had assured me I wouldn't have to smuggle cocaine out of Colombia, Eduardo and his father had appeared at our bedroom door. Eduardo looked to Diana – his eyes ceaselessly imploring her to love him — and said, "My father have connection. For tomorrow."

Diana barely saw Eduardo. She looked at me. "We can drive to a different city," she said. "We'll go to Medellin or Bogota. Those are beautiful cities. You'll love them. We can drive there and then fly out from a different city."

I paused.

"We'll be okay if we fly out from another city. We can still do it. We'll be safe if we get out of Cali." Diana's eyes were pinned on me, and as she spoke an unreasonable thrill shot through me. I was suddenly excited. I wanted to smuggle the cocaine. I wanted the money and, just as much, I wanted the experience. "You think that will make a difference? Flying out from a different city?"

"Definitely. It'll be okay from a different city," Diana said.

"Are you sure?"

"Yes, I'm definitely sure." No, she wasn't.

"Okay, yes." But I was going to do it anyway.

Eduardo and his father followed our conversation with confused expressions, but they understood the yes, and looked relieved.

"Will you go with them tomorrow to pick up the stuff?" Diana asked me later, as we were getting ready for bed.

"You want me to go pick up the cocaine?" I asked, surprised but not surprised.

"Well, you don't have to do anything. Just go with, you know, keep an eye on the money."

"Sure," I said.

The Cali streets were jammed with cars and pedestrians. The father steered his taxi through honking cars, then abruptly pulled over to the side of the street, got out and stood on the corner next to the taxi, lit a cigarette, his dark eyes darting down the street in both directions. Eduardo and I sat in the back seat silently. Five long minutes later the cigarette was finished, flicked to the ground. The father got back in the car, drove another ten minutes, stopped again for another cigarette, another shift of smoking and scanning the street. He flicked the cigarette away, got back in the taxi, and started to drive. Glancing in his rearview mirror, he made a startled noise and pulled over. A police car pulled up behind us.

"Oh shit," I murmured, looking at Eduardo, whose eyes had widened. The father got out of the taxi. There was a rapid exchange of Spanish. I looked at Eduardo who whispered, "He get ticket."

I nodded. Just then the police officer stuck his head into the window, scrutinizing Eduardo and me. I played bored passenger, glanced at the officer with what I hoped was a disinterested look. Then his head disappeared. More rapid Spanish.

"My father tell him we are his children," Eduardo whispered.

"Oh god," I whispered. That meant I should know Spanish. If the officer stuck his head back into the car and said something to me, I decided I would just stare out the window like I was mad, refusing to talk, and dad

Jolette

and brother would have to come up with an explanation. I saw the father pull out his wallet, hand pesos over to the officer. The taxi door opened, and the father slid back into the driver's seat. His face sweaty, he turned the key, and we sped off.

"What was the ticket for?" I asked Eduardo who looked bewildered. He shrugged, his eyes still wide. He didn't do this often I couldn't help but notice. We rode around for about fifteen more minutes before the father parked next to a sidewalk teeming with little kids and adults. The father turned my direction. I opened my Q-tip box, pulled out the wad of bills. He stuffed them into his pocket, got out of the car and strode up to a small house. A door quickly opened, he disappeared inside, and the door shut.

Eduardo and I sat in the backseat. We didn't speak. My throat was parched, my heart a speeding locomotive. I fastened my gaze outside where life appeared normal. The scrambling kids had moved down the sidewalk. Cars careened down the street, population control undoubtedly helped by numerous fatal car accidents, as evidenced by the multiple crosses decorating multiple locations. The sky was bright blue, accessorized with pretty cotton clouds. On the sidewalks were people strolling to destinations unknown. We sat and waited and did not speak. Time crawled like a dying man.

Thirty or sixty or ninety minutes later, the father emerged. He walked quickly, jumped into the taxi, turned and tossed me a clear plastic bag of white powder. Stunned that the bag was clear, more stunned he didn't stash the bag in the secret compartment I assumed must be in the taxi, I shoved it into my purse. We sped back to their little casa, which seemed suddenly familiar and reassuring, like an old friend, and entered the living room where Edo tottered. He looked at me, laughed, plowing towards me. I couldn't help picking him up, twirling him around while he squealed. I then set his chubby little body down, patting his curly head, and went to deliver the drugs to Diana. She was reclining on the bed, sedentary as usual, but energized when I entered.

Jolette

"Where is it?" She shut the bedroom door, her eyes bright as a kid at Christmas. She dabbed her small finger into the powdery fluff, tasting it. She quickly laid out a line, rolled a dollar bill and snorted. She turned to me, "You want some?"

"No thanks." I wasn't attracted to cocaine one single bit. Seemed to me that I needed to be alert for life, not altered.

"Okay, well," she sniffed, rubbing her nose. "We're taking two taxis to Bogota tomorrow night. We'll be in one taxi and the coke will be in the other taxi with their dad. That way we'll be safe. Eduardo will come with since he speaks some English. We might need him. Then we'll meet my friends in Bogota. They'll take care of hiding the coke in your suitcase. You won't even know where it is. My friends there are so much more fun than these people," she said.

Her words were trustworthy as a rattlesnake. And I liked these people. These people were nice. The next morning, I went with the mother for a walk down to the corner mercado. She touched me on the arm while we were walking. She stopped, pretending to lift something from the sidewalk. It took a minute, and then I got it. She was pretending to lift a suitcase from the sidewalk. Then she touched my arm again. Watch me, I knew she was saying, and she carried the pretend suitcase with her chin up, walking like she didn't have a care in the world. She stopped. Pointed at me.

"Claro," I said, smiling. "It's okay. I'll be careful."

She looked at me, put her hand under my chin, lifted my face, and said, "Ten cuidado, mi joven amiga, actua como si no tuvieras nada que ocultar. Confia en ti."

I knew what she said even though I didn't really know what she said. I nodded my head and smiled. "Gracias, muchas gracias por todo," I said. "I'll be careful. I will."

As the evening sky darkened, Diana said it was time to leave. We would travel all night, make it to Bogota shortly after dawn, she said. Laying out another line, she snorted it into her perfect nose. "One for the road," she said.

Jolette

Our two taxis pulled in front of the little casa. Edo looked up at me with dancing eyes. I touched his dark silky curls, rested my palm briefly against his head. "Bye bye, sweet boy," I murmured.

His mother and grandmother smiled. "Gracias, muchas gracias," I said, taking the mother's hand.

"De nada," she replied, holding my hand a moment.

Diana strode by everyone, got into the car, and called impatiently from the back seat, "Come on! Let's go!"

I got in beside Diana. The father and Eduardo climbed into the other taxi and we all pulled out onto the road for the nine-hour drive. We had just left when Diana turned to me, "You speak Spanish don't you?"

"A little," I said.

"I know you speak it fluently."

"No, I don't. Hardly anything. Why?"

Diana started to whimper. "Why are you doing this to me?" she whined. "Why are you doing this?"

"Doing what? What are you talking about?"

"You're setting me up, aren't you? You work for the police, don't you?" Diana continued to whimper.

"What is wrong with you? What's going on? No, of course I don't work for the police."

"Why are you doing this?" Diana repeated. "Why are you doing this?"

"What is wrong with you?" No one had ever told me paranoia was part of the cocaine high. It just seemed as though she were suddenly insane. It was contagious. "Do you have my plane ticket?" I asked, anxious.

"Yes, I have your plane ticket. Why? Why do you want your plane ticket?" Then, her voice shrill, "What are you going to do to me?"

"I want my plane ticket. Is it in your purse?"

"I'll give it to you later," Diana said.

"I want it now."

"No."

"Give it to me!"

"No!"

I grabbed Diana's purse. She held onto it, and we both clamped onto the purse and struggled but I couldn't wrest it from her. I let go and turned towards the driver. "Senor, por favor, halto otro taxi immediamente." The driver glanced at me, perplexed.

"Halto otro taxi ahora, immediamente. Halto otro taxi. Immediamente! Immediamente!"

"See? See? I knew you spoke Spanish fluently! Why are you doing this to me?" Diana was out of her mind.

The taxi driver began honking his horn. When the other taxi pulled over, I jumped out, raced as fast as I could to tell Eduardo and the father how crazy Diana was.

"Diana is loco. Diana is loco!" I cried into the window of the backseat where Eduardo and his father sat. They looked confused. "Diana is loco!" I was vehement. They remained noncomprehending, but got out of the car. On cue Diana opened her taxi door, slowly got out, and easily walked towards us. "What's going on?" she asked, yawning as if she'd just woken up. She looked extremely relaxed. I looked loco.

Eduardo's eyes adoringly attached to Diana as I spoke to the father. "I'm not getting back into that taxi with her. No gusto. Ella loco. I'm riding in this cab. Aqui mucho mejor." I climbed into the father's taxi, stared straight ahead, ignoring the puzzled looks.

"Oh well, I guess she wants to ride with you," Diana laughed, speaking to the father as if he understood English. She didn't even try to speak Spanish, just spoke English as though she didn't need to lift a finger to make any effort, her life story, I was sure. She turned to Eduardo and batted her eyes. "Would you ride with me," she said, giving the prettiest smile.

Eduardo blushed, stammered," But, yes…of course." Then nervously laughed as she took his arm and they strolled like a couple to her taxi.

I stared out the window. We were on the road again, our new seating arrangement in place. Me, the father, and the pound of cocaine in one taxi, and Eduardo and Diana in the taxi behind. I stared out at the shadowy fields that extended into deep darkness, resting my head against the window. A few hours passed. I got sleepy, slipped into slumber.

I surfaced back to consciousness gradually, then remembered and jerked my head up, glancing at the man driving the taxi and the father sitting beside me. It all came back to me and I took in the father. I hadn't seen him much at the little casa as he worked endless hours. He was wearing a long-sleeved t-shirt and jeans and had carried a black leather bag, which sat next to him on the floor. A black leather jacket lay beside him. He felt my look. I gave a small smile. He gave a small smile back. I sat back, wondering how long I'd slept, when a sudden bright light appeared in the distance. We were aimed straight at it.

"Que es?" I asked the driver.

"Estacion de inspeccion," he replied.

"Inspection station?" I repeated. No one had told me anything about an inspection station. "Oh my god." I looked at the father whose face revealed nothing. "Oh my god," I repeated. There was no choice but to sit tight as we sped toward the light. It was a searchlight, and as we got closer the bright light grazed the front end of our taxi, then engulfed us as we arrived at the inspection station where a throng of soldiers converged. The glare stripped away the easy darkness and a flood of fear broke through my veins, nerves, and muscles. My knees began violently knocking together. I did the only thing I could think of. I closed my eyes to hide the terror that I was sure had filled my eyes. I leaned against the back of the seat, pulled my sweater close around me and feigned sleep, a chilly sleep to justify the uncontrollable knocking of my knees. They were banging together like a crazed wind-up toy. I couldn't make them stop.

Our driver rolled down his window. I heard an onslaught of Spanish, one soldier asking questions that our driver answered. I yawned, shifted in my pretend sleep. The soldier was easily placated, and allowed our taxi through as we sped back to the relative safety of the dark highway.

Jolette

The first five inspection stations followed the same pattern. A few questions asked by a soldier, answers given by our driver. My knees went berserk each time. It became a nightmarish routine until the sixth and final inspection before entering the city of Bogota. Within a few short moments it was clear that the sixth inspection station would be much more intense than the preceding five. Our taxi was immediately pulled over to the side, and our driver blasted with a rapid staccato of Spanish from several soldiers surrounding our cab. I became extremely vested in pretending I was sleeping and was very cold. I shifted so that my hair fell over my face, hopefully camouflaging my eyes, which were pressed shut but beginning to twitch. I summoned all my abilities to withstand what was apparently the start of a very serious search.

The trunk of our taxi was opened, sounds of rummaging accompanied demanding Spanish voices, the language normally so beautiful, now ominous. Another vehicle pulled up behind us. I heard car doors open and the nervous laughter of Diana. Our trunk remained open and it sounded as if several soldiers stayed to question our driver, but the majority of soldiers seemed to flock towards Diana's taxi. I heard voices, Spanish, and again the nervous twitter of Diana. Turning to press my face against the backseat, under the long dark veil of my hair, I dared to crack open an eye. The father's profile came into view, his darting eyes following the soldiers. I could smell his nervousness. He looked even more nervous than I felt, if that were possible, and I saw him pull on his black leather jacket, slip his hand into his black bag. I nearly fainted when I recognized the clear plastic bag he pulled out and slipped inside his jacket. He opened the car door with a nonchalance I knew he did not possess, stood next to a ditch, pulled out and lit a cigarette. I understood immediately he was prepared to toss the bag of cocaine into the ditch in an instant.

Forty-five minutes passed. Maybe. An hour. Maybe. The inspection dragged on. I could hear the soldiers. I could hear the taxi drivers. I could hear Diana's high-pitched voice, her babble and irritating laugh. Lucky for me, I was never questioned. No one woke me up. No one made us get out

Jolette

of the car. Voices wound down, the father returned to sit beside me, still in possession of the plastic bag full of cocaine, and finally came the sound of trunks slamming shut. Our driver got back into the car and we returned to the dark highway. No one said a word. Silently we each registered relief.

Bogota at daybreak brought a reddish tint to the sky, dispelling a portion of the fear from the night's journey. Our taxis pulled up to a well-tended hotel. We all gladly broke free from the vehicular confines, streamed out onto the sidewalk, stretching and yawning. Diana came up to me and smiled, "I'm better now."

"Thank god," I said, refusing to smile back. She paid the father and the drivers but not Eduardo who looked at her with the stupefaction of one betrayed. "You say you pay me," Eduardo said.

"I already paid enough," retorted Diana, not batting an eye.

He looked flabbergasted.

"I told you, she's not nice," I murmured to Eduardo as Diana turned to the hotel and a bellboy came to take our suitcases. We unceremoniously parted ways with the still stricken Eduardo and his father, and a half hour later Diana and I were ordering breakfast on a beautiful patio of the Bogota hotel restaurant.

"I want my ticket," I began.

Diana had returned to her normal composure, no longer racked with whiny, paranoid accusations that I guessed came along with the cocaine high, which made me wonder who would want that. Instead, she was bright-eyed and chipper, having made it through the harrowing night, her drugs and mule still intact and onboard. "Let's just wait until later today, after breakfast. Let's just enjoy our breakfast, "she chirped.

I grit my teeth. "I want my ticket now."

"Aren't you happy?" she asked. "We made it! And don't worry. Everything is fine. We'll see my friend here. You'll love him, and he'll sew the stuff into your suitcase. You won't even know where it is."

"I want my ticket."

"Oh, alright. Here, have your plane ticket." Diana pulled my ticket from her purse. I tucked it into my bra where it would live for the rest of the trip.

I didn't watch Diana's friend sew the cocaine into my suitcase. He wasn't really her friend. He had a price tag, and he wasn't so great. But he did iron the bag of powder flatter than the flattest pancake you've ever seen, and sewed it somewhere into the lining of my suitcase. I didn't want to know where. We stayed only a few days in Bogota, tucked into a large house with a huge formal dining room, the table long and gleaming with polished wood. I much preferred Edo and my little family in Cali.

Within a few days we were flying back into the United States – sitting separately — and I was so relieved and happy to be going home, that I didn't care if I got caught. Prison in the United States would be so much better than in Colombia. My giddiness kept me grinning and when the customs agent asked me what I was doing in Colombia, I said, "Visiting amigos, but I am so happy to be home. There's no place like home." I would have clicked my red shoes had I been wearing any. When the customs agent in Miami opened my suitcase, he smiled at me as his hand swept against the lining. "Well, welcome back, young lady. Welcome home." He closed my suitcase and I stepped back into the US, happier than I'd ever been in my life to be on American soil.

Jolette

29

Minneapolis and Tucson, Arizona, 1976

Around a flowering tree there are many insects.
Guinean proverb

My cocaine-lined suitcase was resting comfortably in the plane's belly as it lowered into Minneapolis, where Diana still lived. We were exuberant, safe on the ground in humdrum Minnesota, no soldiers with AK-47s in sight, the airport nearly empty, an unpeopled terrain in sharp contrast to the bustle of Miami and Colombia. Outside a cloudy sky blanketed a hushed, gray landscape. It was just as I remembered. Still and melancholy.

Diana hailed a cab, decided on a quiet restaurant in the affluent suburb of Edina, not far from my parent's home and close to where Diana lived. We ordered lunch, then pulled my suitcase into the restaurant's bathroom. Wielding a sharp restaurant knife, Diana slit open the lining, revealing the flattened plastic bag of white powder, immediately helping herself, laying out a line on her makeup compact mirror. "Just a sec and I'll give you your money."

"Okay. You have powder on your nose."

"Do you want some?" She rubbed her perfect nose with her perfectly manicured finger.

I shook my head. Not in a million years.

Diana dug into her suitcase, and pulled out twenty-one hundred dollar bills. She counted them, then handed them to me. Then the ice princess with a surprising sprinkle of sweet girl, embraced me in a goodbye hug. I hugged her back, departed into a cab and startled my family with a visit.

Their home, a stately two-story house, was propped atop a small hill across from a handsome green park, a tennis court ensconced at one end, a gurgling creek winding throughout. I dragged my violated suitcase up the steep stairs that traveled to the front door of my parent's home and knocked. My father, who thought I was busy at school in Tucson, opened the door, his eyes brightening as he exclaimed, "Jolette!"

And though I hadn't been absent from my family for very long, I noted change. There was new gray at my father's temples, the addition of reading glasses resting on his nose, a few extra pounds on his belly. Some things really do not change, however, and that would include my father's dress style, a maroon vest over a green and white-checkered shirt with plaid slacks. Discordant yet never disfiguring, for he always cut a handsome figure.

"Surprise!" I grinned.

"Well, well," he laughed. "Jolettie! What are you doing here? It's nice to see you!" My dad put an arm around me. "Look who's here. Eleanor. Look who's here." He turned towards the TV room.

"What? Who is it?" My mom's voice came from a reclined position on the sofa.

"Hi mom, what's happenin'?" I strode into the TV room where she scrambled up.

"Oh, for Pete's sake! Jolette! What are you doing here?" My mom was shorter than I remembered. "How did we get so lucky?" She placed a hand on my arm and peered into my face.

"I decided you missed me terribly, so I came to visit." I patted her hand, disengaged and walked through the house. Familiar. Reassuring. The upright piano, the same one I used to practice on, my mother's sheet music, *To Dream the Impossible Dream*, the small black and white TV currently

Jolette

featuring Lawrence Welk, the kitchen, always the coldest room in the house, formidable in the winter. I opened the refrigerator, each shelf a smorgasbord of food. This was the land of plenty. Safely middle class.

"I was just in Colombia," I said, immediately kicking myself for opening my mouth. Stupid.

"What? Colombia! What were you doing there?" my dad asked.

"I just went with a friend. She paid for the trip. She just wanted me to keep her company while she visited her boyfriend," I lied.

"She paid for the trip?" My mother doubtful.

"Yeah, she's rich. She lives here, so I thought I'd come back with her and say hi to you."

"Who is your friend?" my mom asked.

"Diana, she's friends with Bonnie. I'm hungry, mom. What's there to eat?"

"Colombia? You're kidding. Where did you go down there? I've always wanted to see South America," my dad said.

"Do you want a peanut butter sandwich with chips?" my mom asked.

"Yea, that sounds good. We went to Cali. That's where her boyfriend lives. Have you ever heard of it?"

"Cali. Cali. I'm going to look it up on the globe." My dad who had always wanted to be a geographer or a geologist and instead got stuck cleaning teeth, went to his globe, which stood in the dining room corner. He twirled it around to South America, I went to stand by him.

He jabbed a finger. "There it is. It's right there, Well, what do ya know, our little girl is a world traveler. That was awfully nice of your friend to pay."

"Yea, it was." I sat down with my sandwich.

"Your friend paid for the whole trip?" my mom asked again, gazing at me with scrutinizing eyes. "What have you been up to, girlie?"

"Nothing, just sightseeing mostly. It was really dirty and poor, but I really liked the people." I completely ignored her questioning look.

"Well, alright, as long as you're here, safe and sound," she finally relented. "How long are you staying?"

"A couple of days."

By the end of my second day in Minneapolis, I was depressed. The skies were dismal gray. They sat on my head, stirring up old feelings I thought had vanished but really had just slipped under the surface.

My mother succumbed to a migraine, which, as I would learn over the years, would occur by the third day of my visits. My visits seemed to promote tension. Her shoulders and neck would tighten, constricting muscles, restricting blood flow, causing a migraine so severe all lights and sounds were banned. It brought back memories of growing up with a mother maddened by pain and life, stricken with pounding headaches, seething in a dark house. A scary place where her voice lashed out, or she mumbled, or was silent, all of them equally discomforting.

My mother was in bed, her face drawn, eyes barely able to open. She lay motionless in dim light. I murmured sympathies to her, brought a cold washcloth for her pounding head. It wasn't her fault she suffered the infliction of migraines, but I blamed her. Somewhere inside I thought she knew what she was doing. Making the house miserable for everyone. She wasn't happy, so no one else could be happy either. I tried to quiet my internal accusations, held her hand and sat beside her. We were still and quiet. My feelings of discomfort fixed to everything about Minneapolis. Even the pretty little skyline made me uneasy. I felt slightly ill each time I was in the Midwestern city of nice people. Its reputation of nice falsely perpetrated if you ask me. They weren't really that nice.

It was with relief when I bid farewell, returning to Tucson where the sun was like a warm caress. I returned to school and was zealously writing for the campus paper — story ideas flying to me like bats in the night sky — when I received a letter from Marion. He would arrive in a week.

The great thing about not being madly in love with a husband is that when things are lousy, you don't fall flat on the ground and can't get up. We'd had a rotten time in Alaska, but it fazed me only mildly, and I had kind of forgotten about him while I was in Colombia. We communicated through infrequent letters and by the time he appeared at my Tucson apartment, I was even happy to see his familiar face. He seemed happy to see me too.

"Hi Jolette," he said, his face widening into a grin, a split in the middle of a big bushy mustache and beard, his hair long, arms much more muscular than I remembered.

We rekindled our union. He came prematurely as usual, but it was still nice to be with him. It would be years later, after some call girl education, that I learned how to deal with premature ejaculation. First a hand job until ejaculation, then re-arouse and continue on to vaginal penetration. Pre-emies last longer if they get their ultra-excited climax out of the way, potentially then permitting a more enduring intercourse. Takes a bit of effort, but that's one way to do it.

Marion dealt with his frustration by gradually avoiding sex altogether. It didn't matter to me either way. As with food, I fed myself according to whims and desire, immediate gratification the priority, monogamy, in this case with only Marion who I was somewhat attached to but definitely not madly in love with, went unheeded.

The days fell into a pleasant rhythm, the months slid by easy as a whistle. I relished the moderate warmth that eased the strain of winter. There was no bundled clothing or bite of freezing wind in Tucson. Its mild winter winds from California and Nevada keep the environment a pleasant seventy to eighty degrees, the air dry and comfortable. But come summer it gets really hot due to a shift in winds which suddenly enter from the Pacific Ocean and the Gulf of Mexico, hitting Tucson with moisture. That moisture, along with the rising heat of the summer desert, creates a high-pressure ridge over the area, shooting temperatures up past 100 degrees. Too hot for me and my Midwestern metabolism.

"I'm not going to be able to handle the summer heat," I complained to Marion.

"Let's go back to Alaska for a while. Just a little while," he said. He wrapped an arm around me.

I hesitated. "I don't like small towns."

Marion nodded. "I know, but we won't be there long. And it's Alaska. It'll be a good experience."

I paused, then agreed. I'd finish school later. I said goodbye to Tilly, who told me to send stories about Alaska and they'd publish them in the Aztec Campus News. I probably won't be able to write in Alaska, I thought as I packed. As if being able to write was relegated by region. Alaska, the last frontier, could be interesting but I didn't like the country and hated small towns. My expectations were low as a grave.

30

Ketchikan, Alaska, 1976

Do you not see how necessary a world of pains and troubles is to school an intelligence and make it a soul?
John Keats, English poet, 1795-1821.

The sun appears more frequently during the summer months in Alaska, warming the grateful recipients of Ketchikan, which includes not only the locals but also the onslaught of tourists let loose from cruise ships prowling southeastern Alaska's waters. Small port towns burst in population with the arrival of the ships. Sidewalks fill with talk and laughter and the less audible but more significant sound of money and trade.

Although I'd spent almost a week dancing at the Shamrock, I hadn't gotten to see much of Ketchikan. This time, I couldn't help but recognize the force of its raw beauty. Just the ocean's tidal action was enough to make you stop and really notice. Every six hours, the tide rolled into a high tide at thirteen feet, then rolled out, low tide, to one foot. The variance of twelve feet was extreme. An effortless display of immense power.

The tidal extreme would also reflect my life for the next two years in Alaska. Like the low tide, there would be a period of quiet dormancy, followed by high tide, an event of magnitude.

There would be four such events.

Marion was quick to secure a job as a deckhand aboard the *Magnolia*, a fifty-eight-foot purse seiner, with four other male deckhands and a captain, a similar scenario replayed probably a hundred million times since 1905 when commercial salmon trolling began in Southeastern Alaska. Until 1950, salmon trawling was unlimited and continued year-round, salmon hooked by small trawlers or hauled up by the behemoth nets of large seining vessels, up to 20,000 fish at one time in as little as forty-five minutes. Salmon populations declined immensely due to the extensive fishing, were driven to near extinction in some locations until, finally, state and federal restrictions were instated and the slaughter of salmon became seasonal.

A small room for rent in downtown Ketchikan served my immediate purpose. I emptied my backpack, then wandered the streets in search of a job. What I found was Jimmy, a transplant from Wisconsin with long dark hair and eyes topaz blue, his physique taut and strong, he reminded me of a beautiful stallion. We exchanged glances on the street, which led to conversation. He told me he'd been in Ketchikan a year. I told him he reminded me of a stallion. He tossed his mane, invited me to his house, a place I would return to again and again. I was quickly smitten with Jimmy, but so was everyone else. His company desired by multiple women. He told me later that he was having sex with up to three women daily.

Sometimes I was sandwiched in between his morning and nighttime gallivants, he said and laughed. I laughed too since he didn't tell me this until about fifteen years later when I was living in Los Angeles and he called me out of the blue, long after I'd left Alaska behind. By then I was much wiser in terms of how significant sex really was. Not very significant, I can tell you that. Don't be fooled by propaganda overstating the importance of friction, nerve endings, lubrication and joined parts. The engagement a mere conduction of mechanics, nerve endings strategically placed to ensure excitement, inviting repetition, thus propagating the species. Also useful in terms of releasing built-up tension. Emotions to be added at the discretion of the involved humans. Men already know this.

Jolette

Women remain more vulnerable to societal brainwashing that admonishes their sexual freedom and steers their ovaried bodies towards nesting.

Jimmy was gorgeous. He occupied the part of my mind that liked to daydream. It was hard to keep my mind off him. I barely thought of Marion, who was gone for a month. When I mentioned to Jimmy that I needed a job, he told me to go to the docks, get a job on a fishing boat. "You'll get hired. You don't need any experience. Believe me."

I strolled down to Thomas Basin, a harbor near the Shamrock Bar, my dancing alma mater, where a zillion fishing boats were tied to docks, gently rocking. There were a number of men around. I stopped to ask if anyone was hiring. "Yea, try the Kuiu," one scruffy-faced man said and pointed. "Tom's looking for someone. He's leaving tomorrow."

Tom was a slim man with disheveled blond hair, pants and shirt that had seen cleaner days, somewhere in his late twenties. He looked up as I steered down the dock, knew my inquiry even before I opened my mouth, was nodding yes even as I asked, "Are you hiring? I'm looking for a job."

"Do you have any experience?" he asked, giving a friendly smile, making the corners of his eyes crease.

"No."

"Oh well, that's okay. Do you cook?"

"No, not really."

"Oh okay, well we leave tomorrow at sunrise."

I wore jeans, tennis shoes, and a long thrift store dress that hung past my knees, waist cinched with safety pins. It was an unlikely outfit for salmon trolling. Still it was my favorite and that's what I wore the morning I appeared at the Kuiu at 6 a.m. to begin work as a deckhand.

Tom was moving around in the back of the boat — that would be the stern. She was twenty-six-feet long, freshly painted white, with *Kuiu* painted in black on either side. He looked up when he heard me clomping down the dock. A cup of black coffee was cradled in his hand, his fingernails black with dirt.

"Good morning," he grinned. "You ready to go fishing?"

"Good morning, sure," I grinned back.

He glanced at my dress, didn't say anything. "You need some coffee?"

"No thanks."

"Okay, we're almost ready to go. Come onboard."

Each summer, lured by the promise of adventure and potentially tons of money, hordes of people — mostly men — flock to the thin coastal shores of Southeast Alaska looking for deckhand positions on trollers, seiners, or jobs in the canneries, a thankless twelve-hour daily grind. The thin strip of land referred to as Southeast Alaska, runs the length of British Columbia and is surrounded by thousands of islands, which protect inside waters from the rough outer seas, hence the inner waters are referred to as the Inside Passage. That was where we would be fishing.

"We'll be out for a week or two, then we'll sell to the cannery in Hydaburg," Tom said.

I remembered Hydaburg, the small town with the slow speakers. "Oh. Okay. What am I supposed to do?"

"Mostly you clean the fish and throw them in the hold." Tom opened the lid on a hole in the deck's floor. Below was a large area with ice.

"Okay. I don't know how to clean fish."

"It's easy. I'll show you."

The ocean spread out, a fan-like stretch of water and waves, my eyes glancing over its darkened surface at the horrendously early hour of 4 a.m. when we got up to cups of black coffee and a few eggs cooked on a Coleman stove. Then the start of the engine and soon we were slugging our way to Captain Tom's spot where he determined there were tons of fish just waiting for the chance to be caught and placed on dinner plates. The poles were baited and thrown out, the boat began its steady crawl, back and forth for an insufferable ten to twelve hours a day. I sat, brandishing a knife, grimly enduring the endless sputter of the loud engine.

Captain Tom was a nice enough man. He steered his boat. I sat in the stern, never able to escape the wet, always slightly chilled, unless we were lucky enough to see the sun, the warmth soothing, almost magical, and it dawned on me that we had very little control in this land where the elements of nature were clearly in command. The potency of the ocean, the cap of sky, the ruthless rain. Whenever the sun appeared it was like the arrival of a celebrity. Look! There's the sun!

Captain Tom and I took a short break during the afternoon, pushing peanut butter sandwiches past our salted lips, compliments of ocean spray, the salted water impossible to escape. Occasionally I'd have to stand, stretch my cramped and cold body. Then I'd carefully slide along the narrow path against the boat's side rails – a sudden lurch could easily topple me into the dark waters below – until reaching the miniature door that opened to a teeny toilet. I would carefully aim, void contents, then carefully press myself against the boat and slide back to the stern, resume my seated fish-cleaning position. I felt our insignificance very clearly. We were a mere speck between ocean and sky, our lives utterly inconsequential midst the surrounding enormity.

At dusk Captain Tom would anchor us in a protective bay, shut down the engine. With that stillness came relief, my shoulders relaxed as my ears emptied of the engine's voice. Then the startling silence, the gentle arrival of quieter sounds. Water slapping the sides of the boat. The call of birds. The rustle of a soft wind. Our steps oddly loud. Finally into bed, a wide berth with a few sleeping bags. Tom stretched his arm towards me the second or third night, who knew, the days and nights blurred, but at some point his arm stretched towards me, and I automatically responded. It was at least better than cleaning fish.

We'd been on the ocean for a solid week. Seven long days. In the same fish-gut-spattered clothes every day. I also wore fish guts in my hair until Captain Tom pointed it out and helped me spray a gush of water — precious unsalted water — to rinse the innards of the poor fish out of my dirty hair. From the yawn of early morning to the day's retreat at dusk, I sat and cleaned fish. It was tiresome and miserable.

Cleaning fish isn't pretty and can only be done by someone insensitive to the suffering of other living entities, for there were times that the fish were still alive when the tip of the knife was pointed into their belly, then sliced open, their organs and intestines pulled out with one yank. You had to be at a certain level of consciousness or unconsciousness to kill and rip the guts out of someone. For the fish were someone, just as certain as you and I. That perception though, that the life of a fish held value, was still decades away. In those days, I remained a neophyte in terms of any thoughtful, more advanced understanding. Animals and sea life were remorselessly killed so I could eat them. I subscribed to this notion as a matter of course with no additional thought. Just like most people.

One day a distal point on the sea's surface moved. I stared at the dark blob that appeared to be getting larger.

"What's that?" I yelled to Tom over the engine. "What is that?"

He turned to look. "It's another boat. I'm not sure who it is." We stood and stared until the unmistakable form of a large fishing boat emerged.

"We've got company," Tom said and broke into a grin.

"Company? We do? We're going to see someone?"

"Yea. It looks like the Ketchum II. She's a halibut boat. You'll get to meet Zoie. She's the deckhand."

We began waving at the vessel. She slid ever closer, then the engine was cut on the Ketchum II and she skated towards us.

"Grab the boat," Tom said. "We're gonna tie up."

"Okay," I said, and readied myself to try and grab onto the fifty-eight-foot long vessel. I reached out to a hand coming from the Ketchum II. A man with dark curly hair smiled at me.

"Hold on," he said, and we all pulled the boats together.

Captain Tom and the dark curly-haired man threw ropes, wrapped them around the skeets, and I saw how it was done. This was how you got to visit people when fishing out at sea. You tied yourselves together. Kuiu's engine was silenced, the two men made man sounds, there was a moment of overjoy, basking in the wonder of other people after so long at sea. Then

Jolette

Captain Tom turned and said, "This is Major. This is Jolette." His face brightened, smile softened, "And this is Zoie."

Zoie was a marvel to my eyes. With jeans, knee-high rubber boots, her brown hair extraordinarily short, her blue eyes intelligent, she smiled, and I climbed over the sides of both boats to join her.

"Hi, are you a deckhand too?" I asked. Thus began a friendship which would endure the years.

This was event number one.

In later years she told me I had been wearing a dress when we first met. "You were wearing a dress!" she laughed. "A dress on a fishing boat!"

"No, what do you mean, a dress. Of course I wasn't wearing a dress," I admonished, then hesitated. "Oh, that's right, it was a long dress over my jeans. I liked wearing those old dresses way back then."

She remembered my dress. I remembered the salvation of meeting a like-minded soul in a vast surround. She was from California, she said. Santa Cruz.

"Santa Cruz? California?" California was the oasis of the world as far as I was concerned. Immediately Zoie was elevated. I was star-struck.

"Yea, I went to school in Santa Cruz," she said. "You wanna cup of tea? Let's go below."

I followed her slim form down four steep steps. We submerged under the deck to the living quarters, which included a kitchen with a small stove, a counter, a sink.

"Oh, this is so much better than the Kuiu," I said.

"I know," she said. "I worked on the Kuiu with Tom for a while when Major was fixing the boat."

"Oh! You did! That's why Tom looked at you the way he did."

"Yea. I think he likes me."

"Did you sleep with him?"

"No, I'm with Major. Did you?"

Jolette

"Yea. I'm married but my husband person is somewhere on the *Magnolia*."

"You call him your husband person?" She laughed.

"Yea, it's because we only got married for convenience and it feels weird to call him my husband. I don't like the label anyway."

"I don't like the label either. That's why I don't call Major my boyfriend. I hate that word."

"Me too. It's sounds so stupid."

"Yea."

"So, what do you call him then?"

Zoie handed me a cup of tea. "Do you want honey?" she asked.

Honey in my tea seemed suddenly exotic, so entranced was I. "Yes, I'll take some honey. Thanks."

"Well, I call him my lover," she said.

"You do? Hmm. That sounds sorta okay, but sorta weird too."

"I know," she said. "There's really not a good word."

"No, there's not."

"So, your husband person, what's his name?"

"Marion."

"Marion? That's different. What boat is he on?"

"The *Magnolia*."

"He's on the *Magnolia*? That boat hasn't been doing too well. They haven't gotten many fish. I think they docked in Ketchikan last night."

"How do you know all that?"

"Major has a walkie-talkie. Every boat does. That's how it works out here."

I absorbed Zoie like a dry sponge to liquid, and when Captain Tom called for me and it was time to go, we gave each other a hug.

"Can we stay in touch somehow?" I asked.

"Yea," she said. "I'll write to you General Delivery Hydaburg okay? That's where you're selling fish right?"

"Yea, I guess so," I said and climbed back onto the little *Kuiu*, the powerful thrust of the big boat causing waves that rocked us. I steadied myself, held my arm high, waved and waved, the Ketchum II shrinking in size until it was no more.

We pulled up to the dock in Hydaburg the next day to sell our fish. On this, my second visit to Hydaburg, the dock appeared wondrous. It led to stable footing on glorious land and public indoor showers, the shower one of the most desirable inventions ever. On this occasion it was nothing less than euphoric, water cascading over my fish-scaled, aching body. Restorative. The shower. Something you never think about until it's absent. In this rustic land, the basics became paramount. Survival an edge where life balanced.

Tom paid me a sum of money, which I took to the only store in town, a small affair down a winding dirt road, the store with ten or eleven spare shelves, food selection slim, candy and potato chips plentiful, however, and I stocked up. A bright shiny jukebox in the corner of the store accepted the quarter I slipped into its mouth, playing *Love Rollercoaster* by the Ohio Players three times in a row, reminding me of a world far beyond fishing in Alaska, steadying my wilderness-dazed senses.

I wandered back to the *Kuiu*, where I was met with good news. "Your husband just walkie-talkied. He said you can stay in a cabin that's vacant here if you want, and he'll pick you up in a couple of weeks. Did you want to do that?" Tom smiled. "I know you don't really like fishing."

"Yes! Yes!" I couldn't believe my good luck. "Is that okay with you?"

"Yea, sure. I can find another deckhand. I'll walk you to the cabin. I know where it is."

We walked through the meager town of Hydaburg to its far end, then turned off onto a small trail, through thick trees and brush, a sprinkle of yellow wildflowers, to a small wooden cabin sitting a few feet from the slap of waves on the shore.

"It's high tide now," Tom said. "It won't come any closer than that." Then he was off to find another deckhand, which were a dime a dozen even in Hydaburg. Everyone in Southeast Alaska had fishing on the brain.

I pushed open the cabin's small door. There was a sink and counter to the left. I turned the faucet. No water. I opened a door to the right. There sat a toilet, which was just a toilet seat over a hole on a giant box. An outhouse but placed indoors.

Past the sink was a small room with a wood-burning stove, a pile of stacked wood, a small cot, and a desk under a window, a log serving as a chair. I dropped my backpack and gazed at the simple room. I could write at the desk, sit on the log, look out the window to the ocean, its immense body of saltwater dominating most of the earth. This felt a little wonderful. I was content. At least for the time being.

31

Hydaburg, Alaska, 1976

Alaska has long been a magnet for dreamers and misfits, people who think the unsullied enormity of the Last Frontier will patch all the holes in their lives. The bush is an unforgiving place, however, that cares nothing for hope or longing.

John Krakauer, American author and mountaineer b.1954.

I kicked through the dirt on the winding potholed road that led from my cabin through the sparse town, houses scattered like windblown debris off to the sides. The road curved, took me from the small store to the post office. An older, slow-moving man handed me a letter when I asked if I had mail. I hastily opened the envelope and unfolded a letter from Zoie. She was coming to visit me at the end of the week. She'd heard I was staying in Hydaburg and would visit me for three days while the Ketchum II was being repaired. She couldn't wait to see me. I couldn't wait to see her either.

Zoie radiated intelligence. From the minute she stepped off the Ketchum II onto the Hydaburg dock where I stood to greet her, we couldn't stop talking. Our conversation continued for the entirety of her three day visit. I was sure she was the most insightful, keen person I had ever met. I gazed at her while she spoke, while she shared her views, her perceptions. Her blue eyes didn't miss a thing. She was well-read, had a degree in linguistics, spoke fluent Swedish, had lived in Sweden, a language and place I had never even considered. Her first boyfriend had committed suicide, which credited her immediately with wisdom and the strength of endurance. She spoke with knowledge and I latched onto her every word. We agreed we didn't like television. We much preferred reading.

"Television is so mind-numbing. It's for people who don't live life, they just watch," she said.

"Yea, that's what I think too," I said.

She spoke for at least two hours about Major, the man she was madly in love with, the captain of the Ketchum II, his every nuance reflected upon.

"And then, even though he said he loved me, he looked at me with a degree of uncertainty. You know, I felt sure that he really didn't mean what he said but thought he should say it. I could see it in his eyes."

We sat on the sandy shore outside of the little cabin and talked. We walked through the bushy trails of Hydaburg.

"Try this." Zoie plucked a red berry from a bush. "It's a salmonberry. It's good."

I hated anything berry but was enamored of Zoie, so I put the berry in my mouth. It was sweet. "Oh, it's good!"

We made salmonberry pancakes for dinner and sat sipping tea with honey for the rest of the night, talking for hours, until, finally sated, we slipped into our sleeping bags – Zoie insisting the floor was fine — and fell asleep.

In the morning, the sun caused us to stir, and I suddenly remembered the mama cat, a smallish gray tabby who'd moved into the cabin the day after I did, her tail swishing as she purposefully strode through the open cabin door. I put a blanket behind the stove for her, which she evidently liked because it was where, a day later, she birthed a litter of six kittens. I'd heard tiny mewing and looked behind the stove. Mama cat looked up. There were small heads latched onto her belly. She was purring.

Initially, I didn't want to disturb mama cat and her kittens. I left them alone for a day, just gazed at them from afar, then sat down beside them to take a closer look. Upon inspection a problem was revealed. For although the tiny kitten heads were mewing and latching onto mama's nipples, and although their front legs and upper half of their small bodies appeared quite normal, there was something most wrong with their lower bottom half. They were ensnared together.

"Look. There's a cat. This is mama cat. And her kittens. Look at the kittens," I said to Zoie. "There's something wrong with them. They're all tangled together. What do you think that is?"

We sat on the floor and curled around the stove to get a closer look. Mama cat decided it was time for a break and walked away. The kittens mewed. Zoie pet a little gray striped tabby. From its waist down it was somehow attached to the rest of the kittens, so enmeshed, the problem was impossible to decipher.

"What do you think that is?" I repeated.

"That's so strange. I don't know. What's holding them together?"

"I don't know. I can't tell. Do you think it's the umbilical cord?"

"It seems like more than the umbilical cord. It's so weird."

"It's like there's a massive piece of fur in there, winding around them somehow. There's no vet here. There's nothing here. Not even a doctor. Should we take them to someone's house and see what they say?" I asked.

"Yea. Maybe that's a good idea."

We walked together down the dirt road, the kittens cradled in my sweatshirt inside a small box. A man stood in the yard of the first house we came to. He looked at the kittens, shook his head. "You can't fix this. You have to drown them."

"Drown them? We're not going to drown them! Can't we just get them apart somehow?" I said.

The man shrugged. "There's no animal doctor here. The cats will grow. They're just gonna die like this."

We went to another house and another. Everyone shook their heads. "This is Alaska. It's not a good place for animals," one woman said. She shook her head too. "The best thing to do is to drown them. There's nothing else you can do."

Zoie and I went back to the little cabin. Mama cat came back, laid down in front of her kittens and they began to nurse. "Maybe I should cut the umbilical cord on this one," I said, petting a little dark head whose umbilical cord came out from the bellybutton and disappeared into the mass of fur, going somewhere, impossible to follow.

"We could at least try that," Zoie agreed.

I took a pair of scissors, snipped the umbilical cord, and tried to pull the kitten free from the tangle, but the kitten was still connected to the rest of the group. It was maddening. There was no way to detangle them.

The kitten whose umbilical cord was snipped began to weaken. Within twenty minutes, he was completely limp. "Oh god, did he die?" I asked. "Is he dead?"

"Oh no," Zoie said. "I think he did die. He's dead." We stared at the dead kitten, limp in my hand, still attached to the others. "Oh god. Now what?"

"I don't know. This is bad."

"This is really bad."

This was Alaska at its worst. A beast not caring one whit of another's suffering.

On that day in 1976 in Hydaburg, Alaska, where medical care for humans and animals was unavailable, where medical care of any kind required flying to a larger city in Alaska, most places having no medical care for animals, drowning was the only option we knew of.

Zoie put the kittens back in the box, and we walked silently to the water's edge. "I can't do it," I'd already said on the way to the beach.

"I'll do it." Zoie was grim-faced. With her knee-high rubber boots, she waded into the water and looked back at me, and I saw the hesitation on her face. Saw immediately how this had to work. She could physically do it. I couldn't. But she needed me to talk her through each step.

"Put the box in the water and put some rocks on top of it," I said, my voice becoming the support she needed. I saw the box disappear under the water, bubbles immediately surfacing. Zoie struggled with the box.

"I can't get the box to stay," she called, her face tense.

"Hold it down," I said. "Hold it down. You have to keep it down." I kept my voice strong and certain. The bubbles multiplied, covering the water's surface. "Keep it down. You have to keep it down. Keep it down. Hold it down. You can do it. Hold it down." Zoie's eyes were locked into mine until the bubbles dissipated, then vanished.

She stood up, her arms soaking wet, and slowly made her way to the shore. We walked back down the dirt road, stunned and silent. Back to the small cabin where we quietly built a fire in the wood stove and stirred some soup over its heat.

"That was horrible," Zoie said.

"Yea, it was terrible," I said, looking at her. This will bond us forever, I thought. She will still be my friend when we are old and gray. I entertained a brief vision of two white-headed women, heads together while conversing intently over hot cups of tea with honey.

That was event number two.

We spoke very little that evening. I fell asleep uneasy, disquieted by the drowning of young lives. We woke early the next morning to another day in Alaska where brutality and inextinguishable hope wrestled. Neither winning. It was always a draw.

32

Ketchikan, Alaska, 1976

An adventure is only an inconvenience rightly considered. An inconvenience is only an adventure wrongly considered.
            G.K. Chesterton, 1874-1936, English writer, philosopher.

The Frontier Saloon was famous in Ketchikan. The bar bragged the only live music in town, its doors open til 4 a.m. On the weekends it was packed to the gills, so to speak, with locals and tourists. I pushed open its doors and let out a sigh. There were tables and chairs, a floor covered with carpet, a long bar, a dance floor, a stage, and real restrooms. Immediately I felt relief. I was back in civilization. When I left an hour later, I'd been hired as a cocktail waitress and part-time bartender. I then located a small attic apartment — its ceiling so low standing fully upright impossible — in a house far up a steep hill. I moved in with only a few belongings.

Marion had arrived in Hydaburg a few days after Zoie departed. She and I had grimly accepted the fate of the kittens. We'd spent endless hours talking over hot cups of sweet tea, had dissected our romantic relationships thoroughly. When the Ketchum II had been repaired and Zoie rejoined Major, I was left alone but happy to have such a vibrant friend. Who, just knowing you had such a friend, made life better.

The Ketchum II had disappeared into the long stretch of sea, to the rough outside ocean waters where Major and Zoie would lower skates, an approximate 600-foot-long line baited with morsels of octopus and other things halibuts like to eat. Garnished with hundreds of unappetizing hooks. Not a pleasant meal for the poor halibut, who were overfished in both the Pacific and Atlantic Oceans, driven to near extinction in the Atlantic.

Marion and I had left Hydaburg together. We flew back to Ketchikan, a cosmopolitan urban center compared to Hydaburg. Marion never made the big money promised to so many. Alaska didn't bring out the fisherman in him, but it did bring to life the alcoholic.

I was waitressing at the Frontier Saloon, and as the fishing season wound down, Marion became a frequent visitor at the bar. For he'd found a new pastime. To drink as much as humanly possible. It would begin when my shift started. He'd settle at the bar counter, pouring rum down his gullet as if filling an empty tank with gas. Shortly after, he'd begin to morph into something unpleasant and sneering. One busy Friday night, the live music so loud it vibrated every cell, the night manager, Joe, who was a gentle and kind man, approached me. He leaned towards my ear, and said, "Could you get Marion out of here? He's getting obnoxious. He's at the bar." I nodded and turned to push through the dense pack of hot bodies. Holding my tray high, I called out, "Coming through, coming through, behind you, behind you." I couldn't see Marion anywhere. Then suddenly a form slid from a barstool to the floor, the facial features only somewhat recognizable. Marion. He landed in a heap. Joe was by my side, "I'll help you get him in a cab."

I bent over the heap. "Hey, Marion, get up. Hey, get up, get up!"
Marion's face was puffy, his eyes slits. He sneered at me. "Phhucoff."
"Get up, Marion. I gotta get you home, get up."
Joe and I managed to scrape Marion off the floor. I steered him into a taxi. He fought me the entire way. His brown hair, straggly and long, pulled back into an unkempt ponytail, his beard full and scraggly, his face, never handsome to begin with, was now distorted and ugly. "Phhucoff, jus phucoff," he slurred, spittle trailing out the corners of his mouth.

I got him into our attic apartment, no easy feat since it was up a tremendous number of stairs, and Marion resisted the entire way. It was like trying to wrest an unruly child. Except he wasn't a child. He was an unruly man who was becoming something I hadn't seen before. I managed to shuffle him into the apartment, and left him lying on the floor, still muttering angrily. Then returned to the Frontier Saloon to finish my shift. My favorite band was playing, The Clouds. They were up from Los Angeles and I had a crush on the lead singer. I walked back into the swarm of people, looked up to the stage. The singer spotted me, smiled, warming me to the core. I smiled back.

Marion was not only slugging alcohol down his throat as fast as he could swallow, he was also pushing me around. The two seemed to go together. Just a few days earlier, I'd come home from work early. It was a quiet weeknight. Marion had friends over. When I walked in, he stared at me, his eyes hot with hostility, then strode towards me, pushing me backwards. I stumbled but didn't fall.

"Where you ben. Where you ben."

"Working, I was working. I'm home early," I tried to tell him, but he pushed me again.

"Hey, Marion, hey man, don't push your lady." One of his friends placed a hand on his arm but Marion angrily brushed it off.

"Where you been?" His face twisted.

His friends dispersed, scattering like frightened minnows out the door. Marion knocked me to the ground and sat on my chest. I looked up at his head hanging over me, his hair oily, hanging forward, his face misshapen, a deformity of the man I knew. His arm lifted and he slapped my face. Then slapped again. And again. It happened so fast and he slapped hard, so hard I couldn't think. So hard I couldn't feel. My first thought was that I was surprised it didn't hurt more. Odd that it didn't hurt. I noted this even as I lay stunned on the floor. After another round of slapping, he suddenly stopped, got up and drew away grumbling. I lay still for a short time, then slowly got up and went wordlessly to bed.

He had slapped my head into a wall only a few weeks earlier. He was drunk and irritable that time too. I'd staggered from the slam to my head and from his astonishing behavior.

This made three times he'd been violent.

The first was in Minneapolis. Right after we got married. In the front porch of our second floor apartment, after he had been drinking. Angered by some inkling of injustice I had supposedly inflicted. He slammed my head into the wall. It happened fast. Leaving me stunned. Wordless. The next day brought many apologies, promises to never do that again. The template for abusive behavior, an arena I knew little about.

Conflicting emotions swelled. I knew his father had been abusive with him as a child, had made him eat dinner for a year sitting on dark basement stairs while the rest of the family gathered around the dining table. I knew his drinking increased his aggressive flailing. I allowed these excuses to mitigate the offense, my feelings mixed.

There were several nights that Marion was on the edge of becoming violent, his drunken anger palpably building. Those were the evenings I left. One night was spent on Joe's couch, the kind manager of the Frontier Saloon. He and his beautiful wife from Kentucky – I knew she hated Ketchikan too, just like me, for I had begun to detest the confines of the small town – tucked blankets into their couch where I found refuge.

Another night I checked into the only hotel in downtown Ketchikan. Marion found me as I walked down the street near the hotel, aggressively pushing me. An onlooker called the police, who arrived to a belligerent Marion. The police threw him to the ground where he was roughly handcuffed, permanently injuring his wrist, an injury I silently rejoiced. He deserved it but then I felt bad for him. Marion was thrown in jail for being a public nuisance. Not spousal violence which was considered normal.

I endured him, wished his monstrous side would vanish, called a domestic violence hotline later but resented the point-blank advice — leave him. It was so easy for someone to say, "Just leave him." Advice usually given by women who had no experience. I didn't feel like leaving him because he hit me. I might leave him eventually because he was boring. But for now, it was easier to not make it a big deal. It was easier to stick with him.

This was event number three. Which may have caused event number four. It was a distinct possibility. But ultimately hardly mattered.

Fall makes Ketchikan weep, the rain ceaseless. There are only around 100 sunny days a year in Ketchikan, leaving 265 days of precipitation. My naturally curly hair sprang with joy. I did not.

With fishing season officially over, Marion was hired as a bouncer at the Frontier Saloon, which meant he had to stay sober to work, resulting in a decrease of drinking and the violent aftermath. We continued our desultory relationship. At least he wasn't pushing or hitting anymore.

The closest I came to writing was to meet a news reporter from the Ketchikan Daily News. We had a brief affair, nothing exciting. He was not good looking but he did have a daily byline. That was enough. Marion was not as oblivious about my affairs — which were really only a few, the singer, the reporter, and Jimmy – as I thought. Like many people who have a sense their partner does not apply fidelity to their relationship, there was no real proof, yet the feeling pulses as real as the beating of the unseen heart. His undercurrent of anger resided with us, my undercurrent of frustration adding to the stew.

I didn't like Ketchikan and didn't much like Marion anymore either. He wasn't pushing me around anymore but he was no longer the captivating student I had found him once to be. Our relationship had devolved to exchanges of unexceptional barbs.

"Would you read to me?" I asked him one ordinary rainy night.

"No, I don't like reading out loud."

"But you used to like it," I mildly protested. "You used to read to me all the time."

"But I don't like to. It makes it less relaxing for me."

"Okay, well, I don't want to take away from your relaxation. God forbid."

"And now you have to be sarcastic."

"I'm bored and I don't want to live here anymore. We've been here almost two years. I want to leave. I want to move to Hawaii."

"Hawaii?!"

"Yes! Everybody else from here goes to Hawaii. Why don't we? Let's get out of here."

"I like it here."

"I hate it here. I wanna leave. Two years is long enough. I'm wasting my life here," I said, irritated, giving a mild slam to the door as I trudged off to work.

One night I was especially tired after work. I'd just spent seven hours serving drinks, the night busy and long. I'd cashed out, cleaned my section, and started my walk home at 4 a.m. But something was wrong. My head wasn't right. All around me were dollar bills. On the ground. In the trees. In the sky. Hundreds of dollar bills everywhere. I figured I was exhausted, my mind seeing things. I got home, fell into bed, slept hard.

I was under a heavy blanket of murky fog. I tried to swim up, towards the surface, but I was lost, my head hurt, it was a bad headache, pounding. I moaned, then heard a voice, Marion's voice, saying something, over and over, but I couldn't understand. I strained, tried to engage my ears but they weren't working right. Tried to open my eyes, they weren't working right either. A flicker, my eyelids pulled up, fell back down, flickered up again, everything was a blur. There was a head, a blurry head. Marion, he was talking, the sounds rapid. Rhh rhhh rhh. My eyes on his head were finally able to focus. Marions face, his glasses, beard, mouth opening...rhh rhhh rhhh? Rhh rhh rhh.

Finally, the words, "Are you okay, are you okay?"

I tried to speak. "Head…hurts…."

"Are you okay?"

"Head hurts."

"Do you want some aspirin? I'll get you some aspirin."

I began to sink under my eyelids, under the surface.

"Here, let me help you sit up. Here's some water…here, open your eyes. Take some aspirin. Jolette, are you okay?"

My body was pulled upward. I worked hard to lift my eyelids, caught a brief glimpse of Marion's blurred face. "Here, take these."

I fumbled. It was hard to move my hands to take the aspirin. I worked hard to make my hand pick up the pills. I couldn't do it. It was too much.

Marion's voice. "Here, open your mouth." He put the aspirin into my mouth. "Can you swallow? Here's some water."

A rush of liquid fell into my mouth. I swallowed. The pills went down and my body was released back onto the bed. Marion sat down beside me, took my hand. He was excited. "You had seizures last night. Five seizures."

I'd seen him excited before. Fishing. Watching football.

"You had five big ones. Here, look at this."

He went somewhere and came back. It was hard to keep up with him. It was a lot of work to stay on the surface. The gray murky depths were right on my back. I had to cling to the surface. I had to cling every second. It was a lot of work.

"Here, look," he said and pushed something in front of my face. I blinked and looked. I could see a lot of red on something.

"Its my sheath. My knife sheath. I put it in your mouth so you wouldn't swallow your tongue. It's full of blood. Look at it." He was as excited as if a touchdown had just happened.

"Seizures?" I managed.

"Yea, you had five big ones. One every hour."

I couldn't hold on anymore. I fell back under the surface. To the world of sleep where I knew nothing.

This was event number four. Its repercussions would reverberate far into the future.

There was no hospital in Ketchikan. The Ketchikan Medical Clinic was open during the day from eight to five. The doctor a limp white man, a flop of brown over his head, glasses, expressionless face. "You were poisoned most likely," he said.

"Poisoned?" I asked. "What do you mean poisoned?" It was two days later. I felt slow. My head vacant. My eyes blinking, unable to make sense of visuals. Like a newborn. The world unfamiliar. The five seizures had effectively lobotomized me.

"You work at the Frontier? You're a cocktail waitress?" limp doctor asked.

"Um." Was I a waitress? That seemed familiar, but was I? I felt like I should know. I should know this.

Marion nodded. "Yes, she waitresses and bartends."

"Someone probably slipped something into your drink." The doctor was matter of fact. No emotion. No nothing. "Anything can happen at that bar."

"Seizures though?" I asked. What was wrong with me. I couldn't make my brain work right. I tried hard, but it wasn't working. I had to work hard every minute to try and make my brain work right. If I didn't work hard, I would slip back. I knew it. I concentrated. "Why seizures?"

"Probably it was a drug. Probably someone thought it would be funny to slip a drug into your drink. Your blood pressure and temperature are good. You'll be okay in a few days."

"Okay, thank you Doctor," Marion said, and took my arm to lead me out of the small-town clinic. Out the front door where the world hit brash and rough. I winced.

"Are you okay?" Marion asked.

"We're going home now? Can we go home?"

"Yes, we're going home. You'll be alright." The only good thing about having seizures was how nice Marion suddenly was. He got a cab, opened the back door and steered me in. I fell back against the seat and looked out the window. Where was I? I didn't recognize anything. I was glad Marion was beside me. I moved closer to him. He felt warm. Strong. The cab pulled into traffic and the world outside blurred.

I went back to work a week later. My brain's revival was slow as ketchup from a bottle, but by the week's end I was at least able to attach a name to a familiar face, then remember how to get home from work, and finally could recall drink orders. I returned to my routine schedule, appearing normal but struggling internally, an invisible struggle where each minute I clung to the cliff's edge of normalcy, a yawning abyss below, the abyss I had just managed to crawl out of, the fear of falling back into that abyss present every second. It would take weeks to feel normal again. The definition of normal, according to Webster, was functioning on an average or typical level. An average state-of-being. Which was suddenly desirable. Not such a bad thing.

Marion was still treating me very kindly. My seizures must have really affected him.

"Do you want me to read to you?" he asked.

"Yea. Okay."

"Here let me rub your feet."

"Okay."

"Do you still want to move to Hawaii? Honolulu? I'm ready if you still want to move."

"Yes."

The events that occurred in Alaska, far-reaching and dynamic for me, reflected something of the great state itself. Strong, rough, where nature reigned magnificent and profound consequence resided. It had wrenched me and I was happy to leave but it would not be left. It would linger forever in my bones.

Jolette

33

Honolulu, Hawaii 1977

Mohala i ka wai ka maka o ka pua.
(Unfolded by the water are the faces of the flowers.)
Hawaiian proverb, date unknown

The banyan tree on Keeamoku Street in Honolulu was twenty feet in diameter, a gargantuan display of solid tree, its roots diving under the ground, the deep sprawl causing the sidewalk to buckle, creating an undulating, haphazard place for feet to navigate. If I were walking down Keeamoku Street I could never just walk past the banyan tree. I would have to stop and gaze at it, reach out to at least touch its skin of bark, sometimes press my body against the rough-hewn of its trunk, an attempt to soothe myself with the power of its presence.

The banyan trees, part of the fig family, have graced Hawaii's rich landscape since 1873 when missionaries from India brought a banyan tree to the island of Maui. The banyan trees eventually found their way to all seven of the inhabited Hawaiian Islands – there are approximately 130 Hawaiian Islands that are not inhabited. The largest banyan tree sits in Lahaina, Maui, stretching over 1.64 acres, which is about a city block, its circumference a quarter mile with sixteen trunks and over sixty-feet tall. If you can even digest that monumental vision.

Jolette

I'd jumped on a plane without Marion nor a backward glance at the rudimentary forty-ninth state. Marion hadn't been aggressive for months. That chapter seemed to have closed. I didn't know much about abuse patterns, but he stopped drinking and seemed normal again. We both decided that I would go first to Honolulu, get settled and he'd stay behind to tie up loose ends, drape his sobbing body over a clump of fishing nets in farewell.

I found an apartment on the beach in a small community called Maili Cove, thirty miles northwest of Honolulu. The apartment complex curled around an apostrophe-shaped pool surrounded by gently swaying palm trees. From my door, I could look down to the clear body of pool water, then turn my head to view the beach, a series of foamy waves nudging the shore then retreating in an infinite relay race. The sigh I gave was one of contentment. The tropical terrain was the perfect antidote for my Alaskan rain-drenched soul.

Annie was the first neighbor I met. She was Caucasian, though thoroughly browned from perhaps years of leisurely sunning. She laid, ample and comfortable, on an air mattress in the middle of the pool, was very chatty and immediately introduced herself. I noticed a big diamond ring on her left hand.

"You just moved in?" she asked, raising her head to look at me.

"Yes, I moved from Alaska. From Ketchikan. Do you know where that is?"

"God no," she laughed.

"It's the southeastern-most town of Alaska. About an hour and a half from Seattle."

"Alaska! Did you like it?"

"No, not at all. Do you love it here?" I asked.

"Yes I do! I absolutely love it!" Annie exclaimed and proceeded to tell me at length about her husband of twenty years, who was a local, and their two daughters. They owned a cab company. Aloha State Cab. She said I could be a taxi dispatcher if I needed a job. And I did. It paid $20 per shift.

Jolette

"My husband is looking for someone to dispatch and of course you'd have to learn pidgin but that's easy. I'll call him today."

Aloha State Cab was in Honolulu, an hour's bus ride from my apartment. It inhabited a dusty dirt parking lot, filled with taxis and two small trailers, one of which held the dispatch office. I was hired for the graveyard shift, midnight to 8 a.m., which was so quiet it was hard to stay awake. Until 5 a.m. when the phones began to ring. Then came the morning rush and a mad scramble. Everyone spoke pidgin. I couldn't understand them.

Pidgin, a mix of Cantonese, Japanese, Filipino, Hawaiian, and English, created in the 1850s by immigrants working the sugar plantations of Maui, was the favored local idiom. It wasn't easy at all. My tongue, lips and teeth, which together choreograph sounds from the throat to make words, tried but could not deliver. "Eh, calling 3 puka, I like you go 139 puka 7 Kaaheaniua St.," I said, halting and unsure, into the dispatch mic. I sent multiple drivers to wrong addresses on my first shift.

The Hawaiian language itself, lovely and euphonic, presented an even larger challenge. Consisting of eight consonants and five vowels, the vowels were strung together, each one to be pronounced. Aloha Cab, for example, was located on Kaaahi Street, each 'a' pronounced. Ka..a...a...hi Street. Which was easy, but take a street like Pakiluania Street. For a fucking haole like me – haole denoting a white foreigner, I never heard it issued without its adjective sidekick, it would be remarkable if I pronounced it correctly.

As the weak wore on and my pidgin did not improve, the drivers, a group of mostly Hawaiian and Samoan, big, brown, muscular, dark-haired, dark-eyed men, became increasingly disgruntled. But it was a rail-thin older Filipino man, Achipeto, who was most irate. Full of smiles to my face, he became a demon over his walkie-talkie. "AAAWEHHHHH," he screamed in disgust over the dispatch mike. "Kaekeeke or Kaeleka?"

"Um. The first one I think."

"AAAWEHHHH!"

"Achipeto?" I pressed the lever down to open my mic but couldn't get through because Achipeto had his microphone button pressed down. He was making sounds of disgust.

"AAAWEHH!" You bad dispatch lady," it sounded like he said. Fast forward a few years, he'd be found dead in the driver's seat of his cab, his neck cut, artery severed, the result of a robbery, maybe for five bucks. But for now, he sat on his mike so I couldn't get through to anyone, screaming at me. "AAAWEHH!"

"Eh, howzit?" I warbled as I walked past a group of drivers chatting near the taxis, some red-eyed and tired from a shift of driving, others fresh, coffee in hand. They were friendly, smiling as I passed, then muttering when they thought I was out of earshot. "Cannot speak da kine." They were frustrated. I knew I wouldn't last long.

Marion arrived a few weeks later. He liked the colorful billow of the Hawaiian shirts worn by tourists and locals alike. The sun put sparkle in Marion's hair, the daily breeze lifted its ends. He turned to me and smiled. Hawaii looked good on him. We moved to a slender apartment on Spreckels Street, in the Punahou area, close to the University of Hawaii where I was beginning classes and getting back on track writing. I'd started reporting for the campus newspaper, *Ka Leo* – The Voice – where I also became the assistant arts editor, which meant I got to go see lots of plays and films and then write my opinion as if it mattered.

Aloha State Cab hired Marion as a driver. He liked the night shift. Mostly he was downtown Honolulu where many mahus, or drag queens, worked the streets.

"They like me, the mahus," Marion said. "I just tell them they're pretty and take them wherever they need to go and wait for them until they've finished their business."

Many of the mahus were Filipino, slim, with almond eyes, and quite beautiful. Sometimes I was in the cab with Marion when he was working. I would turn from the front seat to smile at the slender forms that slid into the backseat, young men dressed in soft dresses, makeup enhancing their already beauteous features. They gave shy smiles to us, the fucking haoles in the front seat, and I was generous with compliments. I never lied. They were frequently gorgeous.

Marion usually drove me home at dawn, after my morning replacement, Leila, arrived, rescuing me from the tsunami of early morning calls, the onslaught of miscommunication where I had little idea of what was being said. I would sleep a few hours before classes. One morning, I had to get up to finish a review I was writing of the just-released film, *And Justice For All,* with Al Pacino. My deadline for the *Ka Leo* paper was that afternoon at one. Linda was the managing and copy editor. She was a beacon of intelligence, the brightest, most articulate person in the campus newsroom and was holding court when I scurried in that afternoon.

"Cut that, delete, delete," she said, marking the piece of copy she was holding. "Tie these together. Cut this by twenty words," her words like a command coming from the Bible. She handed the copy back to the writer.

"Hi, I finished my piece," I said, breathless after rushing, handing her my review.

"Good, follow me." She snatched my paper and walked into an office with a few desks, glancing over my words. "Okay, good, alright. What are you working on next?"

"The students are putting on Lysistrata. I thought I'd do a story on their rehearsal process and then review the play."

"Okay. That sounds good."

I watched ABC News every night. Knowledge of current events was a must. I wondered what country I'd be reporting from first as a foreign correspondent. I turned on the TV, sat cross-legged on my living room floor. "Hi Frank," I said to Frank Reynolds, the news anchor who spoke each night so earnestly, reporting the daily horrors. He was always serious but looked especially concerned tonight. The Iranian hostage crisis was upsetting much of the world. On November 4, 1979, over sixty American diplomats and citizens were taken hostage at the American Embassy in Tehran by Iranian college students who supported Ayatollah Khomeini and the Iranian Revolution. The students were angry at the US for allowing the former Shah of Iran, Mohammed Reza Pahlavi, into the US for medical treatment and refuge.

The evening news did two things paradoxically. First, it detached the viewer from the news events by its mere mechanics. It placed both far from each other. You are in your safe surroundings, tucked inside, watching horrendous events way out there. Somewhere far away. (That was where I would come in. I would be the foreign correspondent who wasn't afraid to venture into dangerous places, willing to pursue information and knowledge whether it meant riding a camel through the sand-stinging Arabian desert or traversing dark caves to reach clandestine interview locales or dodging down bullet-riddled streets in war torn towns. I would go anywhere. I couldn't wait.)

Second, the news made it clear that the world was a frightening place where nothing was meted out fairly, with no measure of justice. The world was plain ruthless. Catastrophes hit anywhere and everywhere, survival depended on our physical body. Either it still worked or it didn't. Which made me wonder who designed our bodies and why weren't they made more durable and why did there have to be so much pain. Of course, many people believed that God made us. My dad didn't believe in God. He declared himself an agnostic. "What's agnostic?" I asked him when I was thirteen.

"It's not knowing what existence is or where we go when we die," he said.

"Well, where do you think we go?" I asked.

"I don't think there's anything after this. I think it's just nothing when we die."

"That can't be true," I wrinkled my nose. "We're made of energy and that never dies."

"But energy disperses," he said. "It's the First Law of Thermodynamics. Energy disperses when changing from one state to another." To which I had no smart response. But I knew there was more after death. There just had to be. That's all.

I'd just settled into the horrific news of the day, the Iranian hostage situation, when Marion walked in the door. He wasted no time, went directly to his bong, tapped in a few buds, and took a toke.

"You're always stoned," I commented, glancing his way. It was just an idle observation, no judgment. I didn't care.

"I'm never stoned," he countered. "Pot just makes me normal."

"It's day forty-eight," I said. "Carter doesn't know what to do. What should he do?"

Marion exhaled a cloud of smoke and walked over. "They should send in the Israelis. Those guys are kick-ass tough. We should have never been involved with Iran. It's all greed. Oil and greed. They're pissed that Carter let him in, plus they're pissed at the U.S. because we basically put him in power, so he'd be favorable to us, so we'd get oil cheap," Marion said, pushing his rose-tinted glasses up with his forefinger, like he did when he got serious. "I mean I'm not in favor of them taking the hostages, but what did they expect. The problem with people is that they don't understand history. They don't understand the history of the region and they don't respect the ideology. It's a big mistake," he said.

"So what's gonna happen do you think?"

"I don't know. Carter let the Shah in for cancer treatment. The Iranians want him extradited so they can execute him, but Carter won't do that. I don't know what's gonna happen." He shrugged, took another hit from his bong.

One thing I did know. I'd be fired sooner or later from Aloha State Cab. I had known the day was coming. When it did, the owner of Aloha State Cab was gentle. "You know, Jolette, I just don't think it's working out. You're sending the drivers to the wrong addresses and you know, the locals, they think you don't understand them," he said.

"I know. It's because I don't understand them," I said. "I'm sorry."

Not only was I without a job, but Marion announced that he was going fishing for the summer in Alaska. "I'll just be gone a few months. I'm leaving next week."

We woke up to rainy, dark skies on the day Marion was leaving. We'd been in Honolulu for eight months, had created a comfortable routine of watching the news together every night. I'd gleaned insights from Marions point of view, which I respected, he was still very succinct. Sometimes I used his opinions as my own. We went to movies. Explored Honolulu's restaurants. But I was glad he was leaving. I was looking forward to being on my own.

A black cab pulled up. I went with Marion to the airport. The rain hit the cab hard. We didn't say much, our hug goodbye was casual. I yawned, went outside to catch a cab home and found the sun shining through parted clouds. The rain had vanished. I laughed. The exit of dark clouds equaled Marion's departure, the shining sun an omen of good things to come. I was sure of it.

34

Honolulu, Hawaii, 1977, 1978

To the moralist, prostitution does not consist so much in the fact that the woman sells her body but rather that she sells it out of wedlock.
Emma Goldman, political activist, writer, 1869 -1940.

I had $5 in my pocket and that was it. I went to a movie, then was completely broke. That was better. Sometimes it's good to have nothing when starting fresh. I walked down Kalakaua Avenue. Even with no job I was exhilarated. Hawaii was beautiful.

There were about two restaurants per block on Kalakaua, and I went into each one, filling out waitress applications, then walked the two miles home, stopping at my banyan tree on Keeamoku Street, my fingertips brushing the bark. The Ficus benghalensis, its scientific label, had become my anchor, its presence reassuring.

I walked back to Waikiki the next morning, went into at least ten restaurants and could not get a lousy little waitress job.

"There's a lot of people who want these jobs," one restaurant manager informed me, as he glanced at the tattoo on my wrist. I followed his eyes. There it was. Blue ink making a cross topped by a circle, a symbol for eternal life, also a symbol of feminism. I'd done it myself, one afternoon when I was thirteen, had taken a bottle of Indian ink, a needle and thread, stabbed the topside of my wrist repeatedly with the threaded needle — the thread acting as the ink carrier — leaving a homemade tattoo. This was before tattoos had attained the normalcy they have today. It was instead a stigma associated with bikers or criminals.

"A lot of people want to waitress in Waikiki," the manager said pointedly, nodding at my tattoo. "We don't like that kind of thing."

Jerk, I thought as I walked out of the restaurant, tired and hungry. That $5. Maybe I should have kept it. I walked slowly down Kalakaua, turned right on Lewers Street, and, just as the waning day turned to dusk, a flicker of red caught my eye. I looked up. There was another flicker. It was a red neon light in a second-floor window. It flickered again and this time stayed on, spelling out Foxy Lady. I stared at the red neon light – Foxy Lady – and wondered what it was. I knew it was something. Probably sexual. I bet they'd hire me, I thought. I found a back alley set of stairs leading up to the second floor, took them all the way up, ignoring the sudden tremble of my knees, and pushed open a door where a small room held a desk, behind it sat a woman with curly red hair and bright green eyes. Her face lifted into an immediate smile. "Hi," she said.

"Hi," I swallowed, nervous. "Um. Are you hiring?"

She casually glanced me up and down and said, "Yes. Do you want to start now?"

"Oh no!" I gasped. "I mean I can't right now but would tomorrow be okay?"

"Yea, that's fine. Your shift will be 8 p.m. to four."

"Four in the morning?"

"Yes. We're open til four."

"And this is a massage place?" I asked.

"Sure."

"Do I need to know how to massage?" I asked.

"It would be nice, but don't worry about it," she smiled and said, "I'm Allie."

"I'm Jolette."

"You might want to use a different name. Like Danielle or something."

Jolette

"Oh. Okay. I'll be back tomorrow night. Thank you."

She smiled and I gave a slightly unnerved smile back, then scrambled out like I was fleeing a fire. My heart was pounding and only slowed once I was back on Kalakaua Avenue. I started to walk home. I was so happy I had a job. It wouldn't start until the next night. I had a whole day before I had to actually do the job, whatever it was. I stopped for a minute at my banyan tree, placed my palm against its trunk.

Allie was sitting behind the desk the next night when I showed up at Foxy Lady. Her red hair was a triangular shape of tight curls and one of her green eyes looked off in a slightly different direction, but even with the lazy eye, she was striking. Her arms toned and brown, her torso slim. "This is Lila," Allie said, smiling, nodding towards a diminutive dark-haired beautiful girl. "She'll show you around. Ask her anything you want to know."

Lila had a ready smile and spoke with a thick Japanese accent. She walked me through Foxy Lady's living room, shabby with two bedraggled couches, a brown shag carpet and dirty white walls. A splash of red paint over one of the walls spelled out Foxy Lady. There were four small massage rooms just past the living room and a balcony that looked down at the thriving street life of Waikiki.

We returned to the office where a tall man, blonde and blue-eyed, stood in front of Allie's desk. He handed her money and she nodded towards me. "This is Danielle. She'll be your masseuse." The man's eyes landed on me and he smiled. I smiled weakly in return and looked towards Lila.

"I take you. Come this way," Lila said, and we followed her to the back rooms.

"You go that room." She pointed and the man who said his name was Mike, obeyed.

"Take extra towel with you. Crean up," she whispered to me, shoving a couple of towels into my hands. "Make sure he gib you extra. Fifty dorros hand job. More anything else." Then I joined Mike in the exceedingly small room.

"Should I just get on the table?" he asked.

"Um, yes. Take your clothes off, okay?"

"Sure, are you going to take your clothes off too?"

A nervous laugh. "I don't think so."

"But you're not sure." Mike laughed easily as he pulled off his shirt, slipped off his jeans, lay on the table. "What's your name?" he asked.

"Danielle," I answered, fussing with the bottle of oil.

"Is that your real name?"

"Um, yes." I poured some oil onto his chest. It shot out fast. "Oh shoot. That's too much oil!"

"It's okay," Mike laughed. "So how long have you been doing this?"

"Today. You're my first person."

"Oh, for Christ's sake. Do you know what you're getting into, Danielle?"

"Sort of. It's fine. I couldn't get a waitress job. It's really competitive here. Do you want to turn over so I can massage your back?"

He turned and I began rubbing his back for what seemed like a long time. He quieted, then I rubbed down his legs and he stirred. "That was really good. You give a good massage."

"Do you want to turn over now?"

"Sure." He turned and an erect penis waved at me. "Can you help me with this?" he asked.

"Um. That's extra."

"How much extra? I just want a hand job."

"Fifty dollars."

"Okay." Mike pulled a $50 dollar bill from his wallet. I tucked it in my purse then splat a bunch of oil on his penis and began moving my hands up and down his shaft.

"Not so hard, Danielle. Easy."

Jolette

"Oops, okay." I lightened my touch.

"Slower, just nice and slow with a lighter touch."

"Okay, "I pursed my lips and concentrated on taming his boisterous penis. I slowed my movements, lightened up and when I went over the penis's head, I heard Mike's breathing change. So I went over the head again and then all the way down the shaft and up again, slowly, this time pausing a second before going over the head. He moaned and I stayed on the head, slow and steady, light but firm. Suddenly he jerked forward and a fountain of come shot all over my hands. I moved my head just in time.

"Oh my god, that's a lot," I exclaimed.

Mike's head was back on the table, his eyes closed and he took a moment before he said, "I needed that. That was great, Danielle. Do you want to go out sometime? I'm here for a week. I'll take you to dinner."

"Oh no I can't. I'm married."

"You're kidding. Does your husband know you're doing this?"

"No. Not yet."

"He's in for a surprise," Mike laughed, dressed and I walked him through the Foxy Lady living room to the front door.

"Thank you, Danielle. Maybe I'll see you later this week."

The door closed, I sighed. My first client.

"Everything go okay?" Allie asked.

I nodded, "Yes, easy."

"I have another appointment for you at the Hawaiian Village. He's from Australia. He wants to see a thin brunette," she said. "Be sure to look at his ID and plane ticket and collect the fee upfront. You need to make sure he is who he says he is. And that he's not a cop. And make sure you really look at the name and dates. Sometimes the police get fake tickets."

By 4 a.m. I'd made $400, a far cry from the $20 per shift at Aloha Cab, and it wasn't a big deal. It was only sex. I could definitely do it.

Jolette

35

Honolulu, Hawaii 1978

The prostitute is not, as feminists claim, the victim of men, but rather their conqueror, an outlaw, who controls the sexual channels between nature and culture.
Camille Paglia, b. 1947, feminist, academic and social critic, professor of at University of Arts, Philadelphia since 1984.

In the whisper of early evening, after a day of writing for the *Ka Leo* campus paper, of sitting in the University of Hawaii classrooms at the Manoa campus, which should have been profuse with perfumed flowers, given the island's beautiful foliage, but was surprisingly barren, I went to work. I skipped down my apartment building's four flights of stairs wearing a Hawaiian halter dress, sweater over my arm, heeled sandals, and walked around the corner to Keeamoku Street, where I made a point of touching my banyan tree, then stepped onto a bus that delivered me to Waikiki.

My first orgasm happened one night in Waikiki at the Moana Hotel when I was working. It snuck up, hit me by surprise. "Oh my god, I just had an orgasm, " I exclaimed. The Japanese man whom I'd exclaimed to was nothing extraordinary, was slight in body and penis size, decidedly detached in demeanor. He looked at me with disbelief. I was three weeks into working at Foxy Lady and had gotten over the initial nerves that went along with having sex with strangers, checking their ID to make sure they

Jolette

weren't police, and making sincere conversation with them, all done in under an hour. The Japanese man had raised no alarms, and I'd relaxed, just shifted into neutral going through the normal motions when suddenly a huge wave struck and I was catapulted with sensation. "Oh wow, that was great!" I exclaimed again. "So that's what an orgasm is! Wow!"

The Japanese man looked at me. "You've never had an orgasm before?"

"No," I replied and again saw the look of disbelief cross his face. "It's true, this was my first one!"

He grunted, then slipped off me, raced into the bathroom and spit in the sink. All the Japanese men did the same thing — they ran to the bathroom, spit into the sink, gargled, spit some more, then immersed into a hot shower.

"It's a cultural thing," Allie said later. "They do that with all the girls."

Five nights a week I worked at Foxy Lady and spent much of that time walking to appointments in Waikiki, frequenting the Hilton Hawaiian Village, the Sheraton, Royal Hawaiian, Waikiki Beach Hotel, The Outrigger, or Moana Surfrider. I saw two to four clients a night at $100 per hour and was suddenly making more money than I knew what to do with. I crammed it into a shoebox, kept it on my closet shelf.

One night I got an appointment at 2 a.m., a little later than I liked, down a darkened side street at a small motel. A few dim lights invited me to the front door. No one was at the front desk; the lobby was vacant. I walked down a hallway, found the door with the right number and knocked. Immediately it was opened by a local. He looked Hawaiian, but before I could utter a word, he grabbed my arm, yanked me inside and shut the door. I saw the security badge on his shirt.

"Eh, seestah, howzit?" He was big as a bull, and planted himself in front of the door.

"What do you want?" I said, my hair follicles standing at attention.

"I like me one special visit." He gave a mean grin.

I'd heard about this, about security calling the agency, making an appointment, then raping the girl when she got there, sometimes beating the girl up.

As though there wasn't enough to worry about with clients – determining if they were safe or if they were undercover police – you also had to worry about being stopped by security when walking through the hotel to get to a room. If you were stopped, you'd be questioned and then potentially kicked out, aka eighty-sixed, from the hotel. That was the best-case scenario. The bigger problem was the situation I was in right now. A bullish security guard wanting sex for free. Threatening me. Of course he would think he could get away with it. Because people don't believe that a call girl can be raped.

I looked at the security guard with his mean grin. "What do you mean? Who are you?" I asked.

"Whatchu think I mean?" He looked at me hard.

And I got mad. Not scared. Mad. "Well, forget it. It's not gonna happen." I kept my energy strong, pinned my eyes to his.

He hesitated. I saw the hesitation and pushed. "Open the door. Open the fucking door."

"You give me what I want or I'll call the police. Tell them I got me one hooker. They lock you up."

"Let me out now and I won't send my Samoan boyfriend over here to beat the shit out of you."

"Ha ha. Samoan boyfriend," he laughed then got serious. "You're not leaving til you give me head."

"That gets in my mouth, I'll bite it off. Open the door."

He stared at me, I glared back. We weighed each other.

Statistics show that over fifty percent of sex workers have been raped or sexually assaulted. And that's only the ones reported. For me, on that night in the motel room with the bullish security guard, I only knew that I was mad and not yielding an inch. The security guard did not attempt to physically force me into sex that evening. He did not rape me. But he did call the police and when a young, baby-faced, unsure police officer showed up at the door, I performed well, convincing the young officer of my innocence. "I'm a tourist! I was just walking back to my hotel room at the Marriott when this security guard started talking to me. I thought he was a nice man, but he forced me inside and told me to give him oral sex otherwise he'd call the police. I was so scared! Thank god you're here, officer."

The police officer looked at me. I looked back with sincerity, making myself believe everything I said. The officer nodded. I could see in his eyes that he mostly believed me, there was just a speck of doubt, but he allowed me to leave. The security guard protested as I slipped off into the dark and I realized the key to lying was to truly believe your lie, at least while you were saying it. I wondered if an acting career might be in my future.

36

Honolulu, Hawaii 1978

I would never want to take away the option of sex work from someone, but I would want to create more options so that everyone can make the decision whether they want to do sex work or they don't want to do sex work, and that people who do sex work can do it safely.
Emily Symons, b. 1969, actress.

One night I walked all the way to work, past my banyan tree on Keeamoku, over the Ala Wai bridge, which marked the northern boundary of Waikiki, then sprinted up the back-alley stairs to Foxy Lady, which was beginning to feel like my second home. I grinned at Allie who sat behind her desk and plopped down with my books. I had to study for a Spanish test the next morning.

"Danielle, we have a new girl. Go say hi. She's in the living room," Allie said.

I walked into the living room where sometimes in the early morning hours, the girls and I would grab the white sheets we used in the massage rooms, cover ourselves and try to sleep awhile. If a guy happened to trudge up those back stairs, say at three in the morning, Allie or whoever else was at the desk would tell him to go into the living room and pick a girl. He'd enter the living room excited, like he was at a candy shop, and we'd groggily look up, messy heads of hair poking up from the white sheets covering us like we were cadavers. Our makeup smeared or worn off, our expressions sleepy, manner disgruntled, the new security guard Allie had just hired because of a recent break-in, sitting on the balcony outside, his chocolate skin in clear view, his manner intimidating, which it was supposed to be. So, I guess it wasn't surprising that more than one time the guy would startle as he took in the room, abruptly reverse, mumble something and race out.

Lila and a couple of the girls were painting their nails. They looked up.

"Hey Danielle," Shawna said. She was a tough white girl who'd grown up on the island, was big hipped with a cascade of frizzy curly hair and a manner I sensed she honed to fit in on this island dominated by Filipinos, Samoans, and Hawaiians, a place that didn't exactly welcome white girls. She most often wore an expression of pressed lips and lowered eyelids, and I wondered how many of her clients were afraid of her. She would later leave Foxy Lady to go work the streets, wanting me to go with her. She wanted to work as a team, drug the guys, then rob them.

"Naw, I think I'll stick with Foxy Lady. Be careful out there," I said. A few months after she'd quit Foxy Lady, I saw her one night, sitting on a bus bench on Kalakaua, her eyes like a cat, surveying with intent.

"You doing okay?" I asked.

She shrugged, "Yea, I guess. How are you?"

"Good enough."

Then her eyes went past me to some guy. "Take care," I said and kept walking.

"This is Christina," Shawna said now. Christina's skin shimmered like a bronze sculpture. She was long and slender. Her face turned to me and she smiled. Sort of smiled. Granted the smallest of smiles actually. She wasn't pretty but the lift of her chin, the way her head sat, as though she were wearing a crown, lent an aura of regality. Street regal.

"Hi," I offered.

"Hi," she barely said, and I knew she wouldn't say more.

"Shawna!" I turned towards Shawna. "What are you doing?"

"Painting my fucking nails, what does it look like?" Shawna held up her hands for me to admire.

"Real purty, "I said and sat down beside her.

"You want me to do your nails?" Shawna asked.

"Yea. What color?" I asked.

"Dark red how about?"

"Ok." I looked up, saw Christina watching me.

Christina's back was slightly arched the first week we worked together. I didn't think much of it. She was just that way. Her frost finally melted a bit, and she started asking me questions. "You in school?"

"Yea, at UH."

"What are you taking?"

"Journalism. I write for the school paper."

"Where do you live?" she asked.

"Punahou," I said.

"Wanna ride home tonight?"

"Sure, okay."

Christina took me out for drinks on my night off. We strolled down Kalakaua. She steered me around the group of Japanese tourists who moved together as one unit, a giant centipede with one hundred feet. They took up whole sidewalks, blocking entrances, oblivious to those trying to skitter around or through them. We pushed open the front doors of the Hyatt Hotel, passed a wall-length mirror where I caught a glimpse of us, slim and long, high-heeled and coiffed. We looked like expensively wrapped gifts.

We sat at the bar. "You can make a lot more money than I can," Christina said after we'd ordered, 7 Up for me, Coke for her. "Drinking is not good," she said, approving of my choice. "It interferes with thinking." I nodded, noticed that I suddenly desired her approval.

"You can make a lot more money than me cuz lots of guys won't see black girls. Especially the Japanese. They don't like black at all," she said.

"Oh really? That's not fair." I sounded like a dumb white girl.

"Yea, but that's the way it is. That's not stopping me though. I'm making my money anyway."

"Oh, sure, of course," I nodded.

"This is a working bar," she said, and I followed her gaze around the bar. "See that girl over there? The blonde? She's working him."

I looked at the pretty girl with wavy long blonde hair who sat laughing with a man. He was smiling at her. "Really? How can you tell?"

"See how he's looking at her? How she's looking at him? It's like they're both deciding something."

"You don't think maybe they're on a date together for the first time or something?"

"No. She's definitely working. They'll leave the bar in less than ten minutes. He'll take her to his room."

I watched the blonde with the man for a minute, then turned back to Christina whose strong chin jutted forward.

"And see that guy over there? The one who just checked his watch?" Christina nodded towards a dark-haired man in a dark jacket. "See how nervous he looks? He's doing a drug deal."

"How do you know?" I asked.

"I just know. I can tell. I've been reading people a long time."

Christina looked at me and smiled. She had a nice smile. It completely transformed her, almost made her pretty. "I want you to meet Reginald. He's my husband."

"Oh! You're married!"

"Yea, we've been married seven years."

"I'm married too," I said.

She looked surprised. "You are? Where's your husband? I thought you lived by yourself?"

"He's in Alaska fishing. He's gone for the summer."

"For a few more months then?"

"Yea, another month. It's great not having him here," I smiled.

"He knows what you're doing?"

"No, and he won't know until he comes back."

Christina nodded and said, "We'll have dinner with Reggie tomorrow night. You're off right?"

"Yea, okay," I said and glanced back to the blonde and the man. They were getting up, leaving.

"See? They're going to his room," Christina said knowingly.

I nodded, agreeing with my new teacher, although I didn't know how she could tell where they were going. Still, I nodded, accepted her perception, our new roles in place.

Reggie was short. My eyes shifted down when I opened my apartment door the following night. He was holding a big box, tied with red ribbon. "Hi Danielle," Reggie said. "I brought you a gift." Christina and Reggie entered, assessed my small kitchen, which led to a small living room, and settled on the couch.

"Reggie bought you a dress. Go try it on for him," Christina said and Reggie smiled as he handed me the box. I exclaimed dutifully, went into my bedroom to change even though I didn't like Christina telling me what to do. I let the gauzy black and white dress fall over my head and walked into the living room.

"Turn around," Christina said and I obeyed, irked with my ready compliance. I wore the dress to dinner that evening.

Christina and Reggie took me out to dinner several times the next week. The attention surprised me. I was flattered. Sort of. Suspicious. Sort of. Then Christina picked me up one night without Reggie. We had just ordered dinner when Christina turned to me, her face coming so close I thought for a striking moment that she was going to kiss me. But she didn't. She looked into my face. "Reggie likes you."

"Oh," I said.

"Yea, he likes you. So do I."

I squirmed. "Thank you."

"We want you to live with us. We want to make you family." She gazed at me, her eyes steady as a panther.

"Oh thanks. But I'm good where I'm at," I said and it was too bad my voice didn't come out sounding confident. Instead it was squeaky, sounding like the mouse I was starting to resemble.

"Well, think about it. We could work really well as a team."

She drove me home that evening, I looked out the car window, saw my banyan tree stalwart and patient. I missed it.

Reggie smiled at me from across the table. We were having dinner at a hotel on Waikiki Beach. "Say, pretty lady," Reggie said. I smiled dutifully. Christina glanced at him, then said, "Danielle, we want to talk seriously tonight. We really want you to be part of our family. We could do really well together and we like your place. It would be a good place to work from. We wouldn't have to pay any fees to anyone. We'd just take people to your place. We could do two tricks at a time. And you'd move in with us."

Christina was fluid, her words flowing. I felt that she was trying to wrap them around me. Trying to enclose me with her words. Ensnare might be the better word. I was suddenly happy that I was married.

"Thanks you guys, but it wouldn't work. My husband is coming back to town next week," I said.

Christina's eyes widened. "Next week? I thought you said he was gone for two months?"

"Well, I said that a month ago and he'd already been gone a month."

"Oh. Has it been that long? And he's definitely coming back?" Christina sat up, her lips pressed.

"Yea."

"Are you staying with him?" She leveled a look at me.

"Yea, I mean, he's my husband. We're going to move back to uh to the mainland this year together," I stammered.

"What do you think, babe? Danielle's husband is coming back." Christina sounded mad.

Reggie did a glide around the table, and slid in next to me. "Are you sure you wanna stay with a man like that?" Reggie asked, his voice soft, face close to mine. He looked at me with concern. "Tina said he hit you. Are you sure you want to stay with someone who does that to you? We'd never hurt you," he said.

Shit, I'd told Christina too much.

"Yea, I'm going to stay with him. I'm sorry." I don't know why I said I was sorry.

"We really like you, Danielle. Do you really want to stay with him" Reggie tilted his head as he spoke.

"Oh yea, I mean, he's my husband. I'm staying with him. He'll be back Tuesday." I tried not to gulp but they were making me nervous.

"Because I think we could make a good team. We could make a lot of money." Reggie spoke really softly. I almost leaned towards him to hear better but stopped myself. Had to watch my body language. Do not get any closer, I already knew.

"Oh well. No thank you, but thank you anyway." I was such a Girl Scout with these people. "Are you guys going to stay in Honolulu a long time, do you think?"

Christina wasn't interested in small talk. "Who knows?" she said shortly. She was mad. But Reggie wasn't. He continued to smile in my direction. We ate dinner in silence, the clinking of dinnerware amplified. Now I just wanted to get away from them. I wanted to get back to my banyan tree, which I'd totally neglected while being wined and dined by Christina and Reggie. I wanted to get back to my oceanography studies. I had fallen in love with tectonic plates and how they shifted, changing the entire world, and I wanted to concentrate on my writing. I wanted to get back to my normal world and I didn't want to be in their world anymore. I suddenly missed Marion.

When we left the restaurant, I turned to them." I'm going to take a cab home. Thanks for dinner." Christina didn't say anything. Reggie smiled, I turned, walked down Kalakaua. The night air felt like a soft kiss. My breath came out in a big sigh, and I could feel a release of tension. I was happy to be away from Christina and Reggie. I was happy to be me.

37

Honolulu, Seattle 1979, 1980

Life is a succession of lessons which must be lived to be understood.
Helen Keller, 1880-1968, American author, political activist, disability rights advocate, lecturer.

It was 4 a.m. and Foxy Lady had just closed. Marion pulled up in an Aloha State Cab, and, in my new high heels, I very carefully took the stairs down to the back alley, slipped into the front seat.

"Hi," he said and yawned.

"How was your night?" I asked.

"Slow," he said. "How was yours?" Then looked like he wished he hadn't asked.

Christina never returned to Foxy Lady and Marion had come back from Alaska, resumed his old job driving a taxi, had blanched when I told him I'd gotten a job at a massage parlor. Hadn't loved it at all until he realized the money I could make. "I have a thousand dollars saved," I'd said.

That had made him hesitate. He looked at me. "You do?"

"Yeah. It was easy. I have a thousand. Why don't I save another couple of thousand and then we can move back to the mainland? It'll be easy. I can do it fast, and then let's go back to maybe LA? Or San Francisco?"

Jolette

"I will never live in LA."

"Okay. How about San Francisco?"

"I don't like California."

"Well, how about Seattle then?"

"Okay. Seattle."

"I'll just work until we save up a couple of thousand. That should be enough, don't you think?"

"Yea. Okay. And nobody's ever gonna know about this," Marion said.

"Of course not. It's nobody's business anyway," I said.

The night before we left, I walked around the corner to my banyan tree where it held ground, strong and patient, its lifespan 200 to 500 years. I didn't know how old my banyan tree was but as I pressed against its trunk in a final farewell gesture, I thought it would most certainly outlive me, silently sitting on Keeamoku Street, witness and subject to the surrounding scramble of humans. I murmured a thank you, then walked away.

Marion and I landed in Seattle one cool, crisp autumn evening, the city lights friendly and inviting. We checked into a small motel with our large suitcases, and I took a deep breath. We were back on the mainland after four years. I wasn't sad to leave Honolulu. I was ready. We'd been two years in Hawaii and it seemed like two years was long enough anywhere, unless you loved where you were and felt at home. Which I didn't. Not in Minneapolis, not in Tucson, definitely not in Alaska, and not Honolulu although I did get some good learning experiences at Foxy Lady and at the *Ka Leo* campus paper.

The bridge from West Seattle where we found a spacious ground-floor apartment, stretched about six miles, taking an eternity of twenty minutes to cross over the waters of Puget Sound to downtown Seattle. Dense clouds covered the sky on the day I took a bus to Pioneer Square, a locale of cobblestoned streets, the home of many shops and bars, where I was quickly hired at a club featuring live music. My fling with escort work was over. It was an unspoken given that I would return to a minimum wage waitressing job.

Marion was hired as a cook in a West Seattle neighborhood restaurant and we settled into a routine. On my nights off Marion and I bundled up – the night air cold, crisp, sharpening the senses – and took walks down our quiet street to the end of our new block where we could gaze over the dark waters to view the rise of Seattle's skyline. I could see Marion's breath. My hand clasped in his, deep in his pocket. We walked, our steps in unison, darkness settling around our edges.

I started classes at the community college, and continued towards my goal of a journalism degree, even though I was losing credits each time I transferred, which interfered exponentially with progress towards a degree. We settled into our days and stayed this way until the daily became humdrum, and one night while cocktailing, my eyes wandered to the drummer in the band.

He met basic requirements, long hair, jeans, played music, he liked me. Our mild flirtation remained only that until one night after work I felt in need of a little excitement and went to the drummer's crummy little apartment, messy with strewn clothes, with just enough space for us to pant awhile, find the places where our bodies could join. I left shortly after, depressed. The whole thing had been too much effort with little reward. He was too skinny, his bony hips too sharp. He was not desirably overpowering or strong with that testosterone launch where you can catch a wave and travel to heights not earthbound. It was a listless liaison, yawn-worthy only. I caught a cab and went home. It was late. 3 a.m. Marion was in bed but not asleep.

"Hi," I said quietly as I came into the bedroom. "I went with some of the girls to breakfast after work."

"Oh bullshit you did," he said. The moonlight through the window was enough for me to see the anger spread across his face.

"No really I did."

"I want you out. I want you to move out." His teeth clenched.

I was surprised for an instant then a feeling of relief sped through me. Freedom from a routine relationship. "Okay," I easily agreed, laid down, and fell asleep.

A flat-roofed plain small building squat halfway up the steepest hill in the University District, its front door opened directly onto the sidewalk. From its only window was the distinct possibility of touching any pedestrian passing by. The stooped landlord, an elderly man, turned the key in the apartment door, pushed the door open, allowing me inside. I briefly surveyed the microscopic room. The attached kitchen could fit maybe two people. In the smidge of a bathroom you could just barely shut the door by pressing against the sink. I turned to the man. "I'll take it."

"I got a place," I announced to Marion when he came home from work. "I found one in the University District. I can move in on Saturday. I already paid the move-in."

"Oh," Marion said. He blinked and I was surprised at the flush that crossed his face. He swallowed a few times, sat down at the table, his hand pushed through his hair. I hadn't expected emotion. I was suddenly worried he would beg me to stay. Despite past offenses my heart lurched at the sight of his distress. I hoped he would not ask me to stay. He blinked, swallowed a few times, then nodded. "Okay, good. I think it's best. Don't you?"

"Yea, I do. But, you know, we can still be friends, right? I mean, I want to be friends, don't you?"

"Yes," he nodded. "I do."

"You'll help me move on Saturday?"

"Sure."

Now I could do what I wanted. I quit my waitress job.

I needed to make money and I knew how. Pushing open a filthy phone booth door, I flipped open an enormous, unwieldy telephone book that hung from a wire noose, its body heavy, thick with thin pages permeated with ink — the phone numbers of every single person and business in Seattle. I had to ignore my first instinct not to touch this anvil, this breeding ground of bacteria, evidence of spills and grime smeared randomly throughout the monolithic volume, and submitted my fingers into its midst, finding their way to the yellow pages. There were only two ads for outcall massage. I chose Elite Massage, dialed the number. A friendly girl invited me to the office when I asked about a job.

38

Seattle, 1980

I often wished that more people understood the invisible side of things. Even people who seemed to understand, didn't really.
Jennifer Starzec, b. 1997, student, author.

I was making about $4,000 a month. Enough to acquire a car, and to upgrade apartments. I moved into a bigger, better one-bedroom off Fiftieth Street, near the University of Washington where I was enrolled, doggedly continuing to pursue a degree in journalism though the path was bent and winding and though my enthusiasm had waned. I was a little depressed and wasn't sure why, but I was feeling different. Peculiar. I was waking up with blood on my lips. I leaned towards the bathroom mirror. Small bite marks were visible on my lower lip. I washed the blood off, looked into the mirror a moment longer, puzzled. I must have bit my lip in my sleep. Oh well.

But there were some days I couldn't function, when anxiety filled me and I paced the living room, vaguely aware that I couldn't seem to stop. On those days I didn't leave my apartment. I hadn't yet met Augustus.

The phone rang. Marion. We'd been having dinner together once a week, better as friends than spouses.

"Are you okay?" he asked.

"Yea, why?"

"You seemed odd yesterday when we had lunch. And you hit the car in front of you and the car behind you when you were pulling out of your parking space."

"We had lunch yesterday?"

"Yea," he paused. "Don't you remember?"

I didn't remember at all. I pressed the phone to my ear and as Marion spoke a white filmy curtain fell in front of my eyes. I blinked. Everything was turning white. Something was terribly wrong. I hung up and managed to drive myself to the emergency room at the University Hospital.

39

Seattle, 1980

The brain is deeper than the sea.
          Emily Dickinson, 1830-1886, American poet.

I have little recall of the doctor who diagnosed me with epilepsy on the day I drove myself to the emergency room at the University Hospital. I only recall he asked a few questions and, after hearing about the seizures I'd had in Alaska, knocking a few reflex points with his soft hammer and watching me walk down the hallway, announced, "You have idiopathic epilepsy."

"What is that?" I'm sure I asked because epilepsy was one of those things that of course you knew the word, but when diagnosed with it, you realized you knew nothing.

"Seizures. Multiple seizures. Unknown origin, unknown cause," he probably said. I couldn't remember much about that doctor. The bloody lips in the mornings, the days of intense anxiety, of not feeling right, of fearing any encounter, when I wouldn't leave my apartment, were now attributed to seizures. And because most seizures affect the temporal lobe, where memory is stored, you don't even remember what's happened. You can't piece together all the signs. I only knew the doctor seemed very busy and didn't have a lot of time to explain how I was supposed to live the rest of my life with seizures. I do remember the back of his white lab coat as he swished out of the room, leaving me stunned with only stuporous stumbling thoughts.

Weighing about three pounds, the brain is the size of a small head of cauliflower. Extraordinarily, this smallish parcel, made of very soft tissue, which is composed of about sixty percent fat and forty percent water, with protein, carbohydrates, salts, and an enormous system of blood vessels, oversees communications throughout the body. The brain has about eighty-five billion neurons with approximately 100 million billion synapses. It is the synapse that connects the neurons. It is the neurons that transmit information and, along with the spinal cord, make us what we are.

Depending on what you think we are. At the very least, the brain runs the organism we inhabit from which we breathe, ambulate, and utilize sensory functions like speaking, touching, hearing, smelling, and feeling. Our bodies function using twelve systems that we know of, and seventy-eight organs. Our brain is the wizard, the small unit seated up top, cushioned by fat, its electric circuitry essential to our identity. Identity, according to Webster, is the distinguishing character or personality of an individual. Potentially, whoever we are is determined by how well our circuitry flows.

The electrical current within the brain begins with the neuron, also called the nerve cell. The motion of sodium and potassium ions crossing over the neuron's membrane activates an electric signal or impulse. The impulse then travels through the head of the neuron to its tail, this triggers a chemical burst, and whoosh, the electrical signal leaps from one neuron to another, transferring information. So where exactly does thought originate? No one knows. Neural processing plays a gigantic role in our thought process, and who we think we are, but the origin of thought remains a scientific enigma.

Frequently there is an aberration within this set-up. There are perhaps 600 neurological disorders that affect millions of people. Sometimes the electric circuitry goes haywire, causing electrical outbursts, a misfiring, or an electrical storm within the brain. This misfire is called a seizure and is caused by illness, fever, a traumatic injury, genetics, or is idiopathic, which means no one has a clue.

Depending on the location of the electrical misfiring and which part of the brain is affected, a person will exhibit various responses. A jerking of the limbs, a vacant stare, an amnesiac spell, auras, hallucinations, smells, odd behavior, and odd sounds can all occur.

"We'll put you on medication," that doctor probably said. Because that's what happened. They scheduled a CAT scan and gave me drugs to take. Phenobarbital.

You could jump.

It wasn't a voice but a strong thought.

You could jump.

I was standing on the sidewalk, staring up at an open window on the fourth floor of an apartment building. I had been walking home when I glanced up and saw the open window, it stopped me dead in my tracks and pulled me, drew me in.

You could jump.

So much freedom when jumping, free from all restraints, absolute freedom for one mad moment.

You could jump.

I stared at the window. You could jump. The thought a magnet. It was hard to pull away. I thought about finding an open window somewhere. High above.

You could jump.

It was the drug. I knew it was the drug talking. I forced myself away from the open window, went home and called the office at the University of Washington neurology clinic, where I had just become a patient. Mary answered. She was the receptionist I'd gotten to know over the past month.

"Mary, I'm having a problem with my medication. The doctor put me on valproic acid and I don't like it. It's making me feel weird and I'm hearing something telling me to jump out a window. That's not me. I don't think like that. I hate this drug," I said.

"Let me talk to the doctor. Hold on."

I had already been on phenobarbital. It had sat on me like a 3,000-pound weight, daring me to try and function. I couldn't. I was prescribed valproic acid instead. Mary came back on the line. "The doctor says he's going to switch you to Dilantin. We'll call it in for you."

"Dilantin? How horrible is that drug?" my voice plaintive. "I can barely function on these things."

"You'll adapt, Jolette. You'll get used to the drugs."

"Okay," I said, even though it wasn't okay. It wasn't okay at all.

It had been about three years since I'd had seizures in Alaska, where I was misdiagnosed by the small-town ding-dong doctor who'd guessed that I'd been poisoned. Then, only recently, I'd had the mornings with bloodied bite-marked lips, with odd days spent pacing the living room, so fearful of encountering people that I didn't dare leave the apartment. Convinced I was just in a mood. There were years between the misdiagnosis in Ketchikan, and the odd days in Seattle. At least three years with no hint of my body's malfeasance.

And then a lightning bolt diagnosis. Epilepsy. Given by a doctor who swished out of the room rendering only minimal attention. Handing out a diagnosis and drug prescription as if treating a sore throat. Me a sudden castaway, alone and not knowing how to survive.

Perhaps the earthquake is the macroscopic version of a seizure. Perhaps the tectonic shifting of a planet, its circuitry faulty, snapping along a fault line, far-reaching and unsettling, compares to the faulty circuitry of the brain, whose synapse has shifted, causing a misfiring, snapping along its own fault line, far-reaching and unsettling.

Jolette

Perhaps the similarity continues. Like the earthquake, which hits and, if it hits hard, leaves you stupefied. You walk past the fallen bookshelf, you try to turn on the lights that don't work, you check to see what has been broken. And then you go back to normal. Sort of. Seizures hit hard too. You are stunned, you walk around in a daze, and then you go back to normal. Sort of.

Except with the seizure, there is amnesia. So when you get up in the morning and note your bloodied lip — bloody because you bit your lip while seizing during the night — you don't know where it came from. You pause and wonder why your lip is bloody, and then because your memory and comprehension are nearly destroyed, you only pause a moment and then mentally shrug, go to the kitchen to make breakfast. You go back to normal. Sort of.

Even with the diagnosis of epilepsy, I had little notion of what that really meant. The doctors prescribed drugs. Many drugs. Each one worse than the last. So terrible and behavior-changing were the drugs it was no wonder I had to question identity. What makes a person. If my feelings and thinking and behavior could so easily be altered by chemicals, then what was I?

I missed myself when I was on the drugs. I missed the person I had gotten to know during the twenty-four years I'd been in this body. This - as I just found out — brain-damaged body.

A CAT scan revealed a "slight aberration" in my left temporal lobe. Where memory lives. The CAT scan also revealed seizure activity during the sleep portion of the testing. Also, a reaction to flashing lights.

Epileptic.

Perhaps it was because I didn't really remember the seizures. Perhaps it was because the drugs were preposterously grotesque. Perhaps it was because when I decided to stop the drugs, I got myself back. And when I got myself back, perhaps that's why it was easier to dismiss the diagnosis. To stop the medication and go back to normal. Sort of.

But what about working as a foreign correspondent? What about reporting from a war torn region where I was taking risks? I tried hard to think of a way I could still fulfill my dream. I imagined reporting from the streets where bombs were demolishing the city. I imagined infiltrating dangerous areas for a coveted interview. How could I do it? Seizures were promoted by stress. Seizures abolished the mind. I would never survive. Never. Even if I found a medication which allowed normal functioning, what if I lost the medication? What then? What could I do? Nothing. That is what I could do. Nothing. I'd be as helpless as a newborn. I wouldn't be able to survive. I couldn't think of any way around it. What news agency would hire me anyway? Nobody. Not if I admitted my epilepsy diagnosis. I pushed my brain to come up with a solution. But I couldn't. I just couldn't. My dream was over.

I went back to normal. Sort of. Depression surrounded me. Losing my dream of becoming a foreign correspondent, my purpose, made daily life difficult. I would have to find something else. But that was overwhelming. I was defeated. Plus there was a new resident living inside of me. Fear. Fear of being struck down again. I knew I couldn't trust my body anymore. Even after I continued back to work at Elite, went back to school, back to aerobic classes, back to going out with the girls. An undercurrent of fear rode with me everywhere. I tried to adjust to these new feelings - it was a lot of work - and, after a few months, when I felt more normal, the seizures almost seemed like a faraway event. Almost. I was able to resume daily life, feeling mostly normal again. Except I knew I wasn't.

I didn't know if I would have seizures again. Maybe I wouldn't. Maybe I'd be lucky. I didn't even remember having seizures. I only knew they wiped out my brain completely. Still I held onto a hope that I'd never have a seizure again. And I minimized the diagnosis. When I met Augustus, I only briefly mentioned the seizures. "Sometimes I have seizures," I told him. His response was probably like everybody else's. No one knew what to say. They didn't say much. My family gave such little reaction that I was surprised. My parents had negligible concern. It made me wonder if I was lying. I wondered if I was making everything up. Is that why my family didn't act like epilepsy was a big deal? Maybe it wasn't a big deal. Perhaps that was another reason I minimized the seizures. And perhaps it was because when I felt like me again, it was just easier to go back to normal. Sort of.

40

Minneapolis, Phoenix, Las Vegas, 1982

My sexuality is not an inferior trait that needs to be chaperoned by emotionalism or morality.
                      Alice Bag, b. 1958, American punk rock singer, songwriter, author

After four months of traveling through Europe and North Africa, I was back in the States and out of sorts. A fish jumped out of the bowl. Augustus had returned to Seattle. I could have gone with him. Back to Seattle. But he didn't insist enough. He only casually mentioned once or twice or maybe three times that I could come back to Seattle so we could be closer. I wanted him to gaze lovingly into my eyes and proclaim that he wanted me in his life, in his home. Forever. I wanted insistence. Anything less didn't squash my fears that he didn't care about me as much as I cared about him. (He didn't.)

Being fearful is a funny thing. It makes you react and you scurry around, trying to protect yourself. Usually you do things you don't really want to do as a result. I pulled away from Augustus, and decided to move to Los Angeles. Which I really didn't want to do. But that's what happens when you let fear rule. You don't get what you really want. And the more you run from fear, the bigger it gets. Your best bet is to do whatever it is that you're afraid of multiple times. Fifty times. In a row. Fast. That's the way to deal with fear. And this is what you tell that voice inside that tells you to be afraid. That tells you you're scared. You say, so what. Yea, I'm afraid. Big deal. And then do whatever you're afraid of. Over and over. It's an exercise. The flabby fear muscle will be overtaken by newfound strength. Flabby fear will disappear. I wish I would have known all that in those days.

Los Angeles International Airport was as welcoming as a thorny bush. I got off the plane from Minneapolis and stopped dead in my tracks. The fluorescent lighting, the indifferent clamor, the rush of bodies racing by me. None of it felt right. I wasn't part of the race toward baggage claim. I sat on a cold, hard plastic chair, immobilized. The weight of missing Augustus made limb function difficult.

We had left Heathrow just a week earlier. Had flown into Minneapolis where Augustus met my family and stayed for three days. My mother, turning from unloading the dishwasher after I returned from dropping Augustus at the airport, said he didn't smile enough. She couldn't see his teeth. She was obsessed with teeth. Maybe because her own were small and stained brown. She kept her lips pressed for pictures.

"He was nice enough," she said. "But I couldn't see his teeth." She had just gotten a haircut. It clung around her ears. Her hair never looked great. Sometimes she teased it and used a lot of hairspray. Then she looked pretty. Maybe if she would have smiled more, she would have been pretty more often. Most often, her eyes were clouded, her lips a straight line.

"He doesn't smile much," she said, her form slender under a heavy sweater, in the kitchen where it was always so cold.

"Yes, he does," I protested. I loved his smile. It was one of my favorite things about him. Of course, everything about him was my favorite thing.

Augustus stabbed me with his casual departure. He'd easily turned from me when boarding his plane to Seattle from the Minneapolis-St. Paul International Airport. He was excited to leave and didn't glance back, not once, as he stepped inside the passenger boarding bridge. I stared at his plane, watched it lift, vanish into the clouds, then he was gone. The world instantly dulled. A few days later, my mother, father, and younger brother Mitchell, brought me to the airport and sat with me at the gate. We said our farewells only to have the flight suddenly delayed. We had to sit for thirty more minutes and then had to muster up, once again, heartfelt goodbyes.

I stared out at the runway. It was a sunny day. I'd been in Los Angeles for thirty minutes. I was lonely. I couldn't call Augustus. There were invisible rules that said if someone is happy to leave you, you shouldn't call them right away. I suddenly wondered what Lenny was doing. I knew she was in Phoenix. My hand dug inside my purse and I located Lenny's phone number. I pried myself out of the cold hard chair and found a phone booth.

"Hello," I heard Lenny's voice, familiar as my own.

"Len?"

"Jolette?" Her voice lifted.

"I'm in L.A. and I don't wanna stay here. Can I come see you?"

"Yes! I'm staying in a funky little motel in Scottsdale. I was with Slick but I left him. When can you come?"

"Today."

I didn't leave the airport, just got a ticket to Phoenix.

Phoenix was a fast-growing metropolis, hot beyond belief during summer, a hub for heroin all year round, just over 100 miles from Tucson, where heroin was regularly smuggled from Mexico, the brown heroin usually transported via tripled condoms inserted rectally. I knew this from living in Tucson, that knowledge common as a cactus. Phoenix, amidst the heat of the Sonoran Desert, was somehow a thriving community, good for arthritic humans who needed respite from winter's cold, which caused expansion and contraction of tendons, muscles, and soft tissue, making joints painful, the warmth a haven for rickety limbs.

Lenny was standing by her car outside baggage claim. Her hair was short, otherwise she looked the same, always put together in a well-groomed way that never matched my earlier days of torn jeans and frizzy hair. Still the same large brown eyes, which could shine like the brightest star or go dark as a black hole. I waved, she caught it, and we began to laugh. It had been about three years since I'd seen her.

"I like your hair short! It looks good," I exclaimed as I wrapped my arms around her.

She yielded slightly with a small hug but then pulled away. She'd never been at ease with touch. She had scars still tender from years of sexual abuse at the hands of her father. She didn't know this then, the day she picked me up from the airport in Phoenix. About the sexual abuse. We just knew she didn't like being too close. Sometimes it takes a while for realizations to unfold, even, maybe especially, when they are of magnitude.

"I love your hair!" I exclaimed again.

"I think I look like a dork, but I'm glad at least somebody likes it," she said in her Lenny way.

"It looks good," I insisted and we settled into the front seat. "What happened with Slick?"

"I left him last week. He had a bad problem with gambling," she announced, pulling into traffic, lighting a cigarette. "You wanna ciggie butt?" She turned to me, her brown eyes shining like I remembered they did when she was in a good mood.

"No. I quit smoking a few years ago."

"Oh?" Her eyebrows went up. "Well, good for you. I'm glad one of us is taking care of themselves." But as she said it, I felt the change. The familiar fabric of our past faltered. There was a wisp of sameness. In a way it seemed we'd never been apart, but before I could finish that thought it was replaced by a sense that everything had changed.

"So, what happened with Slick?" I asked.

"Slickie and I did better in Minneapolis when I'd only see him a few days every couple of weeks. I'd be excited to see him and he'd make me laugh, you know, the way he does with that black mouth of his, and we'd spend a couple of really nice days together. Then he wanted me to come down here with him," she shrugged, inhaled. "So, I thought what the hell. It's not like I'm doing anything in Minneapolis."

Lenny paused, took another drag, stared straight ahead through the windshield. "He has a real gambling problem. I never really noticed it up in Minneapolis, at Moby Dick's or anywhere, ya know. But once we got down here, he just got worse. He would lose all his money, be out all night and for a while we had to stay at a real dumpy motel, and you KNOW I don't like that at all." She stopped to give me a look.

"I know you don't," I agreed. Lenny liked nice things if she could have them.

"When I tried to talk to him, he was like, 'Len, I'm taking care of bidness. A man's gotta take care of his bidness." she mimicked him so well, I had to laugh. "So I said, since when does a man gotta lose all his money night after night? And he got all huffy and said, "Len, you just don understand.' And then I just flat out told him, 'I'm leaving you if this doesn't stop.' So he acts all sorry, and says he's gonna stop. Just one more weekend. And I said, 'Okay, one more weekend, then it's over.' And he said, 'Okay baby girl, I'll make it right. You'll see. I'll make it right.'"

Lenny sighed, lit a new cigarette with the old one. "He ain't never gonna change. So that weekend comes and goes, he loses all of his money and shit. It's the same old, same old. But I figure, okay, you say you're gonna change, and maybe you will. Here's your chance to prove it."

"But he didn't." I said.

"Hell no he didn't. That next weekend we were gonna celebrate starting new, and he didn't show up for two days. I waited for him, just to make sure he was still alive, and I didn't say one word when he came back. He tried to be all nice and everything, and I was like, 'I don't care what you do anymore. Do what you want. It's your life.' And he got all upset with that. But we just went on with the week and then one night when he was sleeping, I picked up my suitcase and just left. And that was it. I haven't seen or heard from him since. Course he doesn't know where I'm at. I moved into a motel in Scottsdale, which is where we're going now."

Jolette

"I'm sorry, Lenny. I'm really sorry." Slick had been in the picture for about five years. I was with her the night in Moby Dick's when she'd first caught sight of him. He was king of the pool room then, tall, smiling, and laughing unless he was holding his cue. Then he was serious as a sniper, lining up the stick, the ball, the pocket. He excelled at this game of precision and judgment, running table after table, respected by other players. She'd found her way to his side, turned the sparkle of her eyes on him, fit into him like a puzzle piece.

By the time we pulled up to a modest motel on a quiet street, Lenny had smoked another couple of cigarettes and talked about her dancing career for the past few years in the small-town strip joints of northern Minnesota. We'd been writing occasionally so I knew she'd been dancing but this was the first time I could see her eyes when she talked. Could see the shifting of her body as she spoke. The ease. The discomfort.

"I make my own costumes. For Christmas, I made a Santa Claus little dance outfit. I mean, its stupid shit but I kinda like it," she said.

"Do you like the dancing part?"

She shrugged, made a face. "I can take it or leave it. But I make money, then come back and stay in Minneapolis a couple of weeks, then go out again." She sighed.

"How much do you make?"

"Usually about $400 a week."

"You could be making $400 a night you know," I said.

She shook her head. "No way. I just can't stand the thought of those creepy men on top of me."

"I know, but it's only ten minutes."

"Ten minutes is way too long."

There was a dance contest at a nearby bar. Lenny wanted me to enter with her. I groaned. I don't dance well, I said. So what, she said. First place is $300. She gave me a flimsy green bikini bottom with a transparent top and we went to the bar that night. When she stepped on stage, she grabbed that stage like a champion. I was mesmerized by her stage presence. The applause for her was thunderous. Then I danced floundering like I was on an ice-skating rink, relieved when the song ended, met with lukewarm applause. I hadn't improved since my topless dancing debut in Alaska years earlier. Lenny came in third, which didn't win us any money but was pretty good, considering the other dancers were all skinny blondes.

We went out to breakfast that night, our favorite time for breakfast, and I told her I was going to Vegas. To work. "You wanna come with? We could work the hotels, except I know you don't wanna do that kind of work."

"I can't stomach it, honestly," she said. "I think I'm just gonna stay here a while longer then go back to Minneapolis. I'm gonna ask my mom to pay for my ticket. She's gonna love that." Lenny looked at me. "What's gonna happen with us do you think?"

"I don't know," I said.

"Seems to me things kinda suck. That's what I think," she said.

"Yea, I know. But, well, maybe good things will happen."

"I doubt it," she said, then looked at me, "but who knows. Maybe." I could see she really didn't mean it when she said maybe. She only said it for me. She was already fed up with life. She didn't like it and didn't want to stay long. She'd told me that many times.

She paused. "I love ya, ya know." Her eyes glistened.

"I love you too, Lenny." We held that moment for a few seconds in silence, then she broke it.

"Wanna get some spaghetti tomorrow? Remember how great the spaghetti was at Di Napolis?" she asked.

"So good. Yea, let's get some."

I left at the end of the week. Lenny and I retrieved as much of our sameness as we could and by the time I left, it sorta felt like old times, but mostly it felt like the old times had vanished.

41

Phoenix, Las Vegas, Seattle, 1983

Sex work is work.
> *Norma Jean Almodovar, b. 1951, American sex worker activist, author.*

From my airplane window, I spotted a protrusion of buildings sprouting from the flatland of the desert below.

In prehistoric times, the Las Vegas Valley region was a wet marsh, a 600 square mile basin surrounded by mountains, which gradually dried out, evolving into the parched ground of the Mojave Desert. If not for the reaches of the nearby Colorado River, which eeked out a few tributaries and sent water underground making artisan wells, this baked dirt bed may have remained just that. But with the natural water springs came a lush meadow, which became a landmark and oasis for weary travelers, one of whom named the area Las Vegas, Spanish for The Meadow. In this desolate stretch called Las Vegas, grew a small civilization that would burst like a cactus flower, gripping the harsh topography with tenaciousness, surviving against all odds.

The plane descended and I set forth into the small city where silver was first discovered, where blue jeans had their origin, and where gambling lifted its lion's head.

The strip was a string of casinos 4.2 miles in length. The northern end was where Circus Circus had been built in 1968, just one of many establishments offering buffets of plentiful cheap food for tourists already fat and waddling. I checked into Circus Circus, got a comfortable room with two queen-sized beds, turned on the TV, took a shower, disgruntlement cascading over me with the water. I was unhappy without Augustus whom I hadn't spoken to in over a week. I didn't want to call him. Don't call anyone too quickly if you are crazy about them. Because you don't want them to know. Because then they won't like you as much. Especially if they easily turned away from you at the airport only a few weeks earlier. I sighed and thought about the night ahead. I needed to make some money.

Caesar's Palace was an easy choice. I walked into the vast casino interior, and slipped into an area with a small bar, just a few patrons seated at the counter. It was about 8 p.m., a little early, but what the hell. The bartender gauged me, he suspected something already. I was alone less than ten minutes. A man sat down beside me. His name was Dylan, he said. He was at Caesars for just a few nights, was flying back to Miami the next day. Dylan was a nice guy, in his forties, a good age for appearance purposes. Nothing too conspicuous. The bartender glanced our way several times. I just kept smiling, holding a conversation that went on for about an hour, way too long, a waste of time really, but I had to play it safe in new territory.

When I finally got around to politely inquiring, "Are you interested in some company this evening, in your room," the guy looked mildly surprised. He probably thought I'd be a freebie.

"How much?" he asked.

"One hundred," I said.

"Alright. I'm in room 459."

"Okay, I'll give you ten minutes and then join you," I smiled.

Dylan left. I nursed my third 7Up, placed a $20 tip on the counter. The bartender picked it up, nodded, and murmured, "You handled that well. You can come back."

It was an easy $100. If you can call it easy to have a wet mouth slobber on you, hands pulling at the most delicate parts of your body and 180 or so pounds laying on you, squashing your legs open so one of the oddest protrusions on the human male body can be stuck up inside one of the tenderest parts of your body. Penetration didn't bother me that much though. It seemed far enough away, at the other end of my body. But the nipple squeezing and sucking, that gaping mouth coming towards me, made me grit my teeth, pushing hands and mouths away like a dodging quarterback, my chest the football.

Still, the crummy part was only ten minutes or so, then a polite thank you, have a nice evening, and I was out the door.

I finally decided to call Augustus the following day. He seemed happy to hear from me, his voice lifting in exclamation, my body strained on high alert to his every word. This time, when he asked me to come back to Seattle, to move in with him, I believed he really wanted me to, which made me giddy. I laughed. "Alright! Are you sure you want me to move in with you?"

"Yes, already. I miss you! I love you."

"I love you too," I said, the words an elixir. I was floating. Even the Greyhound bus I had to take seemed cozy and comfortable, a haven from the world for the two days it took to reach Seattle. When the gleaming city came into view, the Space Needle poking the sky, I was tired and grimy but never happier. We entered a garage, the bus doors whirred open, then a wash of bus station sounds. I grabbed my backpack, stumbled off and looked for Augustus. Cue the orchestra. The smile on my face was huge. But I didn't see him. He wasn't there.

42

Seattle, 1982

Truth is, everybody is going to hurt you, you just gotta find the ones worth suffering for.
                        Bob Marley, 1945 - 1981, Jamaican singer, songwriter, musician.

Augustus lived in a sweet small house across from a forested ravine called Ravenna Park, which had its start about 15,000 years ago when the Vashon Ice Glacial Sheet began to retreat and melt, leaving behind Lake Washington, Puget Sound, and Hood Canal. Smaller remnants included Green Lake, its radius now a jogger's delight of three miles, surrounded by trees and homes inhabited by those with six-figure incomes. Green Lake's outflow included a creek that wound a couple of miles to Augustus's neighborhood, traveling deep through the ravine across the street that was banked by steep hills, so daunting they prohibited the advance of the logger's saw in the late 1800s, saving the lives of many Maple trees, Douglas fir, pine and cedar trees.

    I called Augustus from the bus station telephone. He'd been there the night before, he said. Waiting. He'd misunderstood. He could come and get me.

    No, I responded, disappointed, trying not to consider the moment telling. I'd rather not wait, I said, impatient. I took a taxi which sped me through downtown Seattle to the University District, turning into a modest neighborhood with small houses lining one side of the street, opposite was the lush ravine overflowing with green towering trees. We stopped in front of a small white house with a large picture window, a weedy, overgrown yard, and a wide porch. The front door of the house opened and out stepped Augustus. He smiled, causing everything around him to fade, only he remained sharp in my focus. So began our three years of living together.

It started with high hopes. Or at least I started with high hopes. Each morning we got up, and like Augustus had been doing for years, we went to get coffee. We parked on Fiftieth Street, in the very spot where I had once gazed down at him from my apartment window above. We had coffee either at the Grand Delusion or at the Allegra across from the University of Washington campus, which was convenient.

I'd started classes again and had called Elite to start working. Carol had answered, her voice cheerful and comforting as hot chocolate on a cold day. I could see why some regulars called her just to talk. I'd gotten together with the girls again. They all knew I was crazy about Augustus, or just plain crazy as Nadine liked to say.

The living room window in Augustus's small house, looked out at a forest of green. Much of the time it was raining and overcast, keeping at least the trees happy.

Augustus sold his part of the coffee shop and started working as a projectionist at movie theaters. After morning coffee, he'd go straight to the gym where he immersed himself in racquetball, his first love. Or maybe coffee was his first love. Whatever it was, it wasn't me. I rarely saw him. At night he'd work, at some theater or another, winding film through projectors as was the case in the '80s. I wandered through the deep ravine across the street, the quiet making me lonely. Augustus was never around, our relationship bobbed like a buoy in a sea of undercurrents and I floundered with uncertainty, trying to keep my head above water.

Sex seemed to be the only time we connected but he seemed absent even while we were locked in place and I, who engaged in this gesture nightly with many lonely people, was well aware of the act's shallow substance.

The farther away Augustus seemed, the more morose I got, losing sight of any purpose, having lost my goal of working as a war correspondent even though I was still at UW. Still working towards a Communications degree. In a lackluster way.

One night Augustus got home at 2 a.m. I knew his shift ended at 11 p.m. I lay in bed in the small bedroom the little house afforded, my ears alert to the sound of passing cars. When I finally heard the familiar engine rounding the corner, I got up and opened the living room door. Rusty the dog came with me. We walked outside as his Chevy pulled up, then the appearance of his dark head and eyes, which immediately went to Rusty.

"Hi babe," he said to the faithful lab, petting her head. "Hi babe," he then said to me.

"Where were you?" I scowled.

"I had to stay late. A projector broke down. I had to fix it. I'm bushed." He entered the house, threw his gym bag on the couch, went to the kitchen. I trailed close behind.

"Really? Is that really what happened?"

"Yes. Oh god. You don't believe me. I can't go through this now. I'm exhausted. I have to sleep." His face was resigned. He was getting tired of accusations no matter how spot-on they were. Especially when they were spot-on.

"But why couldn't you have called me to at least let me know?" I was still trailing him, from the kitchen to the bathroom. He turned to shut the door in my face.

"Do you mind if I take a piss in private?"

"Why do you suddenly need to take a piss in private, as if you haven't pissed in front of me a million times already. "

"Jesus, because I'd like a second away from you, ok?"

"You have every day away from me. I never see you," I said. "We never spend any time together."

"I'm working every night to try and pay off my Europe bill. I don't get paid as much as you do, ya know."

"You were fucking someone tonight weren't you?" I couldn't help it.

"Don't you fuck someone every night?" He looked straight at me.

"That's different," I said. "You know, that's a ton different."

"Oh really? How would I know that? Are you going to tell me you never enjoy yourself?"

"Oh gross. That's so gross. No, I never enjoy myself. I grit my teeth to get through it. I hate it."

"Why don't you quit then?"

"Because I make good money. And it's not a big deal. And you know what? You're switching the subject. You were fucking that concessionaire, weren't you? The one who called here the other day. Laura."

"I'm just friends with Laura. She needed someone to talk to. She's going through a hard time. She's too young for me. I told her she could call here if she needed to talk. I didn't know you'd go ballistic."

"Goddamn it. I hate this shit. I can't believe you're out fucking around."

"I can't believe you're on my butt every single minute."

"You weren't fixing anything at work." I planted my hands on his chest and pushed. He fell back slightly, then grabbed his jacket and headed towards the door.

"Where are you going?" My voice was high-pitched. "Where are you going now?"

"I'm going somewhere I can sleep. Jesus Christ." He flew out the door, but I was right behind him.

He opened his car door, slid in, locked the door, turned the ignition. Like something from a bad movie, I leapt onto the hood of his car, pressed myself against the windshield, stared at him through the glass. "Don't go," I wailed. "Don't go! I'm sorry!"

He shook his head, pulled the collar of his jacket up, it was starting to get a little cold, not that I could feel anything as mundane as the weather, and he closed his eyes. "I'm sorry," I wailed again. He ignored me and I turned to get comfortable on the hood of his car, pulling my bathrobe around me, my feet bare. It was cold, but I couldn't leave to get a jacket. I settled in, looked around at the quiet dark. Probably the neighbors had heard everything. There were no lights anywhere except for a couple of street lamps giving off an embarrassed glow. I looked up at the dark branches. My breathing was slowing. Suddenly I could feel the cold working itself through my skin. Shit. It was freezing. Summer had fled, fall had invaded with a blast of cold, and there I was planted on the hood of a car, hugging a flimsy bathrobe. I turned and tapped the windshield. "Hey, you wanna go inside now?"

No response.

"Augustus?" I raised my voice. His eyelids flickered open, determinedly shut again.

"Wanna go inside?"

No response. Then I heard an engine round the corner behind us. I turned to look. It was a police car. It rolled up. The officer's window came down.

"Hi officer. How are you this evening?" I smiled, courteous.

"Everything okay here?"

"We just had an argument. It's just a domestic thing."

"Okay. Keep it down, alright?"

"Yessir, we will." And he slid off down the block.

Forty-five minutes later my feet were frozen. Finally I heard a rustling. The car door opened. Augustus sighed. "Jesus, Jolette."

He got out of the car. I scrambled behind him and we went inside where he fell into bed, and I wrapped my arms around him like I was clinging to a life raft. "I'm sorry. I'm really sorry," I whispered into his ear.

"Alright," he sighed, "But I don't know how much more of this I can take."

"Girl, you know he was fucking that candy girl. Don't be so stupid," Nadine said. "You're being all crazy over this fool."

"Well, maybe he wasn't. What do you think, Helen?" I was at the office. It was Friday, money day. Trudy, Lisa, and Nadine were there.

"Baby, I don't know." Helen was behind the desk, looking through papers. "Honey, you're stressing way too much. No man is worth that. You know how they are. They think with their penis, that's all there is to it."

"So you think he was fucking that girl? You think so?"

"I don't know, baby. Just try not to think about it. Men are shit. They are." Helen was sympathetic, and I knew she wanted to put me out of my misery, but everyone knew I was in it deep. What they didn't know and what I couldn't tell them, even though Trudy, Nadine, Liz, Lisa and Helen had all become good friends, were like family, actually much better than family, was that I had been thinking about razor blades and cutting my wrists. My arms. Like a burrowing worm, the idea had become planted in my head, first presented as an option when I went to therapy one day and sitting in the lobby was a young guy, his forearms wrapped in white bandages. His stricken face. His arms, careful in the white, soft, clean bandages, spoke volumes without a sound. The image lingered, cutting my wrists suddenly appealing. Or perhaps it was the idea of being wrapped in bandages. Tended to by someone kind and caring, tenderly tucked safely behind bandages.

I had been going to therapy. Week after week. Finally I quit. It was too depressing, talking endlessly about the past. It made things worse and sure didn't help with the overwhelming distress I felt with Augustus. I didn't know how to get out of the torment I had begun to feel almost the minute I moved in with him. Until I thought about razor blades.

Razor blades and cutting myself. I thought about it for months. Nurtured the thought like it was a young seedling I had to tend carefully, encouraging its growth. And then one day, upset once again over Augustus, I bought a box of razor blades. Carried them around in my purse. I felt better, knowing they were near. Knowing I could reach into my purse anytime and touch the box. Then I threw them away when I felt better. Bought them again when I was upset. I was averaging two boxes a month. Carrying them with me in my purse. Just in case.

43

Seattle, 1983

The first lesson I would learn about love is that it is filled with disappointment. The second thing I would learn is that the search for a cure almost invariably ends up being self-destructive.
    Patricia Weitz, author

I was only buying razor blades, not doing anything with them. I was only thinking about them. I didn't want to kill myself, except briefly sometimes. But I didn't really want to kill myself. I just wanted to cut my wrists. My arms. Still, I didn't do it. I was only thinking about it.

Augustus was late again one night.

"You're late," I said, toneless.

"So what."

This time I didn't shift from the couch where I sat staring at the TV that wasn't on. I pulled a blanket over me, stayed there all night. In the morning he left without a word. I got up, packed a suitcase, drove to a small motel and called Trudy.

"Why are you calling me so early?" she grumbled into the phone.

"I left Augustus," I said. "I'm at the Quality Inn. Augustus is screwing around so much, I can't stand it."

"You just can't ignore it?"

"Does it seem like I can ignore it?"

"He probably thinks since you screw ten men a week, he can at least screw a few."

"I know he does. But guess what?" I said.

"He can't," Trudy finished.

"That's right."

We hung up and I turned to face the room. I turned the TV on. Uneasy feelings flooded through me. I had thrown away my last box of razor blades. I needed them. I grabbed my car keys, drove to a drug store, found a box of razor blades, a bag of Fritos, and a 7Up. Back at the motel, I took a swig of 7Up and looked at the box of razor blades. I opened the box, took a blade out. The blade's edge was covered in a little envelope. I held it for a while, ate some Fritos, put down the razor and called Jeffrey. He'd remained a friend over the past few years, since I met him at my apartment where I first noticed Augustus. Jeffrey was gentle and I liked the way he read to me. He didn't answer the phone. I hung up and thought of Augustus. I thought of the nights he came home late. I thought of him wrapped around other women. I picked up the razor blade, and carefully took the envelope off the blade, trying not to cut myself. Then had to laugh. I was trying not to cut myself as I prepared to cut myself. I held the razor to my wrist. I pushed the tip of the razor against my skin. Ouch. Shoot, that stung. It was really sharp. I hadn't even cut and it already hurt. I put the razor blade down, ate more Fritos, drank more 7Up, then called Jeffrey again. This time he answered. We talked for an hour. I told him about the razor blades. He told me not to cut myself. I said okay. When we hung up, I felt better. I put the razor blades in my purse, grabbed my suitcase and drove back to the house. Augustus wasn't home yet. He would never know I left. I felt like I'd been gone a year.

"Are you hurting yourself, honey?"

Startled, I looked at Helen. It was a money drop day but none of the other girls were in the office. It was only Helen and me.

Jolette

It had been several months since my first motel visit with my razor blades. Since then I'd been to motels multiple times and my cutting had progressed. I had managed to draw blood the last time. I had grit my teeth, pushed the tip of the razor into my skin, puncturing the epidermis, a few drops of blood popping out. I knew already how much it stung when the razor first cut. I had gotten that far numerous times, but the last time, I'd pushed ahead. Managed to cut the inside of my left forearm countless times, my teeth clenched, right hand pushing the razor down into my skin. Cut, release, cut, release, cut, release. Finally the skin numbed and I could cut without pain, the blood now running freely. The angry, upset feelings diminished, then disappeared. I pictured them leaving my body just like the blood. The more I bled, the better I felt.

My arm was still sore from the last time I'd cut. I'd had to wrap it, had to wear long sleeves to hide it. Augustus hadn't noticed, or at least pretended not to notice. He was tiring of my drama. Tiring of me. I was tiring of me too. We'd been living together for a little over two years. Two long years.

"It's okay. I don't want to kill myself or anything." I forced myself to smile. "I'm okay. Really."

"Honey, you need to see a therapist. You need to get some help. Please," Helen said.

"It's okay. Really. I'm fine," I lied.

"Baby, I'm worried about you. We're all worried about you."

"I'm okay. I'm not going to kill myself. I promise."

The days passed the way they do. Dully plodding forward like a forced march. I was disenchanted with school. The seizures had stopped my future, replacing my long-held goals with uncertainty and despair. What was the point of school anyway? I dropped out three-quarters shy of a BA in Communications. I felt angry and depressed most of the time.

One night when I went to bed, my head hurt. I never had headaches but on that evening my head was a brick of pain. I crawled into bed. Augustus came home later that evening, his car rounding the corner, Rusty the dog would have been at the door to greet him as usual, but I didn't know any of that, I was sound asleep. During the night I opened my eyes. A force inside of me was stirring, sending up a wave of odd feelings. A sound may have escaped my lips, then I was knocked down by something stronger than I had ever felt before, and was swept into darkness.

44

Seattle, 1983

Your present circumstances don't determine where you can go; they merely determine where you start.
            Nido Qubein, b. 1948, American Jordanian
            businessman, motivational speaker.

My head hurt. Augustus was by my side. I was in a bed, in a hospital.

"You had six seizures. Three at home. Three more here in the hospital. Can you hear me?" It was Augustus's voice.

"Bad…headache," I could hardly form the words. "Hurts," I mumbled before falling back asleep, the next time waking to a man in a white coat. The doctor. He was talking. I couldn't understand him. He looked at me. He had just asked me a question it seemed. I nodded, which seemed to satisfy him, and he walked away. I fell back asleep.

This time I had more memory of the seizures. They were like riding high waves. Or being pulled into the center of a tornado. A power beyond comprehension forced me to submit. It demanded one yield, though I always fought against its tremendous pull.

I had begun to recognize auras, which commonly occur before the onset of a seizure. For me, the auras brought an extraordinarily odd sense of discomfort, of impending doom. Often the aura included a smell. A smell that seemed to travel straight up my nasal passage into the brain where it pressed into a memory, and pictures from the past would pop up. Strangely compelling but frightening.

Certain smells were triggers. Freshly cut grass and the smell of a creek gurgling through a field or a meadow, giving off an oxygenated aroma were smells that brought me to a dangerous edge. They invited the aura. The dreaded aura would come towards me, engulf me if I didn't fight. I would scramble, mentally try to center myself, try to avoid that smell, avoid other triggers like the way the light hits the water in a certain way. Springtime was the worst. Something about the smell of water and grass, and the visual of light hitting water brought me close to seizures. I could feel it. I dodged, trying to mentally outrun the threatening aura. Sometimes I would run all day.

Children's nursery rooms were also places of danger. I could no more rest my eyes on a small child's crib, or the children's toys, than I could walk through fire. Any visual from childhood threatened a fall into the aura, which would bring the seizure.

Going by myself to a movie theater one Seattle afternoon, I purchased the ticket then went to the candy counter where my eyes fell on a box of gumdrops. I stared at the box. It pulled me in, took me all the way inside a memory from so long ago, when I was five, and played the board game Candy Land with my best friend Mary. In Candy Land was gumdrop mountain. I stared at the box of gumdrops at the candy counter. I could feel it pulling me. I had to yank my mind away from that memory, out of that thought. I stepped back from the candy counter, turned from the movie theater, back onto the sidewalk, the ticket in my hand unused.

The night I'd fallen into bed in the little Ravenna house, where Augustus and I pursued our dissatisfying relationship, I knew I was having seizures. I didn't know how many I'd already had. But there was one small moment where I felt it and remembered. I remember that it lifted me up, pulled me into its vortex and then I was gone.

Jolette

I returned from the hospital to Augustus's house, unable to recognize what used to be familiar, unable to retain anything. My short-term memory was shot. Augustus told me later he had never seen anything like it. I kept repeating the same questions over and over again, he said. A calm presence amidst my swirling confusion, Augustus remained sympathetic and kind during the several weeks it took before I was able to go back to work. Since I was too confused to be jealous, we got along pretty well during this time. After several weeks I felt normal and went back to work at Elite, where the girls inquired with concern, but like most other people, didn't know much about epilepsy or seizures, and could only say so much. There wasn't much to say anyway.

The emergency room physician had started me on a drug called carbamazepine and miraculously I felt better. All the strange feelings I'd been having disappeared. Completely disappeared. The anxiety, the funny smells, the haunting of the auras disappeared. The seizures seemed to have stopped. The drug worked. It was a miracle and I should have been overjoyed. But I was subdued. The physical and mental battering had left me crawling. I'd become depressed.

"You can still be a journalist." Trudy's voice was loud over the buzz of the bar. We were at the Broadway in Capitol Hill, had just ordered a vodka, diet-7 for Trudy, a plain 7 for me. "You can still write stories," she said. "But I can't be a war correspondent," I said.

"Well, so what. You can still write all kinds of stories," Trudy was focused on me for a change, instead of swiveling to drool at all the three-legged specimens nearby.

"I don't want to write about what little things regular people are doing. I wanted to be a foreign correspondent. A war correspondent. I don't wanna be anything else."

"You'll figure out something," Trudy glanced at the new arrivals, I glanced too. Two guys. I turned back to Trudy.

"I'm depressed," I sighed and slumped in my chair. Trudy didn't turn back to me. I saw her eyes grow keen, she took a sip of her drink, sending a smile to the two guys who'd settled near us. "I don't get how you can be so interested in men after working all week," I grumbled.

"You're too negative. You have to get a better attitude."

"I don't have to get anything."

"Okay, have it your way." Trudy sighed.

That evening I threw my clothes on the floor in the corner of the bedroom and went to bed. In the morning, Augustus got up and went to get coffee. I didn't go. I walked over, picked up the clothes from the floor, put them back on. I should wear different clothes, I thought absently but was too listless to make the effort. I sat in the living room, looking out the window at the trees and wondered what to do. I picked up the *Seattle Weekly* and flipped through the ads. They were usually good for ideas. There was an ad for an acting class. Maybe I should try an acting class. I'd gotten plenty of acting experience working as a call girl. I remembered a girl I had talked to at the coffee shop one day. She'd taken acting classes in LA. At the Lee Strasberg Theater. I called directory assistance and got the number to the Lee Strasberg Acting School. The woman who answered said I needed to have an in-person interview before being accepted into the school. I made an appointment for the following week. Hung up and made a plane reservation to Los Angeles.

Jolette

45

Seattle, 1984

Prostitution was not legal but working as a seamstress was. Imagine the surprise of early census workers in the late 1800s who discovered a large number of seamstresses living in Pioneer Square, most living on the same block, in fact, and not a single sewing machine to be found among the reportedly 2,700 seamstresses.

More girls were getting busted due to the 1984 presidential election between Ronald Reagan and Walter Mondale. Prostitution arrests always increased at election time. It was just the way law enforcement worked. They thought it made the officials look better. Nadine, Liz, and I were at the office, Helen was on phones. It was early evening on a slow Monday night and I'd just popped in after my aerobics class.

"Are you nervous to go on appointments?" I asked Liz who was pretty as any model on a beauty magazine cover.

"I don't know. A little, I guess."

"Girls, you have got to be extra careful! You already know they're trying to up their quota of arrests and I told you that a girl from Pleasure got busted at the Westin last week and one of the cops was hiding under the bed! Under the bed! Can you believe that?" Helen said. Pleasure Massage was the only other outcall massage in Seattle.

"Don't these grown-ass men have anything better to do than arrest girls who are just trying to make a living?" Nadine shook her head, crossed her well-toned, aerobicized legs.

"Why was a cop hiding under the bed?" I turned to Helen.

"They always make busts in twos. A cop always has a partner with him," Helen said. She knew most everything. "So you have to be extra careful. I don't want any of my babies arrested!"

"It's always this way around election time, isn't it Helen?" I asked.

"Yes, it is. It's just a bunch of bullshit. They think it makes them look good," Helen said. "It makes it hard on us, but that's the way it is. So, girls, you just need to be very careful. Don't stay with anyone if you get a funny feeling."

"They ALL give me a funny feeling," Nadine groaned.

"Hey, Liz, maybe you shouldn't work til after the election." I worried about Liz. She was the sweetest girl.

"No, I have to make rent. And Jim had his hours cut last week."

"Oh no! He did?" Jim was a building contractor. He and Liz had been together since they were in tenth grade. At night, he insisted on driving her to any appointment in the Sea-Tac area. He was worried about her. Shoot, I was worried about her.

"Yea. It's just slow right now."

"Well, be careful, Lizard. I worry about you," I said.

"I hate it when you call me Lizard," Liz protested.

"Really? I think it's cute," I laughed. "Okay, Liz. Ard."

"Quit it," she threw a crumpled napkin at me.

"Oh, alright," I said. "I'm going home. Helen, can I just check out? Mondays are so dead. I don't know why we're even open."

"Marilyn wants to make every penny she can. Okay, honey. Go home."

"Bye Michelle my bell," Liz said.

"Night y'all. Night Liz. Ard." I heard Liz groan as I shut the door.

Everyone had cops on the brain. So, I had no excuse for not being more careful two nights later when I went to the Doubletree Inn, knocked on the door, which opened to a man slight in frame, with sparse curly brown hair, a big nose, and vapid eyes. Michael Miner was a Washington Highway Patrol Officer and was working undercover that evening for the Seattle Police Department. Little did I know that Mr. Vapid Eyes was setting a trap for me. He showed me his ID. His address was local. When I asked him why he was staying at a hotel, he must have given an acceptable answer because normally being local and making an appointment from a hotel room was a red flag. The truth was that I was careless. His personality had the appeal of a vacancy sign, and I dismissed him and just went on automatic, always a mistake – always! remember that. I was mentally paying off my Nordstrom bill when I pulled out a condom - that was all he needed for evidence – and he made a mad dash to the window, wiggled the curtain and two seconds later there was a knock on the door. It was a police officer who promptly arrested me.

I was convicted of Offering and Agreeing (O&A), a misdemeanor charge. The penalty was a couple hundred dollar fine and I was eighty-sixed me from the Sea-Tac Airport for the period of one year. Which I ignored. The arrest was an annoyance, a waste of time, a way for the city to make a few bucks, and overall was an ineffective method of handling a very profitable business, unreasonably burdened with moral and religious overtones. Been that way since forever.

In the late 1800s, Seattle was a logging town just beginning to thrive with the opening of a paper mill. Due to hints of prosperity, people began to flock to the area. The new arrivals included a young German woman, Lou Graham, who arrived by boat one afternoon and stayed for the rest of her life. Lou opened a luxurious and lucrative house of prostitution on the corner of Third and Washington and became a benefactor to the community. She donated up to a quarter of a million dollars to the Seattle public school system, subsidized the building of battleships, and lent money to families in need during an economic downturn. She ran her upscale brothel a few blocks from city hall and it was said that much government business was conducted at her house of prostitution, rather than at city hall.

Prostitution was not legal but working as a seamstress was. Imagine the surprise of early census workers in the late 1800s who discovered a reported 2,700 seamstresses living in Pioneer Square, most living on the same block, in fact, and not a single sewing machine to be found. Madam Lou Graham, who was also registered as a seamstress, came to an agreement with Seattle's city council. The city was broke. The seamstresses were rolling in dough. A compatible agreement was reached. The seamstresses would pay $10 a week as a sewing machine tax and in return, the seamstresses were free to practice their trade with no police interference.

Reagan won the 1984 US presidential election with a landslide victory and soon thereafter came a decrease in prostitution arrests, and working girls nationwide breathed a collective sigh of relief.

46

Los Angeles, Seattle, 1984

It's a wicked life, but what the hell, the stars ain't falling down.
Bob Dylan, b. 1941, American singer, songwriter, author, artist.

The Lee Strasberg Theater and Film Institute opened on Santa Monica Boulevard in West Hollywood in 1978. You could say the seed for the school was planted when Lee Strasberg was born in Poland in 1901. He and his family immigrated to the United States when he was nine years old. His father found work as a garment presser in Manhattan, and Lee would perform in a few plays as a child, igniting his pursuit of acting. Ultimately, he would become renowned as an acting coach, developing a version of The Method in 1941. His Method embraced personal, emotional work and was based on the Stanislavski method developed by the Russian director Konstantin Stanislavski, whose quest was a transcendence of rote acting.

Augustus had been barely able to suppress his delight that I was leaving him for the summer. I had flown to LA six months earlier for the interview at the Strasberg Theater. Stayed at a nearby motel. My heart pounding like a jackhammer when I walked through the Strasberg Acting School doors, into the big square lobby, a bench surrounding its perimeter, a huge window looking out to Santa Monica Boulevard, and then was shown to the office where a smiling woman graciously greeted me. We spoke for possibly ten minutes. Somehow in that brief time she was able to determine that I would make a fine acting student. I was accepted, signed up, and paid for a summer of acting classes. A 7-Eleven across the street was host to a group of students outside its door, the sidewalk filthy and littered. My pulse was still pounding as I walked into the congested 7-Eleven, got a 7Up, stood outside and surveyed the street. This was Los Angeles. I'd just been accepted into an acting school. I was exhilarated as I stood on the squalid sidewalk, surveyed the unruly street rank with smells and noise, and felt like I was at the center of the universe.

The I-5 Freeway south, flat as a pencil line for most of the three-day drive from Seattle to Los Angeles, was nudged upward by a crowd of green hills as my faithful red Honda Prelude and I neared the City of Angels. My gaze lifted to the surrounding mountain tops as we were swallowed by an increase in traffic. I took an exit and ended up on Sunset Boulevard in Hollywood.

Sunset Boulevard was dense with bright and shiny vehicles, no beat-up slum-dwelling cars on this street, and the billboards advertising the current big films – The Terminator, Ghostbusters, Indiana Jones and the Temple of Doom – were splayed high in the air, immense and mesmerizing. The combustion of frenzied vehicles filled the air. The boulevard a dystopian daycare for automobiles.

I moved into the Travelers Lodge on Hollywood Boulevard and La Brea Avenue. The motel sat back off the road. My room was on the second floor with a window looking out over traffic and across the street to a parking lot filled with even more cars, where a grocery store welcomed consumers. I could get groceries there, I thought, and pictured having a cozy shelf full of groceries in my small musty-smelling room with the queen-sized bed, the big mirror, desk, and TV, which I immediately turned on, my only friend.

Jolette

My white pants were a mistake. I was bleeding profusely. A bright red circle expanded from my crotch, spread down my thighs. It was my first day in acting class and my period was gushing like a geyser. I was cross-legged on the floor in a large studio with twelve other students. The acting coach, a woman with long brown hair and glasses, was very animated. Her arms never still, she gesticulated with fervor. Choose an animal, she said. Close your eyes and inhabit that animal. Feel the animal. I looked down at the bright red invading my white pants and ran from the room, mortified at the bloody mess I was becoming.

The restroom was vacant. I pulled off my pants, running the cold water over the bloody crotch, the bright red water swirling down the drain. I wrung them out, with some difficulty got them back on, and returned to class where I dropped to the floor with my wet pants, closed my eyes, and tried to be a cat, stretching my arms in front of me as if my life depended on it.

Hollywood Boulevard was ugly. The sidewalks, splotched with dark stains, doorways emitting smells whose question of origin was better left unanswered, were receptacles for discarded food wrappers, cigarette butts, and empty bottles that congregated along curbs, gathered up against buildings. Agility was required to dodge the stampeding crowds, mostly tourists, an ensemble of moving arms and legs, food being crammed into mouths, eyes ceaselessly scanning. Street people, hands outstretched, poorly made signs on cardboard, please help, god bless you. It was hot and the heat made everything pulsate larger, especially the stink. I would return to my small motel room after exploring parts of the city, tired, feeling grimy, relieved to fall onto the bed.

Amnon, my second acting coach, was a portly man, his beard, gray and wild as a weedy clump, camouflaged a small mouth that allowed a booming voice. The students flocked near him, hung on his approval like refugees on an overcrowded boat. He had a lecherous gaze that fixed on the beautiful young women in class. Despite his lecherous leanings, I liked Amnon. He was not lecherous with me. I was a mere brunette in this land of blonde beauties. I imagined that when Amnon fixed on me it was with keen interest because he recognized my innate acting talent.

"You're so neat. You're such a neat guy. I wish I would have known you when I was little. Not real little. But at the age where you start finding out stuff. When I was cracking rocks apart and looking at the sparkles inside." I spoke the words to Hans, a kid from Germany. He had an accent and an arms-wide-open style, as if he were trying to take in everything. We were onstage, performing a scene from "Cowboy Mouth" by Sam Shepherd and Patti Smith, written in 1971. Hans was Slim. I was Cavale.

The stage smelled like anticipation. It smelled of bright hot lights and heightened places. It smelled like the unwrapping of a package where you hoped for something special.

"And I got to be the ugly ducking and I had to wear some tattered old black cloth and get shit flung at me but I didn't mind cause at the end I'd get to be the pretty swan and all." I was holding a fake dead crow because Cavale loved her dead black crow.

I liked the hushed moment before the scene started. I liked moving on the stage, my footsteps piled on top of layers of footsteps that had come before me. I liked Cavale's words. I could imagine saying them myself. They felt like me. But the stage didn't feel like home. That feeling I had heard actors say they felt when they got onstage. "I knew right away the stage was my home, where I belonged." Not for me. I was nervous. Really nervous. This can't be right, I thought, as I went to the bathroom for the sixth time before we put our scene up. As my intestines twisted. As I filled the theater bathroom with smells of defecated fear.

Hans was a thunderbolt even with his thick German accent. We finished the scene and the class applauded. Amnon looked at me. "I feel that I'm watching a young woman searching. Searching to find her way in the world," he said and I felt that he was really seeing me. I felt special.

Hans and I went out that night to a club, so loud we had to scream at each other. "Cavale, Cavale," he screamed at me. We danced, he got drunk, falling down, calling out "Cavale, Cavale." The club was loud. It wasn't fun. I missed Augustus. The night raucous with events I didn't care about.

Six weeks went by, the summer hot, making me uncomfortable, my face fixed in a sweaty grimace. My initial buoyancy at summer's start had deflated. The initial gusto waned with deprivation. I wanted to see Augustus and decided to leave two weeks early.

"I'm leaving early," I told Amnon in his office. "I have to go back home to Seattle."

"I'm sorry you have to go. I've enjoyed having you in the class," Amnon said as he came towards me and tried to press his big belly against me. I was overcome with revulsion. He was just a regular man. He leaned forward to kiss my neck, bit down hard on my neck's tender flesh.

"Ow!" I screamed and jumped back. "That hurt!"

"Oh, I'm sorry. I thought you would like that."

"No. No, I didn't like that at all."

Fucking men. I guess I wasn't so special after all. Or maybe he wasn't so special after all.

"I'm coming back this week." I told Augustus over the phone. "I miss you. I'm coming back."

He paused. "Okay," he said, his tone unenthusiastic, which I tried to ignore.

I couldn't drive away from Los Angeles fast enough. I couldn't wait to see Augustus again. Three days later, I excitedly pulled up to the little white house with the wide porch across from the thick ravine of trees. Augustus had gotten a roommate while I was gone. Ben. I knew Ben. He was a good friend of Augustus and greeted me that afternoon when I returned. I knew Augustus would be working until six that evening. I was determined that this time our relationship would be much better. I would be more tolerant. Not so jealous.

It didn't take long before Ben, who seemed to oddly relish the moment, smiled a little and said Augustus had been seriously dating someone.

Someone named Marie. I called Augustus where he was working at the theater, still a projectionist.

"Who's Marie?" I asked.

"How did you already find out about her?" he asked, angry, like I had just spoiled everything.

"Ben couldn't wait to tell me," I answered. "So you're seeing someone named Marie?"

"Yes," Augustus said with some defiance. "We'll talk later."

When Augustus got home that evening, I was meek. I tried to be friendly. "So is she just a friend?" I asked. "Could we all be friends?"

"No."

"You're having sex with her?"

"Yes."

"Are you going to keep having sex with her?"

"Yes."

"So you want me to move out?" It was astonishing how calm I sounded. Incredible that I hadn't crumpled to the ground. That I could propose we all be friends so matter-of-factly.

"No, I don't want you to move out but I'm going to keep seeing her. You always said you believed in open relationships," he said.

"Well, clearly I'm not really able to do that. It's ideal but honestly that won't work. Not with you. Not right now." I must have been in a state of shock. How else could I have sounded so reasonable.

"I'm seeing Marie tomorrow night," he said. "I thought I'd spend tonight with you. Since you just got back."

I was dazed. Stupefied. We went out for dinner and I functioned automatically. Tried to be friendly, wondering if this couldn't just be a nightmare that I would wake from. Augustus was resolute. His face set.

Augustus went out with Marie the next night. I went out with Trudy, Liz, and Lisa.

"Oh god. So he's gonna keep seeing her?" Liz asked.

"Yea."

"How are you going to deal with that?" Lisa asked.

"She's not. She's going to kill him," Trudy said, lifting a glass of wine to her brazen mouth.

"I don't know. I'll see if I can handle it," I said, knowing the answer already. We all knew the answer.

I went home early. Augustus came home before midnight. "Did you have sex with her?" I whimpered.

"No," he said, almost certainly lying. Still I felt relieved.

We lay next to each other in bed that night. He fell asleep. I was awake all night, tormented. What I had to do was inescapable. I knew. There was no choice. Augustus got up the next morning, dressed, and went for coffee. I packed a suitcase, got into my car and drove to Trudy's.

I left Augustus.

47

Seattle, 1984, 1985

I think perhaps I will always hold a candle for you — even until it burns my hand. And when the light has long since gone…I will be there in the darkness holding what remains quite simply because I cannot let go.
                                                Ranata Suzuki, poet

My body was far too small to hold everything I was feeling. I had never felt so tiny before. The immensity of grief dwarfed my physical self. I was too small a receptacle for such an outpour. The universe, a spiteful figure, had, with one flick of its finger, sent me reeling into a bottomless pit of excruciating agony. It was possible I would never recover.

I spent a week on Trudy's couch. She'd stop working at Elite a few months earlier. She was working at Nordstrom, which she loved. She came home in the afternoons to me on her couch fluctuating between overwhelming misery, sobbing, or numbed, empty as a shell. Lisa quit Elite too, got a job at a car dealership where she told me she was making $5,000 a month, which I could hardly believe. Liz started working as a travel agent, which she liked. She got to travel. I was working at several escort agencies by now. There were only two agencies when I started. Now there were five. I was checking in with three of them, keeping busy.

Jolette

A loft apartment in Pioneer Square, a second-floor dwelling with a large room, twenty-foot ceilings, two gigantic French opera windows that swung out over the street, inviting in the music from nearby bars, suited me well. I moved from Trudy's couch a week after leaving Augustus. My mattress lay in the loft area above the bathroom, a purple ladder was propped against the wall. Each night I climbed up the ladder with a book and a precariously held hot chocolate, always a little afraid I might fall.

It was in these surroundings that I nursed my wounds. I worked outcall at night and then opened a massage therapy studio, Studio 22, in Pioneer Square, a legitimate massage studio. I had been certified as a massage therapist a few years earlier through the Seattle Massage School. It was an eight-month course and I discovered that although I loved receiving massages, I didn't much love giving them. Still, I studied hard, parked my car twice a week near Green Lake where the classes were held, sat near Duvita, a real brain who was excellent at memorizing all the muscle origins and insertions. She would pin me with her serious blue eyes. "Did you study last night?" she'd ask.

"Yes, how many muscles does the human body have again? Six million thousand?"

"Six-hundred and thirty-six."

"And we're supposed to know the origins and insertions of each one? Are they nuts?"

"Yea, you have to know each one because who knows what they'll ask on the test. It's not that hard."

"For you. It's a pain in the butt if you ask me."

"Well, I guess no one's asking," Duvita said.

"You're a smart ass you know that?"

"What's the origin of the brachialis muscle?"

"Oh crap."

"Come on."

"Alright. Brachialis is one of three muscles that move the forearm. Origin is the inside of the humerus. Insertion is coronoid process."

"Origin is anterior of distal humerous, insertion is coronoid and ulnar tuberosity."

"Jesus."

In the morning, I walked from my apartment, down the street to my office. Annoyed if anyone on my daytime massage table wanted anything sexual, which I would indignantly refuse. At night, I was annoyed if a client wanted a real massage. The two didn't mix. I'd already complained to Trudy. They were different energies. Sexual service was base. Massage was elevated. I was angry whenever someone wanted to mix the two. I was angry a lot anyway.

Somebody was tailgating me on the freeway. Right on my tail. Motherfucker. A surge of heat raced through me and I hit my brakes, then released. The car behind me swerved. I scowled in their direction. Don't fuck with me, I said out loud. Because I just don't give a shit.

I pressed the gas pedal down, the arrow hit eighty miles per hour. I aimed for a telephone pole, my fingers clenched on the steering wheel. Then cut away at the last minute.

I thought about driving through a storefront window. I pictured smashing through the glass. The impact would take me out of what I was feeling. I didn't like the idea of shards of glass slicing me but I kept thinking about it. And was afraid I might do it. I wasn't sure I wouldn't.

Do I want to die? I asked myself one exhausting day. Having a broken heart is fatiguing. The pain never ends, like a car spinning in a rut. Do I want to die? I asked myself. Because if you do, then just do it. But if you don't, you need to get through this somehow. I thought for a very serious moment and then answered myself. No, I don't want to die. I'm not going to die over this. I just want to stop the hurt.

I found a therapist whose method was behavior modification, the focus on changing behavior, not just sitting and talking, which only made everything worse, at least for me. She worked with acute cases only. She interviewed and accepted me. I saw her three times a week. She had soft dark hair and a pleasant face, her manner comfortable yet demanding. She told me to stay away from Augustus. No phone calls. No nothing. For two months.

"Two months?" I moaned. "Two months. That will be hard."

"It's a matter of life and death. You need to stay away from him," she said.

"I can't stop thinking about him," I said.

"Yes, you can," she said. "This sounds simplistic but it works," she said. "Take a rubber band. Put it on your wrist and every time you think of Augustus, snap it, then tell yourself No! Do this every time you think of Augustus. Keep doing this. It will work. And whenever you feel like hurting yourself, call a friend immediately or call me."

My wrist was bright red from snapping the rubber band so much. But it helped. Not right away and not easily. It took effort. But after two days I noticed it was easier to stop thinking about him after I snapped that rubber band. No! I told myself, snapping the rubber band. No! It helped. A little. Though I frequently backslid and was still cutting my arms. "You can come and sit in my waiting room," the therapist said to me one day when I called her, crying, desperate to escape the mammoth monstrous pain that had moved into all my organs. "I don't have any openings today but you can sit in the waiting room and we can talk between my sessions," she said.

It was 4 a.m. I was headed home from a full night of work. Three clients. All of them at hotels on the airport strip. I was on my way home, crying, as I had been doing daily for the past six months since I had left Augustus. I saw a phone booth and pulled over. The street was dark and empty, the leering phone booth filthy, its glass door scarred with etchings, a far cry from its ancestor of one hundred years ago when it was first constructed with mahogany wood and plush carpeted floors. I put two quarters in and dialed Augustus's number. It rang and rang. Finally a sleepy voice, "Hello."

"What are you doing?" I asked.

"Trying to sleep," Augustus said, exasperated.

"You don't get to sleep," I screamed and slammed the receiver down, slammed it over and over until it broke apart, wires sprouting out of the earpiece. I left it hanging, got back in the car.

A few evenings later, I pulled up in front of the little white house across from Ravenna Park. Augustus's car sat at the curb. It stabbed my heart to see it. Light shone through the living room window, the curtains pulled. I knocked on the door, it opened to Augustus, his face registering surprise, then apprehension. "Hi, whatcha doing?" I chirped like a madwoman.

"What do you want?" His tone defensive.

"I want to meet her. Is she here?"

"Yes, she's here. It's not a good time. We just took some mushrooms."

"Perfect," I said and pushed past him into the living room.

Marie was sitting on the couch. She was slim, with long dark hair and a skinny face with a noticeable overbite. Her eyes green. Attractive but not outstanding. I liked me better. "I'm Jolette," I said to her and sat in an opposite chair. She looked away, her arms crossed. "And you're Marie. Well, Marie how does it feel to break up a relationship?"

She shifted uncomfortably, looked away, and in a small voice said, "I think it was already broken." Then she got up and slid into the back bedroom.

I looked at Augustus. "She's not that great," I said.

He shook his head. "Are you happy now?" his voice mean.

"No, I'm not. I'm not happy at all." I got up and strode out the front door, yanking it open, letting it slam against the wall. Got back into my car and screeched away.

My therapist was concerned. She told me about a new program for self-destructive and para-suicidal women that was starting in a month, at the University of Washington. I would have to apply to get into the program. She handed me the application.

48

Seattle, 1986

Criminalizing adult, voluntary, and consensual sex, including the commercial exchange of sexual services, is incompatible with the human right to personal autonomy and privacy. A government should not be telling consenting adults who they can have sex with and on what terms.

> Human Rights Watch, founded in 1978, a collection of advocates, lawyers, and journalists who investigate and report on human rights abuses worldwide.

Elite closed in 1986. Marilyn shut it down. She got nervous with the sudden onslaught of arrests. Four girls from Elite had been busted. She was sure someone would give police information about her. The girls scattered. Liz, Lisa, and Trudy had already left escort and were happily settled in their new jobs. June graduated from school, became an engineer and got a job at Boeing, where many past clients were employed. Kinda funny. Nadine went to New York to pursue fashion design. "Get yourself together," she said. "Then come visit me."

I had been arrested in 1984, was arrested again in 1986, charged again with O&A, offering and agreeing, a misdemeanor.

My second arrest occurred at the Marriott Hotel. The appointment was made through a new agency I'd just started working for, Classy Girls. The woman who ran the agency had been upfront. "They're trying to take me down. Be careful out there. They're trying to bust me," she warned. She had chalky white hair and a voluptuous figure. She answered phones from her loft apartment in the art district in Pioneer Square, not far from me. She was only a few years older. "If it doesn't feel right to you, just leave," she said.

The evening I went to the Marriott Hotel was much like any other. The parking lot crammed with cars, my heels sinking into the thickly carpeted hallway with empty trays outside doors. A knock on the door which opened to a forty-something man, soft in the middle, nothing outstanding in appearance or demeanor. Much like every other average encounter. I gave myself the assignment I usually gave myself. Learn one new thing. At least one.

His name was Roger. He was staying overnight at the Marriott but lived on Bainbridge Island, a ferry ride from downtown Seattle. He was leaving for Las Vegas the next day.

"Why are you staying here if you live on Bainbridge?" I asked.

"I'm leaving first thing in the morning to Vegas. This is just easier," he said.

"What are you going to do in Vegas?"

"Just relax, play the slots, see a few shows."

"Okay," I said and ran my hand across the closet shelf above his hanging coat. One of the girls told me that sometimes a cop hid a tape recorder on the shelf. "I'm just going to take a quick look under the bed," I said. No one was lurking under the bed. "Can I take a look in your suitcase?" I asked.

"You sure are thorough," he said.

"Yes, I am." I smiled.

He opened his suitcase on the bed. It was filled with jeans and a few shirts.

"Where's your dress clothes?"

"Oh, I just wanna stay casual. I wanna relax," he said.

"But you have six pairs of jeans. What are you going to wear to the shows?"

"I might not even go to a show. I just like laying out by the pool during the day."

"But six pairs of jeans?"

"It's what I like to wear."

"Alright, can I see your airplane ticket?"

The ticket had the correct dates and his name. I called the agency, the chalky platinum blonde answered. "This is Danielle. I'm checking in at the Marriott," I said.

"Everything okay?" she asked.

"Not really," I said in an overly casual voice and hoped she would advise me. I was unsure. "He's going to Las Vegas tomorrow, plane ticket checks out, but he lives in Seattle."

"Oh well, be careful." She said nothing more and I saw that Roger had perked up his ears at my conversation. I had alerted him that I felt uncomfortable.

I hung up and sat at the round table. Made casual conversation for twenty minutes. Way too long. But I was uncertain. When I asked him to put the fee on the table, he asked if I had any, "What do you call those things? You know, those things?"

"I don't know what you're talking about," I said. I knew he was trying to get me to say condoms. I knew it. That's when I should have left. That's when I made my mistake. I should have left. But instead, I asked him to put the fee on the table, then went to the bathroom, checked his toiletries, and found prescription bottles. His name was on them. I had to decide. Leave or stay. Leave or stay. I stayed.

I left the bathroom wearing a black lacy slip, went to him and began the routine. His hands were all over me, squeezing my breasts, roaming freely. I pushed him down on the bed, reached into my purse and pulled out a condom. Then the words, "Danielle, your worst fears have just come true. You're under arrest."

I looked at him angrily. "Shit! I knew there was something wrong. I knew it! And don't flatter yourself, this is not my worst fear. This is just a pain in the ass."

Roger, the soft-bellied police officer, told me he wouldn't handcuff me if I calmed down and acted "like a lady." He said we were going out of the Marriott the back way. I asked him where his partner was. Police always make arrests as a team. He was solo, he said, because he was a sergeant. He could make arrests alone. I didn't know if that was true. I didn't like it. We walked out of the room and took an elevator to the basement of the Marriott Hotel, walked out through the back door where the garbage cans were. No one saw us. No one was around. I didn't like it. He led me to the parking lot and indicated his car. It was unmarked. I really didn't like it.

"Wait a minute," I said. "You have an unmarked car? I'm not comfortable with this. Let me see your ID again."

The Green River killer was still around and active. Girls had disappeared recently. There was a rumor that the killer posed as or was a police officer.

Roger showed me his police identification. "Anyone can get a fake ID," I said. "I need something better."

He was accommodating. "How about my police uniform? It's in the trunk." He opened the trunk, I stepped back from the open trunk, but could see several police uniforms. "You know what, it's easy to get fake uniforms," I looked at him and thought about running. I wondered if he would shoot me. I would have to decide fast. Run or stay. Run or stay. I wasn't sure. Then I thought of the police radio.

"Have dispatch call you on the radio," I said.

He got on his police radio, called dispatch who identified him. "Tell her you're bringing me in," I said. He looked at me surprised. "Tell her," I said again. "Give her my name." I needed someone to be able to link us together. He did as I requested.

"10-4," the dispatcher responded.

"Alright," I relented and got in the front seat. He began to drive. I looked at him. "You touched my breasts. You're not supposed to do that."

He didn't respond.

"Well, at least one of us is professional," I said.

The result was a conviction, a $400 fine and I was eighty-sixed from the city of Seattle. I had six months to leave.

I had hired an attorney who negotiated this plan with the court. I'd already told him I was moving out of Seattle. He suggested we propose an agreement that I would not live in or visit the city of Seattle for a period of one year.

"Fine," I said. "I don't care." I was leaving just as soon as I fully recovered from Augustus who was my Achilles heel. I don't know why I fell apart with that relationship. But it brought me down like a bomb demolishing a house. Brought me as close to emotional and physical devastation as I ever care to get. To crawl out of its ruins would take years.

My plan was to move to Los Angeles. I would pursue acting. Or whatever else might come up that I could love. That's what I wanted. A work I could love. Something that was mine and couldn't be taken away.

> *It was not until 2001 that DNA technology finally caught up with the Green River killer, identified as Gerry Ridgeway who was arrested and convicted and is currently serving a life sentence for the murders of 48 women, most of them prostitutes.*

49

Seattle, 1986

> *According to figures from the American Foundation for Suicide Prevention, in 2017 more than 47,000 people killed themselves in the United States, and as of 2015 more than half a million visited a hospital for self-harm behavior.*
> *From* Building a Life Worth Living, *by Marsha Linehan, b. 1943, American author, and psychologist.*

"Your first assignment is to stop saying two words. Should and can't," said psychologist Marsha Linehan, the woman who developed Dialectical Behavior Therapy (DBT) for parasuicidal and self-destructive people in the early 1990s. When I met her, it was 1986. I was part of the pilot program. We were a group of ten parasuicidal and self-destructive women. We sat around a large round table in a small building on the outskirts of the University of Washington while Marsha welcomed us to the program.

"First, I'd just like to welcome you all to this program. I'm really happy that you are all here. Don't be afraid. Don't worry. It will be okay," she said, standing tall and plump, her shirt short-sleeved, allowing a full visual of her bare arms, a patchwork of scars from her wrists up past her elbows. I glanced with some disbelief at her upper arm where she had cut into tender parts of the flesh.

That had to hurt. Her cutting was much more intensive than mine. I had a flurry of scars on the inside of my forearms, but her arms were mutilated beyond belief. She had inflicted much pain upon herself.

"I understand what it is like to feel terrible emotional pain, desperately wanting to escape by whatever means," Marsha said, who, as a teenager had abruptly plunged from a seemingly mentally healthy high schooler to someone in the depths of despair.

Her acute depression appeared suddenly, seemingly without reason, followed by violent suicide attempts, so severe she was institutionalized at the Institute for Living, a psychiatric institution in Hartford, Connecticut, for two years, attended by psychiatrists who couldn't help her. She broke windows to slash herself with shards of glass. She burned her arms and legs with cigarettes. And she dove headfirst off tables to smash herself onto the floor. She managed to mutilate herself even when under twenty-four hour nurse surveillance. She did not, nor did anyone, know what caused this extreme deterioration. She only knew she could not tolerate the pain she felt every single day. She wanted out of life desperately.

Psychoactive drugs, therapy, and seclusion did not help Marsha. Instead, after months of seclusion, she reached her own turning point. She was praying, she would later say, and had a revelation that she did not want to die after all. It was an astonishing change for she had attempted relentlessly for several years to kill herself. Suddenly she pivoted. She had an epiphany. She wanted to get better. "I had to find a way to stop wanting to kill myself, and I did," she said. With her new determination, she vowed she would fight to have a life worth living and would share her skills of recovery to help others.

And that is what she did.

"Building a life experienced as worth living," said Marsha Linehan, in her memoir, *Building a Life Worth Living*, "is the overall goal of DBT. Even if you can't create an ideal life for yourself, you have sufficient control to live a life that has enough positive elements to it that it is indeed worth living."

It hadn't been easy to get into the pilot program. The questionnaire was extensive, pages long.

How many times have you inflicted injury on yourself? 0 to 50 times? 50 to 100 times? 100 to 150 times? 150 to 200 times? 200 to 250 times? 250 to 300 times? 300 to 350 times? 350 to 400 times? More than 400 times?

I had no idea how many times I had cut myself over the past several years. It was more than 50 but maybe less than 400. I wasn't sure. I knew that I had some fear of myself. Of what I might do. I wasn't sure I wouldn't drive my car through a storefront window. I was planning it. I visualized it step by step. The image wouldn't leave me. The intrigue, I knew, was that the impact would take me far out of any pain I was feeling.

I'd first discovered this sensation at the age of fourteen. I had been angry with my father, for some long-forgotten reason, so angry I was planning to throw turpentine on him. I was sitting in my basement bedroom of our suburban home, blankets hanging in lieu of a wall, a headband around my forehead, wearing a psychedelic tapestry as a dress, a hole cut in the middle for my head, it swirled around me. I heard my father's footsteps coming down the stairs. I got a bottle of turpentine from his basement workshop, then sat waiting, cross-legged, on the floor, the uncapped turpentine clutched in my hand, hidden under my psychedelic tapestry. He pulled the hanging blanket back and spoke. I saw his lips moving, willed my arms to throw the turpentine. But could not do it. The only thing I could do was to silently spill it over my bare thigh, keeping my eyes on his face. It burned while he spoke, it burned when he turned and left. It burned when I pushed back my dress to look at my leg. I did not wash the turpentine away. I let it sit and burn. It held me somehow. There is still a scar.

I answered the questionnaire, page after page, and held my breath until I knew I had been accepted. Only then could I rest for a minute.

A thin girl had just gotten out of the hospital the morning before. She'd overdosed on pills. It was her fourth suicide attempt in two months. "I can't get out of bed in the morning. I haven't brushed my teeth for a week. I just can't do it," she said. Other girls nodded. Most of them had been hospitalized multiple times in the past year. I felt normal by contrast. I just cut my arms, only fantasized about smashing my car into a telephone pole, or through a storefront window.

We all had to introduce ourselves. Nobody seemed to like the spotlight. We mumbled about our self-destructive behavior, the suicide attempts. Nobody embellished much. It was enough to say, "I would have died the last time but my brother found me. I've tried to commit suicide five times."

"There are two words that will not help you," Marsha said. "The words should and can't. First, the word should. Should is not a realistic word. It doesn't work and it doesn't help. When you use the word should you're not accepting reality."

Marsha suggested replacing it with an alternative word. Or rephrasing the thought. I shouldn't be so upset over this. Replaced with, I wish I didn't feel so upset by this, but I do right now. This feels difficult. Or, for example, I shouldn't feel this way. Replaced with, I don't like the way I feel right now, but I can understand why I feel this way.

Same thing with the word can't. I can't handle this, replaced with, this is really challenging and it feels difficult right now. That's okay. I may not like it, it may take a while but I can get through it.

"Try not to use these words until our next meeting," Marsha said. She talked about self-empowerment through choice of words. It made perfect sense to me. It would take a lot of practice, but I immediately recognized the power and value of this new perception. I believed in this.

At the end of the meeting, Marsha asked us all to agree not to inflict self-harm or try to commit suicide until the next meeting. She asked for a show of hands in agreement. We all raised our hands.

50

Seattle, 1987

Promise me you'll always remember: You're braver than you believe, and stronger than you seem, and smarter than you think.
           A.A. Milne, 1882-1956, English author, Winnie the Pooh.

Puget Sound lay like a sleeping giant along the waterfront of Seattle, the sun glancing off its sparkling surface. I was jogging past Pier 54, home of Ivar's famous fish restaurant, jogged around the clumps of tourists, past Pier 62, all the way past Pier 70 to the waterfront park where I u-turned and jogged all the way back to Pioneer Square, to the cobblestoned streets that were my backyard. I was jogging every morning. Doing free weights an hour each day. Feeling good.

After my two-mile morning jog along the waterfront, I usually stopped at a small coffee shop where I got a banana walnut muffin, then wandered into the Elliot Bay bookstore where the books were piled on tables and I hurried to check out the titles, survey the covers, flip open a book to the first line. If I liked it, I flipped to the midsection, read a paragraph. If it caught me, I flipped to the end, glanced at a few sentences. I bought a pile of books every couple of weeks. Ellen Gilchrist and Rita Mae Brown were my favorite authors. A new book still as thrilling as it was when I was seven and belonged to the school book club, fresh inky smelling paperbacks handed to me, new and tightly bound, just waiting to be broken open, the world in its pages coming to life in a young mind. Pure gold.

Jolette

I was feeling strong. The pilot program had ended. Twelve weeks, twice-weekly individual and group meetings, role-playing and learning life skills. Like learning how to listen. In the exercise, you listened to someone, then repeated what they had just said back to them. It was tedious.

"I was really angry when she took my shoes."

"So what I hear you saying is that you were angry when she took your shoes."

"Yes, I was angry and I yelled at her."

"So, you're saying that you were angry and yelled at her."

Stuff like that.

Still, I got the point. It was all geared towards self-empowerment and better communication and coping skills for life. Most of it I forgot. But four things stayed with me.

The first was semantics. The importance of the words you choose to think and speak with. It takes effort to catch the words that trip you up, like should and can't. I made effort and paid attention to my internal dialogue. I cut out should and can't. It wasn't easy but I was changing the way I thought. I changed the words I used and when I changed my words, my feelings changed. I started feeling hopeful. I felt better.

The second was to assess a frustrating interaction with the following questions. What's my priority in this exchange? Do I want to win the argument at any cost? Do I want to keep the friendship? There is no wrong answer. The point is to be clear about what you really want. Then, act accordingly. It takes work to be a decent communicative human being. It doesn't come naturally.

Third, I learned the feeling of anger usually had a 'should' attached. *They shouldn't have done that. She shouldn't have said that.* So I had to remember that shoulds never help. The reality is, the person said something regardless of what you might have preferred. That's where you start. Frequently, anger comes from hurt. So you learn to say, 'That hurt my feelings," rather than give a knee-jerk angry response.

Jolette

Fourth, I learned cutting is a real thing. I was unaware that cutting had its own category as self-injury. Very distinct from suicidal. The Journal of American Board of Family Medicine estimates that one to four percent of adults and fifteen percent of teens in the United States engage in self-harm. This knowledge actually backfired. For it didn't deter me. In fact, in a way, it validated the action of cutting. I knew it wasn't supposed to. But in a funny way, I decided to keep it. For when I needed it. Though I had completely stopped cutting now that I was feeling better. Now that I was looking forward to the future. That included moving to Los Angeles. I was leaving in a week.

51

Seattle, 1987

How lucky I am to have something that makes saying goodbye so hard.
A.A. Milne. 1882-1956, English author.

"I know a girl who runs an escort service in LA," Carol said. "I'll call her and see if she'll hire you."

"Great. Thanks Carol."

It had been years since I'd first laid eyes on Carol, that day when I'd navigated my way down the urine-scented hallway to the office apartment after I'd called to ask about a job. She was a stay-at-home mom now that she wasn't answering phones anymore. Her kids were growing up, going into sixth and seventh grade, and she was involved with the PTA and things like that. I smiled at her. She smiled back. We'd worked a lot of nights together, her voice in my ear as I checked in and out of hotels night after night.

There were ten of us sitting at the Broadway restaurant in Capitol Hill, surrounding a huge table. It was a going-away dinner for me.

"Michelle," Liz leaned towards me, she was feeling her third wine, her words a little sloppy. "We're going to come visit you. Okay, guys? Let's go see Michelle in LA."

"Where are you going to live?" June asked. She had the softest voice.

"I already went down and found an apartment in West Hollywood. It's waiting for me," I said. I had flown down, rented a car, and drove around until I spotted a For Rent sign on a street called Hilldale. The manager was a young guy, Mark, an aspiring actor of course, who was very friendly. I gave him a check, he handed me the keys to a small one-bedroom tucked into an enclave of apartments. I glanced around the empty apartment that would be my new home. It would be a new beginning.

"I'm so excited," I said. "All of my furniture is being picked up on Saturday and I'm leaving Sunday. How is Boeing, June? Have you run into any old customers?" We all laughed.

"Do you miss Elite?" Trudy asked June.

"I love my job and noooo, I don't miss Elite," June laughed, the sound as light as a bell. "I don't see anybody. I'm in my own little office. How do you like Nordstroms, Trudy?"

Trudy had recently colored her hair red. It made her green eyes stand out. She looked pretty. She shrugged, guzzled her wine. "I work in lingerie. It's okay but honest to god, I'm getting bored. And I never have much money anymore." She'd had to give up her Corvette. She couldn't afford that kind of car payment anymore on a Nordstrom salary.

"She misses her car," I said.

"That car was a guy magnet," Lisa said.

"It was," Trudy sighed.

"Have you guys heard from Nadine?" I asked. Nadine was in Manhattan, pursuing her dream of fashion design. She had always carried around her drawings of stick-thin women, garbed in her designs. One time she'd had put on a fashion show for us. Lisa and Liz had been the models. We loved her designs.

"She's working in some dress shop and lives with three girls in a small apartment," Carol said. "She sounds good."

"I miss her," I said.

"Have any of you seen Marilyn?" Liz asked. "Have you been in her glass store? She almost fainted when I walked in there." Elite was just one business Marilyn had run. Her main business was a glassware store in downtown Seattle.

"I never knew she ran another business," I said.

"Yea, she's had that glass shop for years," Liz said.

"She might have more businesses. Who knows?" Lisa said.

"Hey, cheers everybody." Trudy raised her glass. "Here's to us!"

"Here's to us," we all chimed, clinked glasses all around.

"Michelle, are you sure you wanna go? We're gonna miss you," Liz said.

"I'm gonna miss you guys too," I said.

We'd celebrated holidays and birthdays every year. We'd played softball every spring, gone to festivals and concerts, and met for countless dinners and drinks. Even when the girls got new jobs, we stayed together.

I looked around the table, everyone was chattering, laughing. Helen met my eye. She leaned across the table. "Honey, I know you think you're leaving forever, but just remember you've got friends here. You can always come back."

Trudy overheard. "She'll never come back," she predicted, lifting her wine glass to her big loud mouth. I was going to miss her. I'd miss them all. If having good friends were enough to keep me there, I would have stayed. But it wasn't enough. It just wasn't.

52

Seattle, 1987

There are things that we don't want to happen, but have to accept, things we don't want to know but have to learn, and people we can't live without but have to let go.
Author unknown

My pace was stronger and faster. I ran along the waterfront easily. I had new muscles, my body felt taut. I had new muscles in my mind too. I was exercising my thinking. Keeping myself on track.

I hit the coffee shop back in Pioneer Square, was standing in line to order my banana muffin, when I heard a familiar voice.

"Hi Jolette."

I turned to look. Augustus. My heart nearly seized. "What are you doing here?" I said.

"I was looking for you. I knew you lived around here somewhere."

I hadn't seen him in two years. He looked the same. The shock of dark hair, the dark eyes now searching my face.

"What's wrong?" I asked.

"I've been thinking about you. Marie and I, well, you know," he shrugged.

"What? You had an argument?"

"Yea. It's not working out," he said glumly.

"You'll make up," I said. "You wanna go for a walk by the water?"

"Yea," he said.

Just as fast as you can say idiot, I was back under his spell. My heart pounding. I tried hard to act casual. We spent the entire day walking and talking by the waterfront. We reminisced over our European and North African trip. He told me everything he was up to. Not much really, still a projectionist, still coffee and racquetball. At one point, he reached for my hand. My endorphins had a field day. I was flooded with feeling. When he left that day, I had backslid. Maybe we'd get back together, a chorus of internal voices sang. My heart pumping furiously, rejoicing. Except he didn't call the next day. Or the day after that. I didn't call him either but I was on edge. The foundation I had slowly been rebuilding, trembled. I filled boxes and got ready for the moving truck. I ran by the waterfront. I thought about my new apartment waiting for me. It was better that he didn't call.

But he did. One day before I was leaving, the phone rang. Him. "You're back with Marie?" I asked.

"Yes," he said.

"I'm leaving in the morning," I said. "I'm moving to LA"

"Can I come and see you tonight to say goodbye?"

"Yes."

"Why are you letting him come by?" Trudy screamed at me over the phone. "You're doing so well. Why are you letting that asshole come over? You almost DIED over him," she shrieked. The girls had been really worried, they thought I might not make it when Augustus and I split up.

"I can't help it," I whined.

"I thought you weren't supposed to use the word can't," she said.

"I forgot."

Jolette

My furniture was picked up the next day. My loft apartment stood empty except for the things I would pack into my car. I would sleep on my blanket on the floor that night, then get up early and leave.

Augustus and I went out for dinner that night at a Thai restaurant down the block from my apartment. He was casual, I tried being casual too. We walked back, he came up with me to my vacant unit. "I can't stay," he said. "But why don't you go down to L.A., get it out of your system, then come back and let's get married."

"What? Married? But you're with Marie," I said.

"I know, but, well, just come back and we'll get married, okay?" He kissed me. "Think about it." Then he left. His bizarre final words had effectively stirred the pot. I turned to face the empty apartment and burst into tears. I sat on my blanket in the corner and sobbed. My chest broke open and the dam let loose. I cried until all the water I had for tears was gone, and then I quieted. Looked around. The twenty-foot-high ceilings, the expanse of French opera windows covering one entire wall. The room completely empty except for me, huddled in the corner on my blanket, sobbing. This would make a good scene in a movie, I thought. And the thought made me laugh.

53

Seattle, 1987

It's time to say goodbye, but I think goodbyes are sad and I'd rather say hello. Hello to new adventure.
Eric Harwell, 1918-2010, American sportscaster.

When the sun is shining, Seattle is a glorious city. It was already up, softly bright when I opened my eyes the next morning and stretched. Augustus showing up had been an unexpected jolt, but maybe that was okay. Maybe it was good to be jolted. Maybe I would go down to LA, not like it and come back. Get back together with Augustus. He'd planted that seed. But probably that wouldn't happen. A small voice said well, maybe it could. But most of me knew it wouldn't.

I was looking forward.

Maybe someday I'd meet Naomi Pearl. She was thirteen now. I'd thought about her often during the years. Every April 20 I looked up at the sky and wished her a happy birthday, wherever she was. The little girl who I'd last seen in a crib in the nursery at Lutheran Social Services, before she was adopted by her new family. I'd called Lutheran Social Services after my epilepsy diagnosis. I'd asked them to pass on the information. I thought Naomi Pearl's family should know. Maybe we'd meet someday. Someday when I wasn't working outcall. When I knew what I wanted to do. When I had more answers. She'd come visit me then. It was too late for her birth father, Albee. He was dead. But maybe she and I could get to know each other. Maybe we could be friends. Maybe that could happen.

Jolette

I packed my car that early morning. Said farewell to my apartment. It had been a good place. I walked out the front door for the last time and jumped into the driver's seat. I would soon be on the I-5 south, and Seattle, the Emerald City, would disappear from my rear-view mirror. I would look ahead. I couldn't wait to see what would happen in Los Angeles. I felt good. Things should be much better in L.A., I thought. Wait wait. Not should. Be more realistic. Life would be different in Los Angeles, and I was ready for new possibilities. It could be stimulating, it could be exciting. It could be great.

I believed in what I had learned. That words carry power. Every word you chose indicates perspective and a choice of interpretation. What words you chose to speak and think with will change perspective, will alter life. Amazing. It's so simple. Relatively simple. It's all your choice.

My foot pressed the gas pedal, I pulled from the curb, drove down the street. Even as I said goodbye to Seattle, I was looking forward. Never straight, always forward, as Maude and I used to say in the old hitchhiking days, raising clenched fists, like we were revolutionaries. Always forward. Into the promise of new worlds.

THE END

Author's Note

Writing this memoir made me relive the past, not a particularly desirous thing. But it's what you must do when you are creating something. You must live with it.

Most of what's written is accurate according to my memory. Some of it is adorned with a bit of creative license.

What is true is that there was much struggle, physically, mentally, and emotionally. Yet I was lucky enough to be able to get back up when I was knocked down. I was extended a hand and taught coping techniques. I was lucky that I could see the value in what I learned. And I was able to finally feel strong and hopeful.

This book ends happily and looking forward. But of course it's not the end. For I am still alive and life has continued doing what it does best. Presenting challenges. As it does to us all.

What has helped me, and what I continually work with, is the power of words. And what I tell myself is, "What words you chose to speak with and think with will change perspective, will alter life. Amazing. It's so simple. Relatively simple."

I have chosen to use a pseudonym to protect my parents from my past, which would undoubtedly give them a heart attack.

J. Mitchell
Los Angeles
January 2023

Thank you, Maia, for so generously giving me a safe place to write and grow when I never believed in safe places.

Thank you, Susan, for forever nudging me with your words, "Keep writing."

Thank you, Kristen Lee, for your unending support.

www.ingramcontent.com/pod-product-compliance
Lightning Source LLC
Chambersburg PA
CBHW070419010526
44118CB00014B/1814